International Screen Industries

Series Editors:
Michael Curtin, University of Wisconsin-Madison and Paul McDonald,
University of Portsmouth

This unique series provides original profiles of film, television and digital media industries in a variety of countries and regions throughout the world. It also analyses how transnational flows of goods, services, talent and capital are shaping the increasingly interconnected global media economy.

Published titles:
European Film Industries *Anne Jäckel*
European Television Industries *Petros Iosifidis, Jeanette Steemers and Mark Wheeler*
Global Television Marketplace *Timothy Havens*
Video and DVD Industries *Paul McDonald*
East Asian Screen Industries *Darrell Davis and Emilie Yueh-yu Yeh*

Forthcoming:
The American Television Industry *Michael Curtin and Jane Shattuc*
The Global Videogames Industry *Randy Nichols*
The Indian Film Industry *Nitin Govil and Ranjani Mazumdar*
Television in India *Shehina Fazal*
Television in Greater China *Joseph Chan*
Latin American Film Industries *Tamara Falicov*

D1365395

To our parents
Aida and Michel Kraidy
Josephine and Fuad Khalil

Arab Television Industries

Marwan M. Kraidy and Joe F. Khalil

A BFI book published by Palgrave Macmillan

First published in 2009 by
PALGRAVE MACMILLAN

on behalf of the

BRITISH FILM INSTITUTE
21 Stephen Street, London W1T 1LN
www.bfi.org.uk

There's more to discover about film and television through the BFI. Our world-renowned archive, cinemas, festivals, films, publications and learning resources are here to inspire you.

Palgrave Macmillan in the UK is an imprint of Macmillan Publishers Limited, registered in England, company number 785998, of Houndmills, Basingstoke, Hampshire RG21 6XS. Palgrave Macmillan in the US is a division of St Martin's Press LLC, 175 Fifth Avenue, New York, NY 10010. Palgrave Macmillan is the global academic imprint of the above companies and has companies and representatives throughout the world. Palgrave® and Macmillan® are registered trademarks in the United States, the United Kingdom, Europe and other countries.

Cover image: (front) Newsroom, Future News TV; (back) *Superstar*, Future TV (19 TV Ltd/FremantleMedia Ltd).
Printed in Great Britain by MPG Books Group, Bodmin & King's Lynn

This book is printed on paper suitable for recycling and made from fully managed and sustained forest sources. Logging, pulping and manufacturing processes are expected to conform to the environmental regulations of the country of origin.

British Library Cataloguing-in-Publication Data
A catalogue record for this book is available from the British Library

ISBN 978–1–84457–302–8 (pbk)
ISBN 978–1–84457–303–5 (hbk)

Contents

Introduction

Arab television burst onto the world stage when al-Jazeera, a Qatari pan-Arab satellite television news channel, scooped leading global news networks like the BBC and CNN with its coverage of the US-led invasion of Afghanistan in the aftermath of the 11 September 2001 attacks on Washington and New York. Al-Jazeera then seized the global imagination by broadcasting video messages from al-Qaeda leader, Osama bin Laden, leading to its widespread perception as embodying the ills of Arab media. Until that point, however, Arab television industries had received relatively little attention from academics, journalists and analysts around the world. Little wonder, then, that even considering the well-known yet unique case of al-Jazeera, knowledge about the historical evolution of Arab television remains scant. This limited understanding extends to the contemporary television industry: when the discussion turns to Arab television, many people around the world, including some of the better-informed journalists and researchers, have tended to think mostly of al-Jazeera. A wave of books about the Doha-based channel has kept it in the limelight, further preventing the emergence of a broader view of Arab television and its stunning diversity. Succinctly stated, al-Jazeera's status as poster child for Arab media in the post-September 11 2001 world obscures further rather than enlightens non-experts who are interested in Arab television.

The growth of the Arab television industries since the early 1990s is a remarkable story of radical transformation. During the last two decades, national broadcasting systems dedicated to socio-economic development, political propaganda and the cult of the leader, have inexorably given way to a pan-Arab satellite television industry whose ownership patterns and politico-economic agendas overlap and compete with state interests and the agendas of non-state actors. This revolution in media affairs has unfolded in a vast geographical region comprising two dozen nation-states, more than half of the world's oil reserves, the historical cradle of Judaism, Christianity and Islam, and some of the most intense ideological, religious and military conflicts of the post-Cold War era.

It is against that backdrop that the contemporary Arab television industries are best understood. In this book we aim to provide a broader perspective on

Arab television, an industry in which a handful of leading institutions, different from each other in institutional identity, political perspective and commercial agenda, drive the industry's growth. Existing models of how media systems operate are not ideal to account for the sweeping transformation that Arab television has witnessed and the ensuing entanglements of business, politics, ideology and religion that drive Arab television today. Because the industry's increasing commercialisation has gone hand in hand with autocratic political practices, it would be inaccurate analytically to locate the industry in the liberal media model developed by Hallin and Mancini (2004). At the same time, because political control is exercised inconsistently and is often directly contested or indirectly mitigated by economic interests, Arab television cannot be labelled authoritarian according to Siebert *et al.* (1956) nomenclature or mobilisation media (Rugh, 2004). Unlike media in post-Soviet societies, national Arab broadcasting systems were not subjected to the standardising influence of Soviet communism; rather television systems in Arab states evolved as discrete entities with minimal overlaps until the early 1990s when satellite technology transformed Arab television into a transnational field, based on a pan-Arab infrastructure of satellite technology established by the Arab Satellite Organization (ARABSAT). Though like film and television in Greater China (Curtin, 2007), Arab television is increasingly driven by twin logics of accumulation and distribution that operate on a transnational scale, the pan-Arab television industries appear to us to be a more integrated single market, under the influence of the shared Arabic language, cultural and religious factors, and the integrative scale of satellite technology. This book will suggest that in structure, content and impact, the pan-Arab television landscape is distinct from both the national systems that preceded it and the contemporary global media system.

We begin this study with a set of fundamental questions the broad conceptual and topical implications of which we address throughout the book, all the while striving to maintain dynamic connections between political developments in Arab countries, the pan-Arab television industries and the global context. This book will address the following questions:

- How have major geopolitical developments affected the growth of Arab television?
- How did various political, economic and religious agendas influence the development of Arab television industries?
- Who are the main industry players?
- Two decades into the so-called satellite television 'revolution', what patterns can we discern in news and entertainment television? Is the industry fragmenting or consolidating, or both?

- To what extent has the introduction of 'new' technologies, from the Internet to mobile telephony contributed to changing television policy, production, programming, distribution and viewing?

As we strive to provide answers to these questions, we will also explore the role of television in shaping recent political, economic and socio-cultural developments in the Arab world, in an approach grounded in the fundamental assumption that the relationship between television and society is relational and reciprocal. Guiding our analysis is a broadly neo-institutionalist approach which considers television industries in their multiple political, economic, social and ideological contexts.

We hope to convey to our readers the extent to which the Arab television industry is pluralistic, vibrant and internally contested. Though al-Jazeera is undoubtedly a leading player in Arab television news and a unique historical development in a global context marked by a long-standing hegemony of Western news media and agencies, this book opens broader vistas on the Arab television industry which as of April 2009 comprises 470 transnational satellite channels, including news networks and channels focused on general entertainment, music, sports, religion and business. These channels cater to multiple audiences within a vast population of Arabic speakers of multiple nationalities residing in a wide geographical swath ranging from Morocco on the Atlantic Ocean to Iraq in the northeasternmost part of the Arab Middle East. The multiple Arabic-speaking diasporic communities scattered throughout the world – North America, Europe, Australia, West Africa and Latin America – also figure in Arab television-programming strategies.

This study has benefited from the two authors' complementary abilities. Kraidy has been writing about global communication and Arab media since the mid-1990s, when Khalil was working in the Arab television industry in Beirut, Rome and later Dubai before returning to the United States to pursue a doctorate. Our approach therefore relies on a dynamic articulation of insider knowledge and scholarly analysis, the former providing otherwise unavailable nuggets of information and an intimate knowledge of industry practices, the latter enabling conceptually grounded analysis based on a wealth of empirical data. Having grown up in the Arab world and come of age as the satellite era was dawning, and then followed careers in which Arab media were a central preoccupation, we occasionally draw on our personal experience with Arab television. We also consulted myriad primary and secondary sources in Arabic. Our analysis is grounded in fieldwork and personal interviews conducted in Egypt (Khalil), Jordan (Kraidy and Khalil together), Kuwait (Kraidy), Lebanon (Kraidy and Khalil), Saudi Arabia (Khalil), the United Arab Emirates (Kraidy and Khalil) and the United Kingdom (Kraidy). The interviews we list at the end of this book reflect a small portion of our extensive interactions with people working in Arab television. We omitted some interviews from the list because their subjects requested not to be named; we also did not mention numerous informal chats, telephone calls and email exchanges each of us has had with industry insiders. In addition to personal interviews, we examined various ratings reports, market research studies, corporate press releases, trade magazines and numerous articles from the Arab and pan-Arab press. As we crafted the chapters, we embedded institutional histories and analyses in broader patterns characterising the industry.

We hope that this volume provides readers with unique insights into the compelling story of a regional television industry that has become the subject of intense political, academic and journalistic interest worldwide in the aftermath of the 11 September 2001 attacks in the United States. Our analysis will seek to accomplish three principal objectives:

1 Our first goal is to identify and explain the main structural patterns in ownership, organisation, financing and programming of the Arab television industries, briefly tracing historical milestones, focusing on key players and taking into account contemporary developments in a volatile regional geopolitical context that has most recently been shaken further by the global economic crisis. To that end we carefully selected key players, examined their interactions with each other and with their political, economic and social environment, without aiming to provide an exhaustive compilation of all television channels operating in the region. For example, we do not cover television in the Arab Maghreb (Algeria, Morocco, Tunisia) thoroughly because it is less consequential to the pan-Arab television industry than actors in the Levant and the Gulf.

2 We also aim to analyse production, programming, distribution and viewing practices, in the context of the formation of a regional market estimated at 250–300 million viewers, and in relation to patterns of consumption, popular taste and cultural reproduction. In light of our consideration of television institutions in their broader social context, we pay particular attention to issues of cultural influence and social controversy, including themes specific to women, youth and religious viewers. We devote Chapter 5 to Ramadan because that intense thirty-day television season captures the complexities of Arab television and brings into focus the articulation of religious observance, television production, programming and viewing, and the advertising industry.

3 Our third major objective is to discuss the impact of national media and information policies and new technologies on the pan-Arab industry. In terms of
   policy, we focus on selected Arab countries – Lebanon, Saudi Arabia, Syria,
   the UAE – because their television policy is either (a) representative of policy environments in other Arab states or (b) influential in the development
   of the emerging pan-Arab policy regime manifest in the creation of free-trade
   zones and more importantly, the Arab Satellite Television Charter of 2008.

RATIONALE AND OUTLINE OF THE BOOK

This book arose from the need to have an accessible introduction to Arab television, *a tour d'horizon* that is nonetheless based in a conceptual and historical
understanding of the Arab television industries, and one that is also grounded
in extensive and recent empirical fieldwork. In contrast to previous studies of
Arab television (Boyd, 1999; Rugh, 2004; Sakr, 2007), our book takes a media
industry approach to understanding Arab television as a pan-Arab industry with
many related parts – ownership, financing, production, programming, distribution, audience research, political and socio-cultural impact, all addressing broad
categories of news and entertainment, and all touching upon the tensions
between the national and supra-national domains. The book is organised in such
a way as to give readers a sense of the history, developments and current patterns, providing the specifics necessary to understand the 'big picture' without
unnecessarily dwelling over small details.

Chapter 1, 'A Short History of Arab Television', provides basic facts and analysis about the new commercial environment of the Arab television industries.
Beginning with a broadly historical approach, the chapter describes early industry players based in European cities like London and Rome, and analyses the
conditions that led to their relocation to Arab cities like Dubai, Beirut and Cairo.
We then move on to explain the various dimensions of the paradigm shift from
national development-oriented television to regional, privately owned commercial media. We discuss the decline of national broadcasting, the advent of
commercialisation and the rise of multiplatform conglomerates. We pay sustained attention to Europe as an early Arab media centre, the persistently
national scope of Egyptian television and Iraqi satellite television as a case study
for explosive wartime media change. The European phase illustrates the
transnational character of the Arab television industry since its formative years.
The case of Egypt seeks to explicate why a country with a long and distinguished
media history has not been a leading player in the pan-Arab satellite television
industry. The tragic case of Iraq connects Arab television with global geopolitics
and violence, describing how the 2003 Anglo-American invasion and the ensu-

ing chaos have led to a turbulent and radically pluralistic post-Saddam Hussein television scene.

Chapter 2, 'Pan-Arab Entertainment Channels', focuses on general channels that include entertainment and news, explaining their development, production and programming strategies, and their political backing. These channels have several important characteristics. They are commercially more successful than news channels and though they seek to reach a large pan-Arab audience, they focus on the Saudi market. They are at the vanguard of integrating the Arab media industry into the global media market. In this chapter we focus on the Saudi-owned, Dubai-based, Middle East Broadcasting Centre (MBC), the Lebanese Broadcasting Corporation (LBC-Sat), a privately owned company, and Dubai TV, the official broadcaster of the Emirate of Dubai in the United Arab Emirates (UAE). These three channels cover the gamut of entertainment channels in the new Arab television industry. First launched in London and then moved to Dubai, MBC is an entertainment leader with a Saudi-oriented style. LBC, originally a militia propaganda outlet during Lebanon's 1975–90 Civil War, has emerged as a leader and MBC's more liberal but nonetheless most serious competitor. Dubai TV is a third regional model for entertainment channels, one that is nominally owned by state authorities but institutionally a hybrid private–state channel.

Chapter 3, 'Niche Channels and Socio-cultural Change', follows up on Chapter 2 to discuss how novel programming genres propagated by the newly commercial channels have entered the fray of debate about social and cultural change in the Arab world. Most important among these genres are music videos, women's programming and religious shows. Whereas music videos have triggered debate about the status of women in Arab society and of acceptable sexual behaviour, religious programmes have contributed to making performances of piety part of public discourse. The chapter pays special attention to gender and youth issues, in addition to hybrid genres that have emerged at the intersection of other kinds of programmes. To that end we examine channels focused on religious matters, music and women. Religious channels cover a wide spectrum ranging from puritanical Wahhabi stations run by Saudi Arabia's establishment clerics to more liberal Islamic channels in Egypt. Similarly, music channels span various genres and audiences, from *tarab* – the classical Arab song repertoire – to Arabic pop. Women's channels target an important niche of customers and include cooking, fashion, beauty, travel and child-rearing programmes.

Chapter 4, 'Pan-Arab News Channels', focuses on leading players and relative outliers. While the Qatar-based al-Jazeera is the most well known, there are several influential channels, chief among them al-Arabiya, set up by Saudi interests explicitly to compete with al-Jazeera. The chapter explains the motivations for establishing these channels, covers milestones in their developments and discusses their continuing rivalry, increased coverage of financial news and the audiences they attract. We then move on to consider a radical alternative to mainstream news channels, Hezbollah's al-Manar (The Beacon), and explore the reasons why this channel has emerged as a model for radical groups throughout the Arab world.

Chapter 5, 'Ramadan: Drama, Comedy and Religious Shows in the Arab Sweeps', zeroes in on the high season of Arab television, when channels air their best productions, corporations increase advertising spending, and Muslim Arab viewers break the religiously required daytime fast to watch television into the late hours of the night. As the industry's most important season, the holy month of Ramadan illustrates like no other phenomenon the imbrications of religion, commercialism and television viewing; by making visible links between production, programming and advertising, Ramadan enables us to better understand the interaction between the politico-economic structure of Arab television and various religious, cultural and national sensibilities.

Chapter 6, 'Television Policy and Regulation in the Arab World', discusses the various state policies that shape Arab media, in addition to the global geopolitical context in which Arab television operates. We discuss how in the UAE economic policy developed Dubai Media City, while other countries with weak states, like Lebanon, spawned a *de facto* media zone. Even 'closed regimes' are on board: the Syrian government recently announced the establishment of a media free zone, and several Arab countries have allowed the establishment of privately owned satellite channels on their territory, though with restrictions. At the same time, a variety of foreign players have entered or re-entered the so-called battle for the hearts and minds of Arabs, including the US government's al-Hurra television, Iran's al-'Alam, Russia's Rusya al-Yawm, the UK's BBC Arabic and others. After discussing national media policies in Lebanon, Saudi Arabia, Syria and the UAE, the chapter concludes with a discussion of the Arab Satellite Charter of 2008, which we take to be symptomatic of the emergence of a pan-Arab media policy regime.

Location

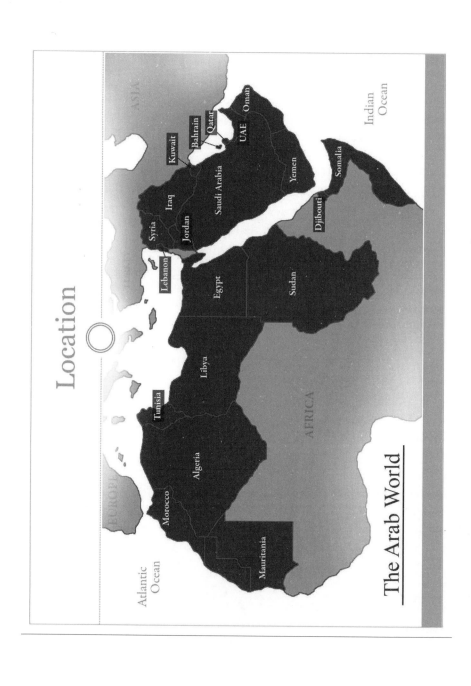

The Arab World

1

A Short History of Arab Television

This chapter describes and explains the historical trajectory of Arab television. It traces major political forces, economic factors and technological developments that have shaped the growth of one of the world's most talked-about regional television industries. The relationship between television institutions and Arab states was from the onset and remains a determining factor shaping Arab television, though increasingly in the new commercial pan-Arab media environment, the role of business has grown to rival the clout of nation-states. The media–state–capital nexus has therefore changed over time: overall, the state's monopolistic power before the 1990s decreased to an important though not-over-determining role in the European phase of Arab television during the first half of the 1990s, to an even smaller role with the advent of Arab media cities, especially Dubai Media City in 2000. These changes have clearly varied by country and region, depending on several factors. In many cases, like those of the Gulf countries, the role of the state in media affairs diminished gradually. In others, like Lebanon during the 1975–90 Civil War and Iraq since 2003, wartime state collapse swiftly gave rise to an anarchic television industry. Surprisingly, such radical ruptures have spawned channels, like the Lebanese Broadcasting Corporation (LBC), that grew from partisan mouthpieces to become leading pan-Arab commercial players. In contrast, in countries like Egypt and Syria, the state remained a paramount actor in media affairs, often to the detriment of national television industries. Egypt's case is especially noteworthy in that regard, as a combination of the state remaining an owner, producer and regulator of television and the interest of Egyptian businessmen who own the few non-state satellite channels in the domestic market, which has prevented the Arab world's historically most productive and influential national television industry from taking a pan-Arab leadership role in the satellite television era.

The following are main questions we begin to address in this chapter:

- What do we mean by 'Arab' television industries?
- How did Arab television industries evolve historically?

- Is there one audience for Arab television or are there rather myriad niche audiences?
- What dynamics between those industries and the states in which they operate shaped institutional development?
- What economic forces impacted the growth and content of Arab media and how?
- What role did technological factors play in the growth of Arab television industries?
- How did all these factors – geopolitical, economic, historical, institutional, cultural – change with the shift in the early 1990s from terrestrial state-owned services to satellite television channels influenced but not directly owned by Arab states?
- What broad institutional growth patterns can be discerned?
- What models of ownership and state–media relationships emerged in the satellite era?

AUDIENCES AND MARKETS

Our analysis focuses on television in the Arabic-speaking countries, two dozen nation-states located in the Levant (Lebanon, Syria etc), the Gulf (Saudi Arabia, Kuwait, etc) and to a lesser degree the Maghreb in North Africa (Algeria, Tunisia, etc). Sharing the Arabic language and with a large proportion of the population adhering to various branches of Islam, the Arab states also have a largely common cultural heritage. Since the early 1990s, these countries have fallen under the umbrella of a single transnational satellite television industry, which has connected them commercially, politically and culturally to a degree that is arguably historically unprecedented. This industry also caters to an audience that is sizeable on a global scale: a 2003 United Nations report estimated the total Arab population at 330 million with an average 80 per cent television penetration (*World Population*, 2003). We have excluded from our analysis countries like Iran, Israel and Turkey, whose languages, Farsi, Hebrew and Turkish, respectively, pre-empt an analytical integration with the pan-Arab television sphere. In some cases, as in post-2003 Iraq where Kurdish channels are important players, we briefly mention minority-language channels in the Arab world. The overwhelming majority of our analysis, however, focuses on Arabic-language television, which also reaches Arabic-speaking communities in the worldwide diaspora via satellite and cable.

Though they share many characteristics, Arab countries and regions exhibit important differences that shape a variety of national and sub-regional media markets. One division is economic, primarily between the wealthy oil monarchies in the Gulf and the other, poorer countries. Gulf societies additionally tend to be more socially conservative than other parts of the Arab world. Another cleavage is between the region's high-density urban areas and scattered rural populations. Another contrast can be found between the demographic heavyweights like Egypt and Saudi Arabia, and small countries like Kuwait, Lebanon and Qatar. Also, a surge in the number of young people, who account for more than 70 per cent of the population (*World Population*, 2003), provides a sharp generational contrast in the audience market. Finally, the rise of religiosity in tandem with the advent of Western-style commercialism is leading to a variety of socio-cultural articulations and disjunctures in Arab societies.

These multiple markers of difference undermine the notion of an Arab mass audience. Though there are a few entertainment (LBC and MBC, see Chapter 2) and news (al-Jazeera and al-Arabiya, see Chapter 4) channels that target a general viewership, a trend towards niche channels specialised in music, youth or women's issues, and religion is solidifying (see Chapter 3). This pattern is exacerbated by the fact that Arab viewers tend to be loyal to individual programmes and not to channels, and by different peak viewing times (primetime) between different countries: for instance, split work shifts lead to primetime viewing during the lunch hour in the Gulf countries and a three-hour time difference between the Maghreb and the Gulf contributes to making them two separate media markets. Weekend primetime varies because the 'weekend' falls on different days in various countries: Thursday and Friday in Algeria, Egypt and Saudi Arabia, Friday and Saturday in the UAE, Saturday and Sunday in Lebanon and Morocco. Diversification is also palatable in the wider scope of Arabic accents typically exhibited on channels, which have expanded from the traditionally dominant Egyptian and Lebanese to include the Khaliji (Gulf) and Syrian accents. Arab television production, which (parallel to the fragmentation of television consumption) has become more specialised, sometimes along national lines, has widened its locus considerably in the last decade. Syria has emerged as a central player in drama production, rivaling Egypt, the former hegemonic force. The Gulf has also seen a timid but perceptible renaissance in local production, with Kuwait and Saudi Arabia producing more drama and comedy in recent years. Lebanon dominates in reality and game shows, and along with Egypt, the Arab music video industry. Some channels in small countries like Jordan, Kuwait and Tunisia, found it less onerous to focus on local markets where they had reliable viewing data attractive to advertisers. More importantly, the television acquisition market is increasingly inter-Arab with less interest in Western programmes (with the exception of some niche and pay-TV channels).

These social, cultural, economic, demographic and creative disparities contribute to shaping Arab television production and markets. One of the main consequences is a strong interdependency between the Arab television industries and the Gulf countries, especially the Saudi Arabian market. For instance, though its population is nearly three times as large as Saudi Arabia's, Egypt lags behind Saudi Arabia as a market for pan-Arab broadcasters because of lower income levels. Additionally, Egyptian television channels broadcast locally produced shows and rarely buy programmes from other Arab producers. In contrast Saudi television, along with the UAE and to a lesser extent other Gulf countries, pays high premiums for acquiring productions. Most importantly, Saudi Arabia is an irresistible television advertising market, combining a large population with high incomes. The country is the largest market in the Gulf estimated at 20 million viewers, 95 per cent of whom watch television at least six times a week, and 23 per cent of whom watch more than four hours of television per day (*Trends in*, 2007). It is no surprise then that the marketing research company MindShare discovered that 80 per cent of Saudi consumers believe that 'television advertising is the most likely medium to influence their buying decision' (Addington, 2005a). As a result, catering to the tastes of Saudi viewers is a priority for the Arab television industries throughout the year, but especially during the holy month of Ramadan when viewership reaches its peak and many channels spend a significant part of their yearly advertising budget (a detailed discussion of the congruence of Ramadan production, programming and advertising can be found in Chapter 5).

Before 1990, the regional advertising market was limited to mostly local consumer items within national television markets. Since the 1990s, the pan-Arab advertising market has expanded with the growth of the media industries. In Gulf Cooperation Council countries (Bahrain, Kuwait, Oman, Qatar, Saudi Arabia, UAE) alone, advertising expenditure rose from US $700 million in 1994 to US $4 billion in 2004 ('GCC Advertising', 2005). Satellite television is perhaps the most important advertising vehicle; in 2006 it captured US $2 billion out of a total regional yearly advertising expenditure of US $5 billion. (The total Arab advertising market grew from US $ 7.7 in 2007 to US $9.9 billion in 2008, a 24 per cent increase) (Hamadeh, 2008). The biggest spenders include both local and global companies, primarily 'fast-moving consumer products' (FMCG), telecommunications and real estate. However, as we explain in detail in Chapter 5, the study of the Arab television market is complicated by a lack of transparency and reliable sources of data.

THE BEGINNINGS OF ARAB NATIONAL TELEVISION

As Arab countries began gaining independence from colonial powers, setting up broadcasting systems was an important symbol of independence and a crucial instrument of nation-building. Broadcasts were privately generated in Morocco as early as March 1954 (a national channel went on air in 1962), and the first state-owned national service opened in Baghdad in 1956 (Boyd, 1999). In the same year, there were French-controlled broadcasts in Algeria (but a state channel was established in 1962). Lebanon followed suit in 1959, after an agreement between a private firm and the state (Kraidy, 1998b). Most other Arab states launched national television channels during the 1960s and 1970s. The Lebanese Civil War spawned dozens of unlicensed television channels in the 1980s (Kraidy, 1998b), which provided a training ground for numerous media workers that later became an important factor in the growth of Arab channels in Europe and the Arab world. The most important of these channels was LBC, which will be discussed in depth in Chapter 2. The last official Arab television service to be launched was in 1994 under the supervision of the Palestinian Authority. Arab state-owned television services on the whole were primarily concerned with forging a national identity, fostering socio-economic development, and serving as mouthpieces for Arab regimes. Table 1.1 below provides details about national television systems.

An authoritarian model characterised most national Arab television systems. Iraq, an Arab television pioneer, represented an extreme version of this model

Table 1.1 Arab National Television Systems (Selected)

Country	Launch year	Original name	Current name
Iraq	1956	Iraq TV	Al-Iraqiya
Lebanon	1959	Compagnie Libanaise de Télévision (CLT)	Télé-Liban
Egypt	1960	Television of the Arab Republic of Egypt	Al-'Ula
Syria	1960	Syrian TV	Syria
Kuwait	1961	Kuwait TV	Kuwait TV 1
Algeria	1962	Entreprise Nationale de Télévision (ENTV)	Canal Algérie
Morocco	1962	Télévision Marocaine	Al-Oula
Saudi Arabia	1965	Saudi TV	Saudi TV 1
Tunisia	1966	Tunis TV	Tunis 7
Libya	1968	Al-Jamahiriya	Al-Jamahiriya
Jordan	1968	Jordan TV	Jordan TV
UAE	1969	Emirates TV	Emirates TV
Qatar	1970	Qatar TV	Qatar TV
Bahrain	1973	Bahrain TV	BTV
Oman	1974	Oman TV	Oman TV
Palestine	1994	Palestine TV	Palestine TV

of Arab television. In 1956, Iraq TV was one of the first national channels in the Arab world, along with television in Lebanon and Morocco. In the ensuing decade, Iraqi television flourished under monarchical rule, but Iraqis' appetite for information and entertainment (as reflected in the Arab saying that 'what is written in Cairo is printed in Beirut and read in Baghdad') was frustrated when the Baath party took control in 1968. At that time, the Ministry of Information, led by loyal regime appointees, quickly gained control over the media through intimidation, repression and the expulsion of journalists. As the authoritarian regime grew increasingly totalitarian, media policy focused on eliminating dissenting voices while mobilising support for the ruler, and educational institutions were training journalists in using Soviet propaganda methods. By the time Saddam Hussein came to power, Iraq's national television had become a full-fledged propaganda tool for the regime. Starting in 1979, under Hussein's rule, the arts, theatre, radio and television were lavishly funded, but tightly controlled, with authoritarian media and cultural policies becoming increasingly totalitarian (Cazes, 2003). Entertainment was explicitly patriotic, praised the regime and glorified its leader. State-owned Iraq TV maintained a monopoly over broadcasting while the government banned satellite dishes and security agents censored news and entertainment.

In line with his self-proclaimed interest in sitting atop his own media empire, Uday Hussein, Saddam's eldest son, became pre-2003 Iraq's single media mogul, establishing his own semi-official media empire. This included, in addition to a radio station and a newspaper, a television channel, Shabab TV (translation: Youth TV). To gain a wide audience among young Iraqis, Shabab TV had slicker production values and featured more cosmopolitan programmes than Iraq TV. Shabab's programming fare consisted of pirated American and French movies, television serials and news. Yet however polished it was on the surface, the channel often resorted to crude didacticism. Movies were often interrupted arbitrarily to broadcast messages or commentaries purporting to analyse the ideological indoctrination coming out of Hollywood. The channel was also an unabashed propaganda outlet for the dictator's son: it scheduled Uday's speeches between, and sometimes even during popular programmes. Uday Hussein established an extremely centralised media structure that gave him an elevated level of control nationally over even local channels: for example, a programme shot and produced in the southern city of Basra would be sent by plane to Baghdad for clearance by Uday or his proxies, and only then would the tape be sent back to Basra for broadcast. Criticism of the regime, even of the mildest sort, was strictly prohibited. Local channels like Basra's television station rarely showed Western films or television series, perhaps in keeping with Shabab TV's monopoly on such international fare. This totalitarian model in which television was centrally controlled and dedicated to the leader's personality cult, we shall see later in this chapter, created conditions that led to an anarchic television landscape when the Anglo-American invasion of Iraq deposed Saddam Hussein and terminated his regime.

If Iraq witnessed the earliest Arab television broadcasts, Egypt developed the most extensive national television system in the Arab world, one that in hindsight dramatically showcases the promises and pitfalls of national television. Building on its radio and film sectors, Egypt launched its national television operation in 1960. Initially there were three services. The first, called the Main Programme, was a mixed format including news, entertainment and educational programmes. The Second Programme carried high-culture content and catered to the Egyptian elite. The Third Programme was directed at the expatriate community in Egypt (Boyd, 1999). During the early years of Egyptian television, Egyptian President and pan-Arab leader Gamal 'Abdelnasser (hereafter referred to as Nasser) utilised television indirectly as a tool of mass mobilisation, televising political events rather than staging political events for television. During the 1967 war with Israel, Egyptian television lost credibility because of its propagandistic coverage. After Egypt's devastating defeat by Israel in the 1967 war, Nasser took responsibility for the defeat and alluded to resigning from the presidency in a speech tailored for the media. After the 1967 war, foreign television programmes greatly diminished and the Third Programme was eliminated altogether. Egyptian television went through years of decline until television drama sales to Arab countries brought in funds and enabled technical upgrades. Its coverage of the 1973 war with Israel was better than its 1967 performance. As Egypt severed its ties with the Soviet Union and completed its *rapprochement* with the West in ensuing years, Western programmes and business activity returned. Egyptian television drama sales to the Arab world increased courtesy of rising oil prices, and the first colour studio became operational in 1974.

Egyptian television, like equivalent services in the developing world before the 1980s, was considered to be primarily a builder of national identity and promoter of national development (al-Bakri, 1999). All broadcasting activities were centralised under the monopoly control of the Egyptian Radio and Television Union (ERTU), under the strict supervision of the Ministry of Information. Television, wrote Abu-Lughod (2005), remains 'a key institution for the production of national culture in Egypt' (p. 7). More than some other Arab countries, Egyptian television from the beginning followed a didactic state-owned development model, focused on national development through the education of citizens. This meant a focus on the state's declared priorities, which over the years have ranged from health and agricultural campaigns in its early history to a dedication to fighting terrorism since the 1980s.

The building of ERTU across the Nile

The country's broadcasting infrastructure clearly reflects the state's widespread dominance over society. The Egyptian Radio and Television Union, whose director reports to the Minister of Information, who in turn reports to the President, enjoys monopoly status over all broadcasting activities in Egypt, by virtue of Law No 13 (1979) and Law No 223 (1989). Into the late 1990s, under both President Hosni Mubarak and long-time Minister of Information Safwat al-Sharif, private ownership of television channels was banned. This was part of the regime's strategy to deny broadcasting resources to non-state actors, including political parties, as reflected in the struggle of opposition political parties such as al-Wafd for adequate media representation. The state denied them licences to launch their private channels in March 1995, and at the same time restricted their access to state-owned channels (Guaaybess, 2005).

Recent developments in Egyptian television are best understood through the prism of the state's economic liberalisation rather than through any meaningful political reform. As Egypt initiated *infitah* (economic opening) policies in the 1970s and accelerated them in the 1990s, a strategy of development realism shifted to one of 'capitalist realism' (Abu-Lughod, 2005). As a result, television advertising began promoting conspicuous consumption rather than socio-economic development and national unity. After several decades during which Egyptian viewers were educated as citizens, they are now being 'trained' as consumers of the commodities that Egypt's opening brought to a largely urban middle class. The concomitant rise of Islamism in recent years has created new challenges for broadcasters who have to consider the extent to which religious content hurts or helps the bottom line (Otterman, 2007). As we will see in Chapter 3, religious channels now constitute a vibrant niche in the Arab television industries.

As a prominent national broadcaster, Egypt also played a key role in the establishment of pan-Arab organisations concerned with television. In 1969, the Arab States Broadcasting Union (ASBU) was launched from Cairo, to institutionalise exchanges in technical and production training among Arab states. But ASBU also reflected Egypt's centrality in the affairs of Arab television in a context of rivalry for pan-Arab leadership between Egypt and Saudi Arabia, two countries that fought a proxy war in Yemen in the 1960s. The Saudis, who did not join ASBU until 1974, retaliated by taking the lead in the establishment of the Arab Satellite Organization (ARABSAT) in 1976, to facilitate the exchange of television programmes between countries (Boyd, 1999; Kraidy, 2002). ARABSAT was conceived for Arab states to share infrastructure and technical know-how, and ASBU to exchange creative expertise and television programmes. Designed as Arab *inter-national* organisations to facilitate exchanges between states, ARABSAT and ASBU instead enabled the establishment of the technical infrastructure for a *trans-national* satellite television industry that consists mostly of privately owned media corporations.

The Egyptian Satellite Channel (ESC), launched on 12 December 1990, was the first Arab national satcaster, with the primary objective of reaching Egyptian troops deployed in Iraq in the Gulf War and countering Iraqi government propaganda aimed at Arab soldiers in the American-led alliance. During the

ARABSAT logo

1990s, the Egyptian satellite television industry was fully owned and operated by the state's media bureaucracy. In 1998, Egypt launched its own satellite, NILESAT, to gain a measure of autonomy from the Saudi-controlled ARABSAT (and from the League of Arab States, the body officially in charge of ARABSAT, whose members boycotted Egypt for making a separate peace deal with Israel at Camp David). With abundant transmission space made available by NILESAT, in 1998 Egyptian authorities launched six Nile Thematic Channels – News, Sport, Drama, Culture, Family & Children and Variety (Yussef, 1997; Sha'ban, 1998). There was also Nile TV, parts of whose schedule are in English and French, a new expression of the defunct Third Programme from the pre-satellite era. The excess transmission capacity reduced the cost of leasing transponders and stimulated the entrance of new players to the satellite market.

These developments notwithstanding, Egypt's role in the pan-Arab satellite television revolution has to date been underwhelming when one considers Egypt's massive national television sector. The primary reason for the inability of Egyptian television to navigate successfully the transition from the age of national broadcasting, which it dominated, to the age of transnational satellite television in which it is a second-rate player, is the fact that the Egyptian state retained a major role in the television industry. In the last decade, however, change has set in, slowly and gradually. In 2001, after the resignation of Safwat al-Sharif, Egypt's long-standing Minister of Information and a staunch opponent of private television, powerful businessman Ahmad Bahgat established Dream TV as the first privately owned channel. The emergence of privately owned channels spawned less cautious, more controversial kinds of programming featuring emboldened talk-show hosts, like famed interviewer Hala Serhan, who after a successful but polemical tenure was sacked by Dream TV's management; or Hiba Qutb, the veiled psychologist who hosts the sex talk show *Kalam Kabir* on al-Mehwar TV, in which she dispenses sexual advice using explicit terms and a direct style of address. These, along with recriminations and soul-searching in the Egyptian drama industry provoked by the rise of Syrian drama as a serious competitor in pan-Arab sales, popularity and critical acclaim, suggest that Egyptian television stands at the cusp of more significant changes, but it is far from certain that the sector will shake off the state's heavy hand and television's heavily national focus in the near future. This is especially the case with Egyptian newscasts, which have limited appeal beyond the country's borders because they are correctly perceived to be a direct expression of government policy (relatedly, see the discussion of the Arab Satellite Television Charter in Chapter 6).

While the Egyptian state remained committed to a model of direct state ownership and operation, other Arab countries, most prominently Saudi Arabia, calculated that they could indirectly project influence over television institutions. Shortly after the launch of the Egyptian Satellite Channel, the Middle East Broadcasting Centre (MBC) initiated satcasting to the Arab world from London. In ensuing years, several privately owned Arab satellite channels were established in Europe: after MBC, Arab Radio and Television (ART) began transmission in 1993, followed by Orbit in 1994 and Showtime Arabia in 1996, all from Italy. These are considered 'Arab' channels because they were owned by Saudi (or other Arab) businesses and featured Arabic-language programmes targeting Arabic-speaking viewers in Arab countries. What is peculiar about these institutions is their location which prompts the following questions:

• Why did these institutions launch their operations in Europe?
• What were the benefits and obstacles arising from this 'offshore' location?
• And what developments led these channels to eventually return to the Arab world?

ARAB 'OFFSHORE' TELEVISION: THE EUROPEAN PHASE
Europe offered an attractive site to establish pan-Arab satellite channels for economic, political and logistical considerations. By the early 1990s, Europe had experienced several years of economic liberalisation and its media and telecommunications systems were witnessing radical changes (Terzis, 2007). The United Kingdom, in particular, had enduring relations with Saudi Arabia and the Gulf states. With its status as a global city, London was an attractive hub from which to launch media ventures. It provided an atmosphere of editorial and creative freedom that was not to be found anywhere in the Arab world. In addition to business and political considerations, Europe was geographically proximate to the Arab world (in comparison to North America) and had attractive logistics and human resources. It is for these reasons that the early to mid-1990s witnessed the establishment of Arabic satellite channels in London and also in Italy: MBC, Orbit, ART, LBC and Showtime Arabia, among others. European Union Euro–Arab Affairs Secretary Jean-Michel Dumont commented on these channels, saying, '[T]hey are privately operated with Arab capital, mainly Saudi, besides being outside of the Arab world. Hence they are offshore Arab television stations, which undoubtedly allow them some independence' ('Arabs Should', 1998). Thus the designation 'offshore' media was adopted to describe Arab television channels based in Europe.

The European phase of Arab satellite television during the 1990s reflected a Saudi model of privately owned but government-friendly satellite channels, based on a convergence of the business interests of Saudi moguls connected to the Saudi royal family on the one hand, and the political agenda of Saudi rulers

on the other hand. After the end of the Gulf War in 1991, a group of businessmen led by Walid al-Ibrahim, a young (in his mid-twenties at the time)
brother-in-law of the late King Fahd, launched the Middle East Broadcasting
Centre (MBC). In order to circumvent antagonism from religious conservatives
who had opposed television on Saudi soil since the 1960s, Saudi authorities did
not object to the establishment of 'offshore' satellite channels. On 18 September 1991, MBC started its satellite broadcasting to the Arab world from London,
gradually expanding to reach Arabic speakers in Europe, Asia, Africa and America, in addition to cable distribution in London and some cities in the United
States. The technical capacities and business stability of London enabled MBC
to make expansion plans: as early as 1994, MBC was planning to expand into a
multichannel network, beginning with a pay-TV package, called MBC1,
designed to run in tandem with the existing MBC service ('MBC to Launch',
1993).

MBC involved other Saudi moguls who later invested in more television ventures. Sheikh Saleh Kamel, owner of the Saudi Dallah al-Baraka conglomerate
whose companies, including Arab Media Corporation (AMC), focus on investments compliant with Islamic law, partnered with the Saudi Prince and fellow
business tycoon al-Waleed bin Talal to launch Arab Radio and Television (ART)
as a pay-TV subsidiary of AMC. ART began satcasting to its subscribers in 1993
in Arabic first from Fucino and later from Avezzano, Italy. Though transmission

MBC Group at Dubai Media City

was based in Italy, production occurred in Cairo, Beirut and Jeddah. In April 1994, another son-in-law of then-Saudi King Fahd bin Abdulaziz, Prince Khaled bin Abdullah bin Abdulrahman, owner of the al-Mawarid Group, launched Orbit on ARABSAT from Tor Sapienza, Italy. At the time, it was 'the first commercial satellite service to use a digital video compression network, enabling it to offer up to 25 channels' (Clark and Palmer, 1994). Orbit's initial objective was to bring Western entertainment to the Arab world, but the company soon decided to expand into news. In 1995, Orbit entered in agreement with the BBC to provide Arabic-language newscasts for ten years (Boehm, 1996). Bankrolled at US $35 million per annum, the contract came under pressure when London-based Saudi dissidents sent faxes to BBC-Arabic shows, and was terminated after the BBC rebroadcast what Orbit's Saudi funders considered a 'racist' episode of *Panorama* aired on 4 April 1996. Called 'Death of a Principle', the programme was critical of Saudi Arabia's record on human rights. In a statement, Orbit revealed that '[T]he BBC's contractual agreement [...] requires them to take account of local sensitivities. This they did not do' ('Orbit Satellite', 1996). Thus the upsetting of Saudi sensitivities dealt a fatal blow to the BBC Arabic contract.

Table 1.2 Europe-Based Arab Satellite Television Channels

Channel	Year and city launched	Year and city relocated	Founding ownership/ Founding chairman	Nationality
MBC	1991 London	2001 Dubai (UAE)	ARA Group International (AGI) and Dallah el Baraka Walid al-Ibrahim	Saudi
ART	1993 Rome	2002 Amman (Jordan)	Dallah Albraka Group 70% Prince al-Waleed bin Talal 30% Sheikh Saleh Kamel	Saudi
Orbit	1994 Rome	2005 Manama (Bahrain)	Al-Mawarid Group 100% Prince Khaled bin Abdullah	Saudi
LBC-Sat	1996 Rome–Beirut	1996 Adma (Lebanon)	LBC International 51% Kingdom Holding Company 49% Pierre el-Daher	Lebanese/ Saudi
Showtime Arabia	1996 London	2004 Dubai (UAE)	KIPCO 80% Viacom Inc. 20% John Tydeman (1996)	Kuwaiti/US
ANN	1997 London	London	Family of Rif 'at al-Asad Sawmar al-Asad	Syrian
Khalifa TV	2002 Paris–London	Channel dissolved in 2003	Khalifa Group	Algerian

Not all the European-based Arab channels were Saudi-owned. In June 1996, a Kuwaiti–American joint venture launched Showtime Arabia from London. The new channel was a subsidiary of Gulf DTH, a media company based in the UAE, 80 per cent owned by Kuwait Projects Company (KIPCO), and 20 per cent by the US Viacom Inc. ('Leading Middle East', 2004). What is significant about Showtime Arabia is that it heralded the introduction of a global media player (Viacom) into the Arab media market. Showtime also entered into one of the very first alliances between Arab television channels (the other being the LBC–ART joint venture). KIPCO stated that it realised the potential of digital pay-TV but 'had to find the right partner who could provide top quality programming and movie content to complement [their] regional knowledge and infrastructure' ('KIPCO Chief', 2000). Showtime Arabia and ART collaborated to offer bundled multichannel packages using encrypted satellite signals; the two channels complemented each other, as Showtime provided English-language programmes while ART offered Arabic-language content.

A European base of transmission was also instrumental to the success of Lebanon's first private television company, the Lebanese Broadcasting Corporation. In early 1996, LBC issued shares worth US $50 million to finance the launching of a satellite channel consisting of 'three separate but affiliated companies: one for acquisitions, a production firm and a dubbing company' ('Lebanon Satellite', 1996). By purchasing the bulk of these shares, Arab Radio and Television's (ART) Sheikh Saleh Kamel became a major investor in LBC, and provided the Lebanese channel with the capacity to go on satellite from ART's base in Italy. On 29 March, the caption al-Fada'iya al-Lubnaniya (The Lebanese Satellite Channel) appeared on the screen under the LBC logo on a test signal made possible through ART's arrangement with ARABSAT. LBC's satellite channel was officially launched in April 1996, transmitting from Italy tapes recorded in Lebanon, and went on to become one of the two top entertainment channels in the Arab world, a story we tell in full in Chapter 2. There were other smaller European-based channels, like the London-based Arab News Network (ANN), owned by the estranged cousin of Syrian President Bashar al-Asad, al-Mustaqilla, a dissident Tunisian channel, and Khalifa TV, owned by an Algerian tycoon, which moved to London after a brief stint in Paris. Clearly, while offering a framework for the development of institutions that would develop into top pan-Arab channels, Europe also served as a playground for less consequential media owners.

ARAB SATELLITE TELEVISION RETURNS HOME AND GROWS EXPONENTIALLY

By the late 1990s, officials at European-based Arab channels began considering moving their headquarters to the Arab world. In addition to the clashes between Saudi political practices and British journalistic norms, their calculations were based on the high cost of operating in London and Rome, the need to be geographically closer to the Arab audience and culturally more authentic, and the development of media free zones in the Arab world which offered attractive *Dubai* logistical and editorial conditions. Both human resources and facilities have a high cost in London, which forced companies like MBC to restructure its staff in 1998, and to relocate to Dubai Media City in 2002, with the objective of cutting 'production costs and boosting efficiency after 10 years in London' ('Arab World's', 2001). In fact, leaving London helped MBC cut overall cost by 30 per cent ('MBC Opens', 2002). Similarly, ART faced challenges from the Italian labour union syndicate, which accused the network of violating the country's labour rules (Ghorab, 1994). After eight years in Italy, ART's owner Saleh Kamel, who believed that 'there is a Western media campaign to undermine [their] Arab culture and traditions' (Ambah, 1995a) ('Divine Inspiration', 1997), was happy to return to the Arab world. In 2002, ART relocated to Jordan Media City, strategically located next to Jordan's Radio and Television *Jordan* building in Amman, at an initial cost of US $8 million paid by the Arab Media Holding Company in an agreement with the Jordanian government ('Sixteen Satellite', 2004).

In 1999, Orbit's then-President and Chief Executive Officer Alexander Zilo boasted that their 'target audience is the entire Arab population in the Middle East, North Africa and Europe' (Abuljadayel, 1999), which motivated them to move to the Arab world to be closer to their viewers. Orbit relocated its headquarters to Bahrain in 2005 and increased its presence regionally with offices and studios in several Arab capitals. In 2004 Showtime Arabia had transferred its equipment and a full-time staff of 500 to Dubai Media City, justifying its move as 'a reflection on the company's desire to identify more strongly with the multi-cultural, cosmopolitan subscriber base' ('Showtime Fully', 2004).

The European phase of Arabic satellite television was prompted by the Gulf War and the development of satellite technology, and it was smothered by a combination of geographic, political and economic factors, to which we must add the events of 11 September 2001 and the resulting climate of tension between Arabs and Westerners which led to a reversal in calculations about the best locations for Arab television industries. While many of the decisions to relocate to the Arab world were taken in early 2001, the events of 11 September accelerated the momentum. At the same time, the geopolitical conflagrations triggered by 9/11 would shape the development of Arab television for the coming decade. Rather than stifling growth, however, these events contributed to the development of a vibrant transnational television industry. Indeed, even before many of

Master control room for ART
at Jordan Media City

the European-based channels returned to the Arab world, some indigenous
channels were briskly establishing themselves as key players from their Arab
location. The year 1996 was momentous in that regard, because it saw the
launch of al-Jazeera from Qatar and the initiation of satellite broadcasts from
Lebanon by LBC (effectively the launch of LBC-Sat). These channels revolutionised how the Arab television industries produced and programmed news (in
the case of al-Jazeera) and entertainment (in the case of LBC-Sat and also
Future TV). The repatriation of leading channels from Europe, coupled with the
dynamism of the indigenous channels, had a multiplier effect, giving momentum to what some analysts have dubbed the Arab media revolution. News
channels like al-Jazeera pushed entertainment channels like MBC to give more
attention to news and later compelled the creation of counterweights like al-
Arabiya. Most of the top channels, which will receive detailed treatment in
subsequent chapters (MBC and LBC in Chapter 2; al-Jazeera and al-Arabiya in
Chapter 4), were not strictly speaking government-owned, but were in the hands
of owners with connections to political power.

The growth of a dynamic commercial industry, nevertheless, did not termi-
nate government-owned television. Eager to a have a voice in the nascent
transnational media landscape, several Arab governments launched their own
satellite services, including Libya TV, Yemen TV, Jordan TV and Syria TV. Currently, all Arab governments have a satellite channel or broadcast their terrestrial
television services via satellite. However, compared to the commercial channels,
most of the government satcasters have low production values and small audiences. Some of the rich countries like Qatar and Saudi Arabia can launch
ambitious satellite channels with pan-Arab appeal while poorer countries like
Sudan or Yemen cannot afford significant satellite investments (Guaaybess,
2005, p. 245). Government involvement in satellite broadcasting has certainly
varied in Arab countries. In the case of Egypt, the state retains an impressive
level of control of television production, distribution and broadcasting in the

country. The Jordanian and Syrian governments have allowed, in principle, private ownership of satellite channels, but in practice have hindered their development. In the UAE, local, i.e. Emirate-level channels (such as Abu Dhabi TV and Dubai TV) remain technically in the hands of local governments, but are in fact managed by other Arabs. These people are officially designated as 'consultants' in spite of the fact that they are in charge, more or less permanently, of management, production and programming (Dubai TV is discussed in Chapter 2 as an embodiment of a peculiar government–private hybrid television model). Overall, throughout the Arab world governments have been relinquishing full control over television, but very incrementally – with one notable exception: in sharp contrast to this gradualism, Iraq has since 2003 witnessed the anarchic growth of a radically diverse television landscape. As an outlier in the development of Arab television industries, Iraq deserves further attention.

VOICES OF BABEL: IRAQI TELEVISION AFTER 2003

Iraq was by all criteria a late-joiner in the Arab satellite television boom of the 1990s. It was only in 1999 that Iraqis gained access to satellite television after the Iraqi Ministry of Information initiated a tightly controlled plan to make that possible. The two-stage plan involved scheduling twenty-four channels including eight local channels dedicated to local languages, education and other specialities. The channels could be received using a locally produced 'box' and a monthly subscription ('Dr Abd al-Halim', 1999). On the eve of the 2003 war, Iraqis had access to five newspapers, one state television and radio station, and Uday Hussein's Shabab Television. State control of television production, distribution and consumption was absolute.

The war ended the state's television monopoly. Channels of rival Kurdish political groups (Jalal Talibani's Kurd Sat and Mas'ud Barazani's Kurdistan TV) had existed since 2000 in the Kurdish-ruled, Western-protected (since 1991) autonomous region in northern Iraq. These channels were broadcasting in various languages including Kurdish, Arabic and English. The Ministry of Information was one of the first targets to be hit during the 2003 invasion, and looters took equipment and files before torching it ('Saddam's Sacked,' 2003). Its staff of just under 7,000 – translators of articles about Iraq in the foreign press, state media censors and monitors of Iraqi journalists, writers and poets – was reduced to fewer than 2,000; then on 23 May 2003, Paul Bremer, the US civil administrator for Iraq, abolished the Ministry (McCarthy, 2003). It is against this backdrop that the post-Saddam television era began to take shape, with al-Iraqiya launched by the new government in 2003. In the next couple of years, many channels went on air, including new Kurdish-owned outlets satcasting in Arabic.

The collapse of state media pushed Iraqis towards proliferating privately owned channels (by 2006 there were approximately sixty Iraqi channels) ('Measuring Security', 2006). Broadcasting terrestrially or via satellite, based in Iraq or abroad, these channels provide a stunningly diverse spectrum of political, religious or social views. The names of these channels reveal their ideological

Table 1.3. Iraqi Television Channels

Channel	Year	Owner	Ideological/Sectarian affiliation	Language
Kurd Sat	2000	Jalal Talibani	Kurdish – Patriotic Union of Kurdistan	Kurdish
Kurdistan Sat	2000	Mas'ud Barazani	Kurdish – Kurdistan Democratic Party	Kurdish/ English
Al-Iraqiya	2003	Iraqi Media Network	Government – Shi'i dominated	Arabic
Al-Hurriya TV	2003	Jalal Talibani	Kurdish – Patriotic Union of Kurdistan	Arabic
Al-Sumariya	2004	Iraqi and Lebanese businessmen	Independent	Arabic
Al-Sharqiya	2004	Saad al-Bazzaz	Sunni-Nationalist	Arabic
Al-Nahrayn	2004	Supreme Council for the Islamic Revolution in Iraq	Shi'i – Sayyed 'Abdulaziz al-Hakim	Arabic
Al-Furat	2004	Supreme Council for the Islamic Revolution in Iraq	Shi'i – Sayyed 'Adbulaziz al-Hakim	Arabic
Ad-Diyar	2004	Faisal al-Yasiri	Sunni focusing on entertainment	Arabic
Ishtar TV	2005	Assyrian businessmen and associations	Assyrian Christian – affiliated with Kurdistan Democratic Party	Assyrian/ Arabic/ Kurdish
Al-Fayha'	2005	Mohammed al-Ta'ee and businessmen	Shi'i (Basra)	Arabic
Zagros TV	2005	Mas'ud Barazani	Kurdish – Kurdistan Democratic Party	Kurdish
Al-Zawra'	2007	Mesh'aan al-Juburi	Sunni/Islamist/ Jihadi – Kirkuk's Sunni Arab council	Arabic

stance, religious affiliation and intended audience: there were regional (i.e. sub-national) channels like al-Sumariya (The Sumari One) and al-Sharqiya (The Eastern One); nationalist outlets like al-Iraqiya (The Iraqi One), al-Nahrayn (The Two Rivers), Biladi (My Country), ad-Diyar (The Homes); sectarian like al-Fayha', al-Zawra' and Ishtar TV (see Table 1.3). Additions to this Iraqi mix include al Hurra-Iraq, funded by the US Congress, and al-'Alam, Iran's Arabic-language satellite channel focused on covering Iraqi issues.

The first US-led effort to establish television broadcasting aimed at Iraqis was through a joint military–civilian operation dubbed Commander Solo. Awkwardly housed in a C-13 military cargo plane, this five-hour daily broadcast included news compiled by a team of expatriate Arab journalists and material from US networks like ABC, NBC, CBS, Fox and PBS (CNN refused to participate, arguing that it was not appropriate for a worldwide news organisation to be associated with the US government) (Chaddock, 2003). This operation was more of an afterthought than part of a strategic plan that foresaw the need to re-establish the Iraqi media; in fact, the Broadcasting Board of Governors, in charge of this operation, was itself instructed to provide the content days after the fall of Baghdad (Chinni, 2003). A number of explicitly ideological shows aired including *Towards Freedom*, a programme produced by World Television on behalf of the British government which included news, a press review and propaganda messages from the Foreign Office (Byrne, 2003). The ultimate purpose of these broadcasts was strategic – 'to counter the negative images being broadcast right now [particularly from al-Jazeera], the incitement to violence, the hate radio, the journalistic self-censorship' (Burkeman, 2003).

The first effort to actually replace Iraq's state television came through the establishment of the Iraqi Media Network (IMN) and its television channel al-Iraqiya. However, this effort was hindered by political intimidation, censorship and corruption. This television station was conceived by the Provisional Authority as a means of communicating with the Iraqis while ultimately wanting to become a PBS-style broadcaster. These irreconcilable missions – propaganda and public service – came to a head at various instances particularly during Bremer's tenure (Gourevitch, 2003). In addition, the notion of public service was anathema to the extreme market-friendly ideology embraced by Bremer and other US political appointees in Baghdad. Once transferred to the Iraqi government, the IMN mirrored the intricate balance of power within a polarised and unstable wartime government. The establishment and management of IMN were also subject to various accusations of corruption. The building of the IMN involved a radio and television network and a newspaper. The American company, Science Application International Corporation (SAIC) was awarded the initial contract for US $108 million, but was unable to finish the work. Harris Corporation took over with a US $96 million contract, in which Harris partnered with the Lebanese Broadcasting Corporation for training and content provision of both radio and television stations (al-Mesmar, 2004; Jaafar, 2005)

Beginning to broadcast on 13 May 2004, al-Iraqiya was initially a mouthpiece for the Coalition Provisional Authority (CPA). Leading up to the January 2005 election, al-Iraqiya moved from the CPA's orbit to come under the influence of Iyad Allawi, a secular Shi'i politician. The nightly fare offered by al-Iraqiya features documentaries on reconstruction efforts, coverage of anti-terrorist activities (some of which is carried live), shows involving interrogation videos with criminals at police headquarters and some LBC-produced entertainment shows. Overall, its coverage of the conflict in the country toes the government's line, which is set by the Prime Minister, who hails from the Shi'i community. Fallen officers from the country's security forces are called 'martyrs', US-led coalition soldiers are called 'multi-national forces' while insurgents are labelled 'terrorists'. Entertainment programmes, including music videos, reflect the channel's overall nationalist ethos. Talk shows host government officials, discuss corruption and reflect people's wartime socio-economic concerns (al-Marashi, 2007).

Operating as a business entity, al-Sharqiya (The Eastern One) broadcasts on satellite and terrestrial from both Baghdad and Dubai. This US $30 million family-owned media holding company is chaired by Saad al-Bazzaz, who launched the channel on 11 June 2004 (al-Bazzaz, a one-time editor of a Baath party paper and an Iraqi diplomat who went into exile, is an aspiring politician). Al-Sharqiya's programming formula consists of three ingredients: drama series, reality shows and news, the latter with a strong nationalist bent. This channel's programming grid is clearly tuned to the pulse of a war-traumatised Iraqi population. With a blend of sketch comedy and dark humour, the show *Caricature* focuses on the daily lives of Iraqis pointing to specific flaws in the conduct of the government, the coalition forces or the insurgents. The team of the show paid a heavy price that came in the murder of one of its actors, Walid Hassan; as a result, actors and crew relocated to Dubai. Focused on community assistance, reality shows like *Labour and Materials* took ABC's *Extreme Makeover: Home Edition* into a different realm. Instead of kitchens, living rooms or bedrooms, the show helps rebuild war-destroyed houses. Using reality-television techniques of handheld cameras and patched editing, *Health and Wealth* is another copycat show for newlyweds. Using sponsorships and advertising, the show covers the wedding expenses of young Iraqi couples. Other similar shows, clearly inspired by wartime privation and insecurity, included *al-Bitaqa al-Tamwiniya* (Food Card/Stamp), *Futurqun 'Alayna* (Your Breakfast Is on Us), *al-Bayt Baytak* (The House Is Yours). The nationalistic policy of the channel goes beyond banning imported films, the exclusive running of Iraqi productions and the absence of religious programming or sermons. Al-Sharqiya's political line is in contrast with that of the state television: for instance, Saddam Hussein is not described as a 'tyrant' but as 'the President' and on the day he was executed, al-Sharqiya's news anchors wore black (mourning) clothes. Predictably, the Iraqi government closed al-Sharqiya's Baghdad office. Another successful business operation is al-Sumariya which claims to be 'the first terrestrial digital network in the region' ('Alsumaria TV', 2007). Available on NILESAT since September 2004, the channel operates across the Arab world primarily in Iraq and Lebanon but also in Jordan and the UAE. Combining Arab and Iraqi productions, the channel provides entertainment, politics and cultural programmes hosted by Iraqis.

The appearance of sectarian-motivated media is a new, post-2003 phenomenon in Iraq. Sectarian channels reflected political changes in a country in which the collapse of totalitarian one-party rule and its centralised television service results in an explosion of narrowly based media outlets representing myriad on-the-ground factions. Channels like al-Fayha' and the pro-insurgency al-Zawra' are examples of politically financed, ideological and/or religious channels whose employees convey the owner's outlook to a targeted audience. For example, al-Fayha' was established by Mohammed al-Ta'ee, an Iraqi migrant journalist. At a cost of US $3 million per year, al-Fayha' is supposedly financed by a group of independent Iraqi businessmen joined by 'their love for Iraq and having suffered from a bad past and from a worse political present' (al-Sarraf and Jasem, 2005). Originally broadcasting from Dubai, al-Fayha' resumed its broadcasts from the Iraqi city of Basra, a Shi'i stronghold. It is not unusual for a sectarian entity like the Iran-backed Supreme Council for the Islamic Revolution in Iraq to support more than one channel to air its views: Najaf-based al-Furat (the Euphrates) and Basra-based al-Fayha'.

Al-Zawra' channel stirred a number of controversies within and outside of Iraq. The channel is infamous in the West for broadcasting insurgency activities and acting as a forum for various groups claiming attacks on US and Iraqi forces. Using the approach of Jihadi websites, al-Zawra' produces programmes like *Juba: Baghdad Sniper*, which compiles various reality-type videos shot with cheap cameras or mobile phones, showing insurgent sniper activities. These videos are edited adding chants, graphics, slow-motion, replays and behind-the-scene activities; they are then relayed to Cairo where they are repackaged and played on NILESAT (Pintak, 2007a). The Bush administration in 2007 asked Egyptian authorities to block the channel's access to NILESAT but al-Zawra' carried on using European satellite broadcasters to satcast to Europe and the United

States (Pintak, 2007b). The public face of the channel is Mesh'aan al-Juburi, a former member of Iraq's parliament who resides in Syria.

In contrast with the Jihadi tone of al-Zawra', Iraqi Christian minorities launched a channel to advocate 'the political administrative and cultural rights of the Christian minorities and to develop their traditions and show their civilization' ('Ishtar Satellite', 2005). Registered outside of Iraq and managed by Dr George Mansour former head of IMN, the channel Ishtar TV operates through an affiliate in Kurdistan and broadcasts in Assyrian, Arabic and Kurdish. Also in the Basra region, a community television channel was established with the support of the BBC Trust Fund. Former employees of Basra TV, civil-society activists and community representatives were trained in television management and production. As a start-up, the channel benefited from financial and material support from the government of the UAE.

As of mid-2009, the media landscape in Iraq remains highly vulnerable to changes in security, political and economic conditions. The variety of television channels reflects different established and emerging voices in Iraq, and as such the appearance and disappearance of television channels on the spectrum is a good barometer to measure the fluid political and security situation in the country. The ability for television to act as a reassembling force in a post-war society hinges upon the strength and availability of an applicable legal framework. In July 2004, Iraq's National Communication and Media Commission (NCMC) endorsed a broadcasting regulation act, the Interim Broadcasting Code of Practice. Television stations became subject to regulation spelling out criteria for licensing, permissible programme content and sanctioning. The difficult security and political situation in Iraq is not conducive, however, to implementing or enforcing the law. Consequently, Iraqi television reflects the country's ideological and sectarian fragmentation where even the public channel fails to represent various social, political and ethnic constituents. Al-Iraqiya has become a propaganda tool in the hands of Iraq's new rulers while privately owned channels are at the mercy of the political ambitions of their owners. In this media environment dominated by wartime political and security imperatives, there are no stable, commercially viable, advertising-supported channels.

CONCLUSION

This chapter has described key transformative moments in the history of Arab television from the beginning of national channels in the 1950s to most recent developments consisting of the mushrooming of television channels in war-torn Iraq since 2003. The 1960s and 1970s witnessed the development of national systems in most Arab states, in addition to the establishment of the Cairo-based Arab States Broadcasting Union (ASBU) and the Riyadh-based Arab Satellite

Organization (ARABSAT), designed to facilitate exchanges of skills, pro-grammes and experiences between official Arab broadcasters. In the 1980s, the Civil War in Lebanon spawned myriad privately owned television channels oper-ating in a regulatory vacuum. The 1990s were a pivotal decade: the Gulf War exposed the unfulfilled need for non-official Arab television news, various Arab television channels were established in Europe, al-Jazeera revolutionised Arab television news, and the Lebanese entertainment television model emerged. The 2000s have thus far seen the advent of Arab media cities, the launch of al-Jazeera arch-rival al-Arabiya in Dubai Media City, and war-induced television anarchy in Iraq.

Countries have undergone distinct yet patterned experiences in the shift from government-owned, nationally oriented terrestrial broadcasting to privately owned, transnational satcasting. The level of development of national television systems before the 1990s has not necessarily predicted the kind of transnational channels that countries have spawned thereafter. Iraq was one of the first Arab countries to initiate television broadcasting. And yet its national system was stunted by the totalitarian grip of Saddam Hussein and his family, leading to the rapid emergence of numerous television channels when the regime collapsed in 2003. In contrast, Qatar was one of the latest Arab states to establish a national channel and that institution was woefully underdeveloped. And yet, Qatar man-aged to launch the successful al-Jazeera, while its national channel remains relatively unsophisticated (this is one reason why the focus on al-Jazeera as a representative of Arab television is misleading). Egypt's sizeable national tele-vision system has arguably been a hindrance in the new satellite era, and the country has allowed the establishment of private channels reluctantly and with excruciating slowness. The anarchy of the airwaves that occurred in Lebanon in the 1980s spawned a major pan-Arab entertainment channel (LBC-Sat, Chap-ter 2) but did not enable the development of a strong regional news network. Though most Arab television systems opened up incrementally, Lebanon and Iraq offer two different consequences of chaotic political and media rupture. In Chapter 6 we explore and compare the regulatory and policy frameworks in which television operates in some other Arab countries.

Together, these diverse experiences have contributed to the creation of a transnational television industry whose speed and scale of growth are remark-able on a global scale. Before 1990, television in the Arab world consisted of isolated national systems that were overall unremarkable and insignificant in the global context. By 2000, there was a solid industry with clear market leaders in news and entertainment. In the middle of 2009, there are close to 470 Arabic-language satellite channels (Abbasi interview, 26 April 2009) targeting 250–300 million Arabic-speaking viewers in the Middle East and worldwide. But the growth is qualitative as well as quantitative, as Arab television industries today boast high levels of technical sophistication, professional capabilities and increased recognition as an important political, economic and cultural force. The chapters that follow will focus on some of the most important players, institutions and trends in the contemporary Arab television industries.

2

Pan-Arab Entertainment Channels

Satellite entertainment channels target a large and multinational audience, though they focus on wealthy Gulf viewers, particularly in Saudi Arabia. More popular than news networks, entertainment channels reflect an influential nexus of economic, political, social and economic forces in the Arab world. They have been industry pioneers in three ways. First, they are at the vanguard of inte- ①grating the Arab television industry into the global media market, through licensed (format) programmes, and pan-Arab production, acquisition and promotion, which lure international partners eager to reach the pan-Arab market. Second, they have spearheaded changes in the Arab media landscape by pro- ②moting relatively liberal social, cultural and economic agendas. A central theme in this chapter is the degree to which socio-political and cultural openness is affected by the channel's ownership, scope of operations and objectives. Third, ③this chapter examines how entertainment channels have driven the commercialisation of the Arab television industries.

Entertainment channels have contributed to a fundamental shift in the kinds of programmes watched by average Arab viewers. In the pre-satellite era, state broadcasters served captive national audiences a mix of social marketing, political propaganda, religious shows and carefully filtered or censored entertainment. Since the 1990s, taking advantage of new operational scales enabled by satellite technology, entertainment channels have expanded the reach of Arab television by targeting viewers in the large expatriate Arabic-speaking communities in North America, Europe and elsewhere, in addition to viewers in the Arab world, where these channels have opened several country-based bureaus and studios. Entertainment channels have also expanded the margins of permissible entertainment – to include bold talk shows, playful game shows, titillating music videos, sensationalist reality shows – that were non-existent in the pre-satellite era. The sharp contrast between the dour and cautious programmes of state broadcasters and the fresh and edgy fare of the commercial entertainment channels caused a massive audience shift from the former towards the latter. By 2000, the popularity of satellite entertainment channels had grown to such an extent that it forced government-owned channels to adapt to the changing

media landscape – an adaptation that for the most part consisted of imitating the practices of the newcomers.

As a result, channels like the Middle East Broadcasting Centre (MBC) and the
Lebanese Broadcasting Corporation (LBC) have shaped – much more than the
news channels – the evolution of Arab television into a commercially driven satellite industry with regionally based production and high production values. Today,
MBC and LBC-Sat lead the pack of privately owned entertainment channels,
while Dubai TV is an intriguing example of hybrid private–state ownership with
a peculiar profile in the industry. Initially established as an offshore commercial
alternative to conservative Saudi state-owned television, MBC has morphed into
the MBC Group, a multichannel conglomerate targeting various demographic
groups. LBC emerged as the voice of a warring militia in the regulatory vacuum
and political anarchy of Lebanon's Civil War, but then shifted to serve specific
Saudi-Lebanese interests. If MBC and LBC-Sat set entertainment trends in the
Arab television industries, Dubai TV represents an alternative model: a local
(Dubai) as opposed to national (UAE) broadcaster morphing from the practice
of typical state broadcasting for the Emirate of Dubai to imitating privately
owned channels like MBC and LBC-Sat to promote Dubai's economic success,
all the while being managed by a quasi-governmental holding.

This chapter aims to answer the following questions about the centrality of
entertainment channels in the Arab television industries:

- Who are the main players in entertainment television?
- How did these satellite channels develop?
- How are they financed and what are their objectives?
- What types of programmes do they acquire or produce?
- What role do these channels play in Arab public life, and how do they relate
  to socio-political, cultural and economic changes?

Two important and related trends define the Arab television industries. First,
the programming policies of Arab entertainment channels provide a measure of
the changing social, cultural, economic and political landscape in the Arab
world. Even as they aim to reach the largest possible audience on a transnational
scale and across demographic groups, general entertainment channels target
specific viewer groups in their programme-scheduling strategy. While daytime
programming focuses mostly on women and children, primetime (8.00 to mid-
night) combines news and entertainment content. Being the largest pan-Arab
demographic group, youth are attracted by variety and reality shows scheduled
during primetime (see Table 2.1).

Table 2.1. Overview of Entertainment Genres and Sources

Activities of general entertainment channels	Countries	Genres
Foreign acquisitions	USA	Movies,
	Latin America	Soap operas,
	Turkey	Series,
Arab productions and co-productions	Egypt	Serials,
	Jordan	Talk shows,
	Lebanon	Variety shows,
	Dubai	Magazine shows,
	Syria	Reality shows,
Format adaptations	Lebanon	Talk shows,
	Egypt	Variety shows

② Second and more important, channels like MBC and LBC-Sat, and to a lesser extent Dubai TV, have pioneered what is perhaps the single most important pattern in the development of the Arab television industries: the rise of multichannel conglomerates that are often vertically and horizontally integrated *reach consolidate* (these groups also include print, radio and Internet companies that we do not cover in depth here because of the book's focus on television). As this chapter shows, the growth of conglomerates like MBC Group and LBC Holding (and later LBC-Rotana) reflects the growing sophistication, commercialisation and specialisation of the industry, leading Arab television into an era where channels consolidated into conglomerates segment the pan-Arab audience into desirable target groups. Though top entertainment channels in the early days of the Arab satellite era now sit at the centre of competing multichannel conglomerates, the growth from single-channel to multiple-channel companies has followed different but overlapping paths. The growth of the MBC and LBC conglomerates have been shaped by different political, economic and socio-cultural forces that sometimes reinforce and other times compete with each other. In the remainder of the chapter, we analyse these institutional trajectories, beginning with MBC, proceeding with LBC and concluding with Dubai TV.

MIDDLE EAST BROADCASTING CENTRE (MBC) – MBC GROUP

MBC's institutional story is typical of some European-born, pan-Arab channels. Such a trajectory moves from formative years in London or Rome, is followed by relocation to the Arab world and an initially uneasy fit within the Arab media landscape, and finally concludes with some channels ascending to pan-Arab popularity and commercial success. Roughly accounting for over a quarter of primetime Arab audiences, MBC has grown from a single satellite channel to a regional media empire with eight free-to-air channels, two radio channels, a documentary production house, a news service and a multilingual news and video portal. This section examines the Group's growth with a focus on the flagship and original channel, MBC1 (known simply as MBC).

When the first Gulf War started, Saudi Television reported Iraq's invasion of Kuwait three days after the fact. As a result, Saudi nationals gravitated towards CNN that they watched through hastily imported satellite receivers. In combination with satellite technology and Saudi capital, this thirst for news unfiltered by state censors was the catalyst for the launch of MBC as the first commercial Arab satellite channel in 1991. MBC's parent company, ARA Group International (AGI) has been in the media business since 1985. In addition to investments in radio and television, AGI's original focus was on news agencies, media agencies and wireless cable. Establishing a satellite television channel was a logical step given the global interest in satellite communication in the early 1990s. Between 1991 and 1995, MBC built a 'seventy-strong newsroom producing over 120 minutes of news every day with hourly bulletins' ('MBC Celebrates', 1996). Trained by former BBC and ITV journalists, MBC's newsroom was a formative space for talent that became the backbone of BBC Arabic's first (and failed) venture, then al-Jazeera and finally al-Arabiya (for more details see Chapter 4). Between 1996 and 1998, MBC faced increased competition, financial problems and lack of access to many national Arab markets ('MBC to Launch', 1993, p. 5). As MBC embarked on a restructuring process in the late 1990s, which involved reshuffling functions and relations between London headquarters and various regional offices, the company made the decision to relocate to the Arab world based on the belief that a successful pan-Arab expansion required on-the-ground visibility.

MBC's decision to relocate to Dubai Media City (DMC) – rather than to Amman, Beirut or Cairo ('Arab World's', 2001) – boosted DMC status as the pre-eminent regional media hub. In tandem with the move, MBC's management revived a three-year-old plan to establish a news television channel and several radio stations. With a budget of US $300 million, the plans for al-Arabiya news channel were underway. At the same time, seeing that English channels available in the Gulf region were government-owned, MBC decided to pursue an English-language channel, known as MBC2, which began transmission on 12 January 2003 (al-Alawi, 2003). One month later, the MBC Group-affiliated news channel al-Arabiya initiated satcasting, promptly rising to become a major challenger to al-Jazeera's seven-year domination of pan-Arab satellite television news (discussed in Chapter 4). Between 2003 and 2009, MBC Group pursued a segmentation strategy based on multiple channels and delivery platforms targeting various market niches on generic, age, gender and linguistic criteria (see Table 2.2).

desire
for
unfiltered
news

Table 2.2 MBC Group

Channel*	Established	Target	Content
MBC1	1991	General audience	General entertainment and news (Arabic)
MBC2	2003	General audience	Western movies (Arabic subtitles)
Al-Arabiya	2003	General (mostly adult) audience	News and current affairs (Arabic)
Text TV	2003	Youth	Text messages (English and Arabic)
MBC3	2004	Children	General entertainment (Arabic and English)
MBC4	2005	Women	General entertainment (Arabic and English)
MBC Action	2007	Male teenagers	Action adventure Western movies (Arabic subtitles)
MBC Max	2008	General (mostly male)	Action adventure Western movies (Arabic subtitles)
MBC Persia	2008	Iran	Western movies (subtitled in Persian)
MBC +	2008	General audience (mostly adult)	Drama series (original or dubbed)

*This table reflects television channels only; all are free-to-air except Text TV and MBC+ which are available through the pay-TV bouquet Showtime Arabia.

MBC1 featured two talk shows inspired by ABC's *The View*: *Kalam Nawa'em* (Soft/Women's Talk), for women, and *Adam* (which last aired in 2008), for men. Both programmes tackle delicate issues like male impotence and domestic violence, and less sensitive issues like social etiquette and household management. Supplying a space to discuss and interpret a range of cultural traditions, social practices and religious beliefs, *Kalam Nawa'em* and *Adam* can be said to provide a platform for reconciling traditional norms with modern lifestyles. In *Kalam Nawa'em*, four women from different Arab nationalities and professional backgrounds present issues, news and real-life stories. Similarly, *Adam* provides a forum to discuss social issues from the perspective of Arab men. Both programmes have focused on issues of general concern using real-life situations as examples. While in their very format the two shows reify gender divisions, they do not refrain from inter-gender interaction and debate: *Kalam Nawa'em* has featured debates between the hosts and religious conservatives on women's issues. One episode in 2006 covered the story of thirty-five Kuwaiti women who had come into contact with an AIDS victim; another in 2007 focused on the ban on women's driving in Saudi Arabia; yet another in 2008 discussed the issue of Arab–Western intermarriage. Similarly *Adam*, by no means a radical show, has nonetheless featured feminist writers, and conversations that questioned aspects of traditional gender roles, for example advocating that men reveal their emotions and be more sensitive to women's needs.

MBC has also been a leader in adapting globally formatted shows to Arabic. In that area, two significant experiences stand out. From November 2000 to 2003, *Man Sa-Yarbah al-Malyoun* (Who Will Win the Million), MBC's version of *Who Wants to Be a Millionaire* (1999–) was a ratings sensation. MBC purchased a licence from the UK-based Celador covering the Arabic-speaking Middle East and North Africa, the only such licence to cover twenty-two countries (Khalil, 2004). One of the Arab world's most successful reality TV/game shows, the programme was first produced in London, then in Paris and later in Cairo as a result of the pursuit of lower production costs and 'authenticity', i.e. an Arab-looking studio audience. The show started with a British crew but by the time it arrived in Egypt, Arab staff had taken over. The host of the show, Lebanese radio personality-turned-television celebrity Georges Qordahi, treated his viewers to a mix of cultural elitism, humorous banter and an overall playful demeanour. Qordahi's ability to position himself as an Arab rather than Lebanese host, MBC's high production values and strategic casting decisions, attracted an eclectic group of charismatic Arab competitors, men and women, the latter veiled and non-veiled (Khalil, 2004). A regional hit for over two years, the show entered the Arab popular vernacular with the catchphrase 'Jawab Neha'y?' – 'Is that your final answer?' From 2005 to 2007, MBC tried unsuccessfully to repeat the success of *Man Sa-Yarbah al-Malyoun*, re-signing Qordahi and doubling the

Georges Qordahi on the set of *Power of Ten*, dubbed *al-Quwwa al-ʿAshera*

prize to 2 million Saudi Riyals (more than US $500,000). The success of this programme genre triggered a regional interest in similar shows including Arabic adaptations of Western formats such as *al-Fakh* (The Trap); *al-Kursy* (The Chair); *al-Halaqa al-Ad'af* (The Weakest Link); *Ya Atel Ya Ma'tul* (Greed); and *Deal or No Deal*.

On the other hand, MBC's version of *Big Brother* (2004–), called *al-Ra'is*, was one of the company's worst investments, and highlighted the perils of adapting Western formats that may prove overly controversial to influential Arab politicians or clerics. Satcast on MBC2 from 20 February to 2 March 2004, *al-Ra'is* (The President) was shut down in a firestorm of controversy. A format owned by Dutch company Endemol, the show, known elsewhere as *Big Brother*, is a popularity contest between a group of girls and guys living together in a purpose-built villa in the island-state of Bahrain, Saudi Arabia's smaller and more socially liberal neighbour. In an effort to accommodate cultural and religious sensitivities, producers consulted with religious clerics in Saudi Arabia and Bahrain who suggested limiting physical contact between males and females, showing the participants praying, and keeping the wardrobe and social etiquette conservative. Inside the villa, producers and participants for the most part abided by these rules. However, a combination of manipulation by powerful Saudi clerics opposed to the programme and anger in the Bahraini parliament would ultimately lead to the shutdown of *al-Ra'is*. The 'official' trigger was cheek kissing between two participants during the first week of the show. Quickly thereafter, *al-Ra'is* became the centre of a heated debate between Islamists and liberals in the Bahraini parliament. Islamists organised demonstrations demanding that the broadcasts be immediately halted, while liberals argued that the programme created jobs and promoted Bahrain as a destination for foreign investment and tourism. The former prevailed by pushing MBC to shut down the programme. The channel's press release stated that

> [T]he decision came following a request from the communications minister of Bahrain, the country hosting the programme. [The decision was made] out of a desire to preserve [Bahrain's] social unity and out of concern lest MBC constitute a reason for disagreement [in the country]. ('*Big Brother*', 2004)

The controversy surrounding *al-Ra'is* illustrates the problems that Arab television channels can encounter when a programme triggers hostile reactions and political resistance. Nonetheless, rather than preventing MBC from making more reality shows, the incident led the channel to search for less controversial formats that did not include physical contact between males and females, of which MBC has produced more than ten since 2003 (for detailed analysis of the *al-Ra'is* controversy, see Kraidy, 2009, Chapter 2).

MBC crew shooting outdoors

MBC Group's global scale contributed to the development of the Arab tele-vision industries. In addition to its pan-Arab coverage, MBC reached Europe, Asia, Africa and the Americas. More recently, it created MBC Maghreb, acknowledging the cultural specificities and viewing patterns of its North African viewers. Organisationally, MBC started as a multinational company maintaining a regional, sometimes global, production network. The Group's workforce is multinational, drawn from various Arab countries in addition to some Europeans, Americans and South Asians. Although Saudi-funded, the number of Saudi employees working at MBC represented no more than 8 per cent ('General Manager', 2006). In fact, MBC's management has been heavily criticised for its reliance on foreign and Arab expatriates; recent efforts to train and develop Saudi talent for employment with MBC in Saudi Arabia or abroad have had mixed results.

MBC has also contributed to regionalising Arab media production through the Group's various bureaux and partnerships throughout the Arab world. Head-quartered in Dubai, MBC has the two biggest studios in the Egypt Media Production City (EMPC), large production facilities in Beirut and Riyadh and partnerships with production companies in Jordan, Syria, Kuwait, Tunisia and Morocco. MBC has also been involved as an outside contractor in the training of staff and restructuring of Bahrain Television (BTV) and Saudi Arabia's al-Ekhbariya. Towards the goal of developing a pan-Arab audience, MBC led the establishment of fundraising telethons that reflected the channel's (and by exten-sion, Saudi Arabia's) commitment to Arab and Muslim issues. During these telethons, MBC dedicated resources and airtime to cover how Saudis rallied to the assistance of victims of wars and natural disasters: in April 2002, a telethon simulcast on MBC and Saudi TV raised US $109 million for Palestinians during the Second Intifada; in 2004, the two channels joined forces in telethons aimed at supporting victims of an earthquake in Pakistan and the South-Asian tsunami.

Buoyed by Saudi investments, an aggressive expansion strategy, adaptations of successful Western programmes and pan-Arab talent, MBC has in the past two decades established itself as a market leader in Arab satellite entertainment television, and is believed to be the only channel or (with LBC-Sat, one of two channels) consistently making profits. The channel's commercial success is due primarily to its effective courtship of Saudi viewers, to which MBC speaks directly. Dependence on the Saudi audience, however, brings with it a set of challenges. As the *al-Ra'is* episode demonstrated, the flipside of this success is that MBC is constrained by Saudi Arabia's conservative social and religious mores. MBC's chief rival, LBC-Sat, has historically had to overcome a different set of challenges, which we discuss in the following section.

LEBANESE BROADCASTING CORPORATION (LBC) – LBC HOLDING
During the 1975–90 war in Lebanon, dozens of private television stations appeared on the airwaves. For the most part, these were ideological mouthpieces launched by warring militias who carved the national territory into self-administered enclaves. These stations were unlicensed, taking advantage of the power and regulatory vacuum created by the collapse of the Lebanese state. The Lebanese Forces, a Christian-nationalist militia, launched the Lebanese Broadcasting Corporation (LBC) in August 1985. LBC was the first of many wartime channels in Lebanon; the channel's ideological bent notwithstanding, LBC emerged as the most successful wartime channel, thanks to a combination of competent management, exciting pirated and adapted programmes and technical sophistication (Kraidy, 1998b). Emerging from the Lebanese war, LBC underwent internal restructuring and was renamed the Lebanese Broadcasting Corporation International (LBCI) in 1992. One of only four privately owned channels to survive the 1996 licensing process based on Lebanon's 1994 Audio-Visual Media Law, LBCI remains the top terrestrial television channel in Lebanon, while its satellite arm, al-Fada'iyya al-Lubnaniyya (the Lebanese Satellite Channel, known in the industry as LBC-Sat), is a leading pan-Arab entertainment channel. Now in its third decade, LBC is the Arab world's oldest continuously operating privately owned television channel.

Since its inception in 1985, LBC has been a national and eventually a pan-Arab industry trendsetter reflecting the rise of American-style broadcasting at the expense of the older European norm. This is reflected in the station's choice of a three-letter acronym name, its focus on entertainment programmes, and its reliance on advertisements. Even as a partisan voice in the Lebanese war, LBC from its early days was run as a business, for example broadcasting special Ramadan programmes for Muslim audiences during the Civil War (for more on the Ramadan schedule see Chapter 5). In the early years, the bulk of the channel's programming grid consisted of foreign programmes. French adventure shows for young people, US sitcoms and police series, British comedy and Egyptian soap operas were early staples.

Since its early years, LBC became known for its creativity in entertainment programmes. Highly successful variety and game shows were locally produced under the supervision of Simon Asmar, who LBC snatched from national broadcaster La Compagnie Libanaise de Télévision. As producer/director, Asmar was behind classic hits such as *Studio al-Fann* (Art Studio), *Iftah ya Simsim* (Open Sesame), *Laylat Hazz* (Night of Fortune), that can be traced to French and Turkish variety-show formats. Two of Asmar's early successes were *Laqta 'al Hawa* (Live Snapshot) and *Qalbi Dalili* (My Heart Is My Guide) moulded after *The Dating Game* and *Matchmaker* respectively (Khalil, 2004). LBC capitalised on Asmar's ability to repackage ideas for Arab viewers; the end products proved to be sites where cultural and social taboos are redefined, gender and class roles are renegotiated. LBC also produced nightly newscasts that reflected the ideological outlook of the Lebanese Forces – advocating national sovereignty from both Syrian intervention and Palestinian power in Lebanon, promoting Christian Lebanese interests, and an overall rightwing political ideology – while featuring innovations in production values, which were slick, and delivery style, which was relatively informal.

In 1996, the transition from a terrestrial Lebanese national channel, LBCI, to a satellite pan-Arab channel, LBC-Sat, involved a careful marketing strategy centred on an ostensibly 'liberated' sexuality. This entailed broadcasting uncensored films, which until then had been the exclusive purview of pay-TV. LBC-Sat was able to schedule late-night films that challenged the codes of pan-Arab, particularly Saudi, morality. But as competition over Western movies increased so did their broadcasting fees. To avoid these ever steeper costs, LBC-Sat gradually limited Western movies. Typical of its use of women as a key marketing ingredient, LBC-Sat scheduled a morning aerobic show featuring Lebanese-Sudanese instructor Haifa (not to be mistaken with Lebanese singer Haifa Wehbi). *Ma 'Elak 'Ella Haifa* (Haifa Is the One) was an instant success with Saudi, predominantly male, audiences attracted by the host's erotically charged movements. Both Western movies and Haifa's show are credited with LBC-Sat's initial success in Saudi Arabia. To maintain this success, LBC-Sat followed with one of the first format programmes, *Ya Layl Ya 'Ayn*, a variety game show originally produced for Lebanese audiences. Inspired by the French programme *La Fureur*, the programme is built around *karaoke* performances by Lebanese socialites and Arab celebrities. Between 1999 and 2002, the show was a major success, featuring 3000 songs, 500 dances, 150 artists, 800 participants and more than US $2.5 million in monetary rewards and gifts from the show's commercial sponsors (Khalil, 2005).

In spite of its success, the odds were not always in favour of LBC's survival, and the channel's management has displayed high levels of political acumen and organisational flexibility over the years to surmount major economic and political challenges. Indeed, the economic challenge of being one channel among fifty others in a minuscule country with 4 million inhabitants was met by putting commercial considerations on a par with political calculations (as demonstrated by special Ramadan programmes, not an expected strategy from an institution owned by a Christian militia locked in conflict with various Christian and Muslim opponents). Pierre el-Daher, LBC's General Manager and the only leader the institution has known in a quarter-century of existence, forged a twenty-five-year alliance with advertising mogul Antoine Choueiri (it unravelled in 2008 as LBC-Sat moved into the orbit of al-Waleed bin Talal's Rotana conglomerate, with its own media sales representative; for more on advertising see Chapter 5). El-Daher also led the development of an alluring institutional brand at the core of which lies a focus on light-hearted entertainment featuring attractive women – a sure profit-maker, in contrast to news, a perennial budget-buster. Last but not least, as will be discussed shortly, LBC established a beneficial partnership with well-connected Saudi investors, earning financial security and political protection. Moreover, LBC-Sat integrated mobile phones and the Internet with television programmes, namely by embedding interactive features – nominating and voting procedures, etc – in its reality television programmes (see discussion of *Star Academy* later in this chapter) and thereby generating new revenue streams.

From 1990 to 2005, LBC and its political patrons faced a hostile political and security climate dominated by Syrian hegemony over every aspect of Lebanese life. Political challenges to LBC's success were addressed by establishing a complex organisational structure that enabled LBC to elude closure or confiscations of equipment. Whereas the terrestrial station, LBC International (LBCI), is registered in Lebanon and subject to Lebanese law, its satellite counterpart, LBC-Sat, is a multinational corporation registered in the Cayman Islands. Since its founding in 1996, Saudis have owned nearly half of LBC-Sat. Saudi mogul Saleh Kamel initially owned 49 per cent of the shares and was known to brag in public of his ability to influence programming content, especially in curbing material of a sexual nature that he deemed inappropriate to Saudi sensibilities. For his own business reasons and also because LBC-Sat management reportedly resisted his meddling, Kamel swapped his shares with another Saudi mogul, Prince al-Waleed bin Talal, a global investor with interests in media companies. Bin Talal bought Kamel's shares for US $100 million in 2000, at which time the company was worth around US $200 million. With this massive influx of equity, LBC-Sat gained the resources to compete regionally, in addition to some political protection since bin Talal was close to Lebanon's then-President Emile Lahoud. The channel that began as a Christian-Lebanese militia television station merged its operations with al-Waleed bin Talal's Rotana music-and-television conglomerate in 2008, the harbinger of a trend towards consolidation in the Arab television industries. While LBC-Sat succeeded in tightening its grip on the Saudi market, terrestrial LBCI is (as of May 2009) battling a legal case over its ownership in Lebanon. The channel's general manager, Pierre el-Daher, stands accused by the Lebanese Forces, the Christian militia (now a political party) that launched LBC in 1985, of embezzlement, for turning LBC into a shareholding company and for selling the majority of the satellite channel's shares to al-Waleed bin Talal. These troubles notwithstanding, in 2009 LBC Holding remains a top conglomerate with a 'bouquet' – industry parlance for a group – of channels focusing on Lebanese, pan-Arab and diasporic audiences, as reflected in Table 2.3.

One of LBC's decisive advantages over MBC is the former's Lebanese location and ownership, which to this day permeates the channel's identity, Saudi ownership notwithstanding. This allows LBC a wider range of content than its

Table 2.3 LBC Holding

Channel*	Established	Target audience	Content
LBCI	1985	Lebanese family	General entertainment and news Focus on Lebanon
Al-Fada'iyya al-Lubnaniyya	1996	Arab youth and women	General entertainment Focus on Saudi Arabia and Lebanon
LBC-Sat			News in partnership with *al-Hayat* newspaper
LBC-Europe	1996	Lebanese expatriates	General entertainment and news Rescheduled LBCI and LBC-Sat programmes
LBC-America	1996	Arab and Lebanese expatriates	General entertainment and news Rescheduled LBCI and LBC-Sat programmes
LBC-Australia	1996	Arab and Lebanese expatriates	General entertainment and news Rescheduled LBCI and LBC-Sat programmes
Nagham	2003	Arab youth	Reality Television Channel Seasonal Music Channel
LBC-Maghreb	2006	Arab youth and women	General entertainment and news Rescheduled LBC-Sat programmes

This table reflects currently operating television channels only, all are free-to-air with the exception of LBC Europe, LBC America and LBC Australia.

rival MBC. At the same time as the *al-Ra'is* controversy was unfolding in Bahrain, LBC was already airing from Lebanon another reality show, *Star Academy*. Both *al-Ra'is* and *Star Academy* are global formats owned by the Dutch firm Endemol and involve contact between unmarried men and women, a practice frowned upon in the conservative Gulf societies. After gaining momentum with their victory on *al-Ra'is*, extremists, clerics and religious zealots, particularly in Saudi Arabia, focused their attention on *Star Academy* because of its popularity and its similarity to *al-Ra'is*, notably since both programmes were promoted under the controversial rubric of 'reality' television. Started in December 2003, *Star Academy* had a successful sixth season in 2009, making it the longest continuously running, commercially successful and controversial pan-Arab reality show.

In *Star Academy*, sixteen or more contestants are selected from several thousand applicants to join the 'Academy', a purpose-built 'house' with ancillary classrooms, kitchen, living room and, more recently, a swimming pool. Contestants live together for four months; they cook, they eat, they interact, they practise together. Paying lip-service to putative 'Islamic' values towards male–female relations, males and females have separate sleeping quarters and bathrooms though they share other areas of the 'Academy'. The students take classes in various aspects of performance art and showbusiness and prepare for

Star Academy wallpaper

a weekly live public performance. Monitored by 300 staff members using sixty cameras, their daily activities are broadcast on a twenty-four-hour channel. A summary of these activities appears on a daily show called *Access*. During the week, the instructors nominate three potential 'students' for possible eviction from the 'Academy'. Every week on Friday, the 'students' and guest stars offer a two-hour 'prime night' of performances and clips of the week's activities. By the end of this viewers vote one 'student' out via text messages (in later seasons peers save another nominee in a public straw vote). The daily *Access* (a half-hour show that summarises the day's activities) and the two-hour Friday 'Prime' are aired on LBC-Sat in addition to a dedicated channel Nagham (Tune), which functions as a substitute for web-streaming by airing activities in the 'Academy' non-stop for the entire duration of the show (Kraidy, 2006a and 2006b).

The controversies surrounding *Star Academy* did not result from breaking any censorship codes; after all, the show abides by the same censorship rules that govern television fiction. In fact, the 'Academy' is a rather controlled environment where sexual activities are ostensibly prohibited, alcohol is forbidden and the students are instructed to avoid profanity and offensive language in general. Conversations about politics and religion are banned, and the dress code is (relative to LBC-Sat's other shows) conservative, though the contestants' attire has become more risqué over the years. In addition, the production is satcast with a thirty-minute delay that allows producers ample time to censor indiscretions. Nevertheless, *Star Academy* created a crisis in countries such as Kuwait and Saudi Arabia where clerics and extremists attacked LBC-Sat, the national participants and the sponsoring businesses for broadcasting the show. Their tools included *fatwas*, religious edicts pronounced by clerics, underground violent sermons by preachers who may or may not be official clerics, newspaper op-eds and Internet-based articles (Kraidy, 2009). In fact, the original sponsor, instant coffee brand Nescafé, withdrew because it did not want to be associated with the show's mixing of the sexes; but the show's sponsorship package was picked up by Pepsi for US $4 million per season.

Since 2003, LBC-Sat has considered *Star Academy* as an important instrument with which to target the Saudi market, especially young Saudi viewers. By including Saudi contestants (only male) in the final group of yearly contestants, by crowning a Saudi national winner of the show in its second season, and by straddling the boundaries between the morally acceptable and therefore ordinary on the one hand, and the morally controversial but therefore titillating on the other hand, LBC-Sat has earned a loyal following among Saudi viewers. In recent years, LBC-Sat has developed several shows explicitly targeting Saudi Arabia, often hosted by Saudi media personalities: *'Eishu Ma'na* (Live with Us) is a Saudi-oriented daily show, hosted by Saudis; spotlighting issues that challenge prevailing traditions and values of Saudi (and other Gulf) citizens. Another programme, *'Ahmar bil-Khatt al-'Arid* (Red in Bold Lines) is a social talk show that touches on hot topics in the Arab world including Saudi Arabia's rules on gender mixing and women's rights. The show stirred a scandal in July 2009 when it featured a Saudi man boasting of his sexual adventures in his Jeddah apartment. In the process, LBC-Sat has become increasingly identified as a Saudi channel, a perception that is bound to grow with LBC-Sat's merger with Rotana.

MBC and LBC-Sat reflect two successful models of advertising-supported general entertainment channels that have expanded beyond their initial spheres of operation and introduced Arab audiences to a wide and expanding range of acquired, adapted and/or locally created programmes. Born in Europe and relocated to Dubai Media City, the Saudi-owned MBC is one of the most profitable privately owned Arab television institutions, due to its diverse programming options and audience segmentation strategy. After emerging as a political player during Lebanon's Civil War, LBC-Sat forged regional alliances with various Saudi businesses, securing political protection and access to the lucrative Saudi market and thereby securing its continued growth. The success of MBC and LBC-Sat has led various national channels to emulate their strategies and practices. The case of Dubai TV stands out as an outlying but striking example of how state-owned television services can emulate privately owned channels, spawning a hybrid model of a state-sponsored but privately operated television.

DUBAI TV – DUBAI MEDIA INCORPORATED (DMI)
In 1969, the Emirate of Dubai, the second most influential in the United Arab Emirates after the capital-Emirate of Abu Dhabi, witnessed the first television signal from a relay station operating under the name 'Kuwait Television from Dubai'. At the time, the Kuwaiti government established and trained the future generation of Emiratis and expatriate Arabs who would then transform the black-and-white channel to the first colour television in the Gulf region under the banner of Dubai TV in 1974 (al-Sheikh, 2007). However, other Arab expatriates were soon brought in to expand the channel's services on behalf of the ruling al-Maktoum family. Palestinian manager Riyad al-Su'aibi transformed the station from simply a transmission facility to a fully fledged channel with production and broadcasting capacities. In the 1970s and 1980s, Dubai TV became a production hub for war-exiled Lebanese producers as well as Egyptians whose political views disadvantaged them professionally in the wake of Egypt's peace agreement with Israel.

The second phase in the development of Dubai TV was primarily engineered by another Palestinian-Emirati, Nassib al-Bitar. Under his leadership, on 27

October 1992, Dubai TV became the first Arab channel to satcast twenty-four hours via ARABSAT and HotBird, covering both the Arab world and most of Europe. By December 1993, Dubai TV's signal also covered the US. Almost 30 per cent of its programmes were in English, but Dubai TV was an early experimenter with live Arabic-language talk shows and call-in programmes. Within a couple of years, Dubai TV developed several free-to-air channels including an English-language channel and other channels dedicated to business and sports. Dubai TV's success came to a halt by the mid-1990s because of what Ali al-Khalifa, former director of Dubai TV, called 'managerial dysfunction which affected the employees' performance levels and the media product presented to the viewer' (Haneyneh, 2005). A traditional state-television programming strategy aimed at pleasing the ruler rather than the viewer hindered Dubai TV's growth. Work politics between rival Arab expatriates and Emirati nationals were exacerbated by competing visions for the channel from within Dubai's al-Maktoum ruling family. In addition, the newly born offshore Saudi channels lured some of Dubai TV's expatriate professionals.

Dubai TV's receding role stood in sharp contrast with Dubai's economic expansion. A highly ambitious economic plan aiming to position Dubai as a global free trade, investment and tourism destination was not complemented by a proportionally significant media expansion. By 2003, Dubai's ruler Sheikh Mohammed bin Rashed al-Maktoum turned his attention to what was then called the Dubai Department of Media, a small-scale Information Ministry. The third, and current, phase in Dubai TV's history was prompted by a 2003 decree to establish Dubai Media Incorporated (DMI) as a government-owned company managed like a trust but with the intention to make a profit, which provided a managerial umbrella for the restructuring of four television stations, as well as three radio stations and a newspaper. According to Ali al-Rumaythy, former Director of Dubai TV, 'the strength of Dubai's name was not accompanied with government-owned visual media. That required a governmental intervention to bring this body to life' ('Refuses Earning', 2006). DMI's target has been for Dubai TV to be the most popular satellite channel in Dubai, and consequently, it started by changing the 'old-school' management because it was 'bureaucratic,' 'afraid of the star system' and 'not flexible and proactive ('Refuses Earning', 2006).

Along with a board of directors comprised of Emirati and foreign professionals, marketers and advertising veterans, DMI hired Ali Jaber, formerly a co-founder and general manager of Lebanon's Future TV, as a consultant to oversee the channel's transformation. With the restructuring of Dubai TV budgeted at US $108 million, Jaber proceeded to recruit former colleagues from Future TV and international consultancies, and to negotiate with programme

Table 2.4 Dubai Media Incorporated (DMI)

Channel*	Relaunch	Target audience	Content
Dubai TV	2004	General	Entertainment and news
'One TV	2004	Arab and expatriates	Western entertainment (subtitled)
Sama Dubai	2005	Emiratis and Arab expatriates	Local news and entertainment
Dubai Sports	2006	All audiences	National, pan-Arab and international sports
Dubai Racing	2008	Emiratis and Dubai residents	Horse and camel racing; hawk-related sports

*This table includes television channels only, all free-to-air

suppliers and format distributors (al-Zein, 2006). The result was a group of tele-vision channels that incorporates a new vision for media – market-friendly, Western-oriented, viewer-centred – in the UAE (Table 2.4), following the pat-tern of multichannel conglomerates established by MBC and LBC.

Dubai TV has to a large extent succeeded in achieving several objectives at once: preserving a state television mission of covering the rulers' activities and enhancing their image, advertising Dubai as a business and tourism hub, and depicting Dubai as a hip and cosmopolitan place in which to live and work. A Lebanese television critic compared Dubai TV to 'a laboratory to produce an identity or image to accompany the experience of the city of Dubai which is busy building itself and shaping its identity and image' (al-Zein, 2006). In so doing, the management aimed to fulfil DMI's mission statement which stipulated that the aim was to 'reach the maximum number of viewers by presenting creative and meaningful television content that respects social, cultural and family val-ues in the UAE, the Gulf and the Arab world' and 'translating into life Dubai's human and cultural diversification' (*DMI Mission*, 2008).

Unlike MBC and to a lesser extent LBC, Dubai TV's internal diversification into several channels does not reflect a strategy of audience fragmentation. To various degrees, all DMI channels fluidly integrate the Gulf, Arab and cos-mopolitan identities of Dubai. The flagship channel, Dubai TV's programming strategy blends Dubai's local, Emirati, Gulf, Arab and international layers of iden-tity. In the words of its one-time director, Dubai TV is 'not a specialised news channel but it is a complete general channel which at the same time cares to pre-sent the right information in all fields to the Arab viewer' ('Director of', 2006). The channel is careful to cater to its national – Emirati – audience through pro-grammes like *Akhbar al-Emarat* (News of the Emirates), which is produced and hosted by Emirati news anchors. This in itself is a symptom of the channel's trans-formation since '[U]ntil recently we were not watching an Emirati male or female presenter on television for social reasons' ('Director of', 2006).

The set of Dubai TV's *Taratata* adopted from a French format

Dubai TV's strategy is typical of Arab channels seeking to be in sync with the commercial global television industry while preserving local traditions. The channel selects 'programmes in accordance with viewers' preferences by providing what is new and modern, and applying the latest international technology but preserving the Arab culture' ('Again from', 2007). Cosmopolitan programmes are juxtaposed with conservative content and international formats are repackaged to fit local standards. For instance, the international format *Change My Life*, dubbed *Ghayyerli Hayati*, has become a show about plastic surgery 'targeting those who suffered from accidents that changed their physical appearance' ('Again from', 2007). Another locally developed reality show, *al-Daw' al-Akhdar* (Green Light) is what industry insiders call 'Islamic compliant', in the sense that two groups compete to execute goodwill tasks in light of Islamic traditions of charitable giving. Such 'Arabised' shows, in which staff gain experience producing new television genres, are consistent with prevailing social and religious sensibilities ('Director of', 2006).

Since its 2004 relaunch Dubai TV has invested in the production of Arabic series, primarily Gulf and Egyptian productions. As a business operation, Dubai TV has opted directly to finance private companies to executive-produce programmes on the channel's behalf. This strategy has provided Dubai TV with benefits on several fronts: the channel is able to control costs, to maintain flexibility in negotiating contracts with production companies throughout the Arab world, and to legally own its programmes. As a result, Dubai TV has felt empowered to pursue the establishment of its own distribution company, since it is

> the largest player in the production of drama both on the Gulf or Egyptian scene, and it will not contract distribution companies for open run broadcast licenses any more, until it establishes its own company at the beginning of the new year [2008]. (Toutounji, 2007)

Productions commissioned by Dubai TV are extremely visible during the Ramadan season but also throughout the year. This vertical integration has allowed Dubai TV to diversify its production, for instance by supporting a local adult cartoon programme titled *Freej* (the name of the main character). In its third season, the show featured an all-Emirati cast and crew and local plotlines: against the backdrop of an isolated neighbourhood in contemporary Dubai, the show is a relatively progressive depiction of the daily lives of four old local women – the animation itself, however, is executed in India ('About Freej', 2009).

Dubai TV is an unconventional entertainment channel. It showcases the challenges and opportunities of a hybrid structure in which the government of Dubai is the legal owner while much of the daily operations is left to expatriate 'consultants', who in effect perform management, production, acquisitions and programming for the channel – recently, however, the government's 'Emiratisation' strategy has increased the number of UAE citizens working for the channel. The channel is an outlier in that it is intimately related to the development of Dubai as a neo-liberal enclave populated by expatriates in which natives are a small minority. The channel's mix of Arabic and English, of Dubai-specific coverage with Emirati, Gulf and pan-Arab themes, gives it a unique flavour. Though organisationally Dubai TV has followed the lead of MBC and LBC in developing multiple channels targeting – in this case, rather symbolically, as we have argued earlier – various viewing communities, the channel remains a distinct, perhaps unique, institution in the Arab television industries.

TRENDS IN PAN-ARAB TELEVISION ENTERTAINMENT

The importance of the general entertainment channels stems from their vast popular appeal. Because of their ability to attract large audiences across demographic groups – unlike news channels, whose viewers tend to be predominantly adult males – entertainment channels have shaped the development of national and regional (pan-Arab) television industries. Since popular appeal in a commercial media industry translates into advertising revenue, entertainment channels have earned considerable politico-economic clout, enabling the production and airing of controversial programmes. In turn, as we have seen in recent years, controversial programmes – including bold *musalsalat* (serialised drama), satirical comedies, sensationalist reality programmes, provocative social talk shows, and titillating music videos – typically generate impassioned polemics, generate high ratings … and the cycle repeats itself: controversial content, elevated ratings, increased revenue, higher production budgets, more controversial content, etc.

It is therefore not surprising that genres known to elicit controversy dominate the programme grids of entertainment channels: talk shows, *musalsalat*, reality shows, etc. As we discuss in detail in Chapter 5, drama permeates programme grids because it combines themes of family relations, cultural identity, national pride and social messages. Recent *musalsalat* have addressed historical, religious and socially progressive issues, targeted new demographics – the well travelled, the religious and the nostalgic – employed multinational on-screen and off-screen staff, and filmed on various locations in the region and around the world. *Musalsalat* aside, one of the important contributions of satellite television has been its reliance on lively, interactive and mostly unscripted television formats. Whether live or recorded, these formats have attracted large audiences.

Talk shows on national channels feature society's opinion leaders, artists, celebrities and intellectuals. In the pre-satellite era, topics were rarely polemical, guests (and sometimes questions) were pre-approved and programmes were pre-recorded and edited by censors. In contrast, today a successful talk show would typically entail a combination of the following ingredients: live transmission, taboo and sensitive topics, a high level of interactivity through calling, emailing or texting, and an aggressive promotion strategy. Shows often involve live or recorded testimonials, expert panels and call-ins, emails or faxes from audiences. Some issues that are routinely addressed by these talk shows include transsexuals, rape, weight loss, domestic violence, globalisation and freedom of expression. In a 2008 episode, Malek Maktabi, host of LBC's talk show '*Ahmar bil-Khatt al-'Arid* (Red in Bold Lines), invited to his studio a number of Arab women holding unconventional jobs including a Syrian truck driver, an Egyptian butcher and a Moroccan train conductor. More controversial, Egyptian celebrity talk-show host Hala Serhan lost her job several times for her bold treatment of issues. In a 2005 episode of '*ala al-Hawa* (On the Air), she focused on female masturbation and took many phone calls from women viewers. However, Serhan's reported April 2009 US $2.5 million contract with al-Libiya indicates that controversy can sometimes be a potent career booster (Daher, 2009).

A talk show's success and survival are largely dependent on the host's ability to address sensitive topics without attracting overt state censorship; the ability to push the envelope without inviting repression is perhaps the most challenging aspect of producing successful talk shows in the region. Another type of talk show combines variety entertainment and celebrity gossip. Celebrity variety talk shows are prime-time fare on general entertainment channels; they have a cross-demographic appeal and routinely attract criticism from cultural critics and religious authorities. Unlike government television, satellite channels promise limited censorship and, in many cases, manage to uphold that promise. Most social talk shows are primarily targeted at women and youth.

Since 2003, entertainment channels have ventured into the production of a variety of reality programmes. Because reality shows include interactive features, offer vast product-placement and sponsorship opportunities, and attract large and young audiences, the advertising industry has encouraged, promoted and in some cases indirectly bankrolled this type of programming. The popularity of reality TV in the Arab world misled many Western journalists to welcome *Star Academy*, *al-Ra'is* and others and praise their 'democratic' values and modern, taboo-shattering themes. Within the Arab world, religious leaders and intellectual and creative elites were critical of the genre, for threatening vaguely defined Islamic values or for low-brow creative decadence. The Arab reality-TV phenomenon was in fact the result of complex overlaps of political, business, religious and representational forces operating locally and transnationally (see Kraidy, 2009). Television and advertising executives welcomed the increase in primetime audiences and the momentous financial windfall of such ratings. In addition, there was renewed faith in a production that could be 'truly' pan-Arab, both in terms of participants and audiences, the Western origins of many reality formats notwithstanding. As we discussed earlier, MBC's experience with *al-Ra'is* led the channel to search for and find socially acceptable reality-TV formats. One result was MBC's version of *The Biggest Loser*, which was dubbed *al-Rabeh al-Akbar* (The Biggest Winner). Given its commercial and popular success with *Star Academy*, LBC-Sat continued to be the sole producer of polemical and live-streamed reality television. Whether the celebrity reality show *al-Wadi* (The Farm), or the designer/model competition *Mission Fashion*, LBC-Sat specialises in reality TV that involves women and men in mixed company under the unrelenting gaze of cameras. In contrast, Dubai TV developed reality-TV programmes locally that enabled it to balance the channel's quest to compete with privately owned channels while maintaining control over the content. Competition in the reality genre between MBC, LBC-Sat and Dubai TV meant that each channel produced at least three shows a year. Reality television has become an established – even ubiquitous – genre in the Arab world because of its popular appeal, commercial success and ability to generate publicity.

CONCLUSION

As the most commercially successful segment of the Arab television industry, entertainment satellite channels set industry-wide trends in production, programming, promotion and financing. Though there are several successful entertainment channels, in this chapter we focused on sector leaders MBC and LBC-Sat, and Dubai TV, which presents a distinct case as a private–government owned institution with a local grounding and a manifestly cosmopolitan identity.

There is enough evidence to suggest that political protection is an essential requirement for the sustainability and growth of entertainment satellite channels. Throughout their history, these channels have sought political protection, financial support and in return projected specific socio-political visions and discourses. MBC reflects a 'modern' Saudi vision, a middle-of-the-road social liberalism (in Saudi terms) that is nonetheless politically agreeable to, even encouraging of, the Saudi *political* (though not necessarily social) status quo. LBC, initially the voice of a rightwing militia during the Lebanese Civil War, negotiated its survival locally and regionally to become – as LBC-Sat – a more socially liberal and Saudi-oriented version of MBC. In contrast, Dubai TV's fortunes are inextricable from the ambitions of Dubai's rulers. This clearly shows that television entertainment is implicated in politics, even if not as directly as television news.

This means that entertainment channels operate within a set of constraints that, although socially or religiously inspired, are politically enforced. The survival and growth of general entertainment channels depends as much on their deft navigation between competing ideological agendas. In order to comply with these boundaries, general entertainment channels are owned and operated like general businesses that are nonetheless closely aligned with powerful political agendas. By maintaining control over production and circulation, owners have ensured the survival and growth of their channels. Nevertheless, recent market growth has challenged this prevailing structure and forced channels to seriously consider new organisational structures, particularly the expansion into multichannel operations. MBC announced in 2009 its intention to become a publicly listed company; LBC-Sat has for all practical purposes merged with Rotana. Following MBC Group and LBC Holding (and in news, al-Jazeera Network, to be analysed in Chapter 4), the Arab television industries are poised for increased consolidation into multiplatform media conglomerates.

One important implication of these developments is that general entertainment channels have driven the integration of the Arab media industry into the global media landscape, with pan-Arab regionalisation being a link between national industries and the global market. Despite audience entertainment preferences, these channels have promoted a regionalisation of production that includes the development of concepts, site or studio production, promotion and distribution. Traditionally Lebanese- and Egyptian-dominated, the industry is now more diverse, with more Gulf media personalities assuming prominent positions, on and off screen. These multinational and multicultural production teams have diversified programming and helped entertainment capture increasingly larger overall audiences through targeting segmented markets via specialised channels. In this endeavour, entertainment channels face stiff competition. As the following chapter explains, specialised channels have emerged to target niche audiences in the increasingly fragmented pan-Arab media market.

3

Niche Channels and Socio-cultural Change: Youth, Women and Religion

Because the general entertainment channels we discussed in Chapter 2 appeal deliberately to the putative 'Arab family', their programming is relatively conservative, conforming to the social and cultural status quo rather than challenging the prevailing order. In contrast, in this chapter we discuss how some relatively new programming genres aired by new specialised commercial Arab satellite television channels have entered the fray of debate about social and cultural change. Gender, religious and youth issues are among the touchiest topics in the Arab world today. Television programmes that question or depict alternatives to established gender roles, challenge the role of religion in public life, or are perceived to have a negative influence on Arab youth have routinely stirred controversy. Most important among these genres are music programmes, religious programmes and social talk shows. Music videos have triggered debate about the status of women in Arab society, about acceptable sexual behaviour and the gender norms and social values to which Arab youth ought or ought not to be exposed. Religious programmes have pulled in the other direction, ostensibly re-traditionalising Arab popular culture by reasserting broadly defined (and contested) 'Arab-Islamic values' through modern media forms that appeal to various demographic groups, including women and youth. Social talk shows feature frank discussion of hot-button issues.

To tackle the relationship between television institutions and social and cultural change from a media industries perspective, we focus primarily on television genres that have spawned dedicated niche channels and generated public debates, and analyse the industry and social trends behind the popularity of these genres. Indeed, in the increasingly specialised pan-Arab television industries, television genres often overlap with niche channels with this chapter's three broad areas of analysis: music videos targeting youth, satcast mostly but not exclusively on specialised music channels; women's programmes, which are the province of niche and general channels, and religious programming, also featured on general channels but also driving a growth in religiously themed outlets. After discussing music, women's and religious channels, the discussion moves to hybrid genres that have emerged at the intersection of other kinds of programmes, including mixtures of music and religion, a contentious crossroads of tensions involving youth, women, religion and commercialism.

Programmes focusing on music/youth, women and religion, and at a later stage channels dedicated entirely to these genres and demographics, have all emerged in a pan-Arab environment marked by anxieties about Western social and cultural influence which have been exacerbated by continued external political and military interventions in the Middle East. Against that geopolitical backdrop, there are other related concerns specific to the media industries. First, the lack of indigenous cultural and knowledge production – books, films, art, etc – has fuelled concerns over Western cultural influence and more recently Western-inspired television content. The crisis of Arab cultural production was detailed in the *Arab Human Development Report 2003*, written by Arab authors and published by the United Nations Development Programme and the Arab Fund for Economic and Social Development. With 5 per cent of the world's population, the report noted, Arab countries produce merely around 1 per cent of the world's books. Only 1000 to 3000 copies of an Arab novel are usually published (*Arab Human*, 2003), despite a potential readership that spans millions of people living in two dozen countries. Theatrical and cinematic production also reflects a dismal situation in the Arab cultural industries at large.

In this environment, television is a partial exception. The 1990s, as we discuss in both the previous and upcoming chapters, have witnessed the development of vibrant Arab television industries that have filled Arab prime-time with locally produced, Arabic-language news, talk shows, drama, music videos, game shows and reality shows. As we explain in more depth in Chapter 5, Arab television drama serials known as *musalsalat* have relied on public–private cooperation and multi-country co-productions to raise the profile and the income of writers in countries like Egypt and Syria and to a lesser extent in the Gulf countries, especially during the holy month of Ramadan which is considered the most important television viewing season of the year in the Arab world. In Ramadan 2008 alone, Egypt and Syria together produced 104 *musalsalat* ('Quick Overview', 2008; Chapter 5 explores the utmost importance of Ramadan for the Arab television industries). But this trend has been thwarted since television officials prefer the low-risk, high-yield strategy of format adaptation. In contrast to drama which can be considered truly local, music videos, women's talk shows and even some religious programmes present adaptations of 'Western' formats, which are often embedded in synergistic strategies including advertising or sponsorship deals, in addition to audio music and music video deals. However, there are multiple ways in which Arab programmers and producers have borrowed ideas from Western productions, ranging from informal inspirations to adapted licensed formats (Khalil, 2004). Most of these programmes which in spite of their Western provenance use the Arabic language and pan-Arab talent, are perhaps best described as hybrid genres, which, as we will discuss in this chapter's conclusion, can be even more polemical than controversial local programmes.

In public debates related to the media over social and cultural change, religion, women and youth figure prominently. Islam is perceived as a source of norms that are sharply different from putative Western values, while women and youth are feared to be the two groups most vulnerable to the seduction of Western values and lifestyles. At the same time, in the new commercialised and transnational Arabic-language television industry, women, youth and pious people form attractive niche markets for advertisers and as a result are conceived of as segmented audiences by television executives. Rival conceptions of these two groups, i.e., that on the one hand women and young people are vulnerable to undesirable Western influence, and that on the other hand, they are both attractive groups of consumers, has driven many pan-Arab media scandals and controversies. Like youth and women, pious people are increasingly targeted by specialised channels that have developed a popular Islamic sensibility in their programmes and marketing. Because of their growing importance, in this chapter we take an in-depth look at music channels, women's channels and religious channels.

MUSIC CHANNELS AND ARAB YOUTH

Popular culture plays an important role in the life of young people, and the media industries are instrumental in shaping young people's cultural consumption and production. Like youth in other parts of the world, young Arabs are eager users of mobile telephones and text messaging, the Internet, satellite television, and avid consumers of popular music. The existence of a clash between global media-oriented youth culture and local social norms across cultures – in the Arab world and elsewhere – is beyond dispute (Kraidy and Khalil, 2008; see also Karam, 2007). However, Arabs experience this clash in particularly acute forms for several reasons. First is the generational gap between contemporary Arab youth and their parents. According to the United Nations Population Fund, around 34 per cent of the population of Arab countries is under the age of fifteen, and the median age for the Arab region is twenty-two ('Overview: The', 2006). While people who are currently eighteen years old or younger were born into the vibrant and diverse commercial satellite television era, their parents are likely to have grown up with one or two staid national channels. Elements of global media culture that are familiar to these children are completely alien to their parents. There are also vast differences in social class and geographical location, both within and between countries: urban middle and upper classes are targeted by commercial pan-Arab media but poorer and rural viewers are neglected; and wealthy oil-based Gulf economies (especially Saudi Arabia, Kuwait and the United Arab Emirates) contain concentrated groups of wealthy consumers in contrast to the mostly less-well-to-do viewers in the Levant and North Africa (especially in the poorest Arab countries like the Sudan in Africa, Syria in the Levant and Yemen in the Arabian peninsula). In this context of economic disparities, the music television industry has aggressively (though not exclusively) catered to the Arab youth segment in wealthier markets.

Music channels are one of the fastest-growing sectors in Arab satellite television. Their number exploded from zero in 1992 to approximately seventy channels in 2009. The growth of music television occurred in three stages; in each of these periods, industry executives developed new business models for music television in response to shifts in demographic realities, economic opportunities and social values. During the first period, which lasted from 1993 to 2001, channels with a high proportion of music programmes began on ART, Orbit and Showtime Arabia which pioneered pay-television, a sector whose struggle for profitability continues to this day. During the second period, from 2001 to 2004, recording producers and distributors underwrote music television to promote artists and albums, liberating music television from the frustrating search for subscription revenues, with for example the case of the Egyptian Melody Hits channel. In the third and current stage, which started in 2005, televised music evolved into a group of niche and commercially viable satellite channels, and international music channels like MTV launched MTV Arabia, whose impact on the music television market is difficult to ascertain at this early stage.

Before the satellite era, variety shows on Arab national television channels included live musical performances or taped segments – these can be considered as precursors to today's Arab music videos. These shows were produced in

Table 3.1 Selected Arab Music Channels

Channel*	Launch year	Owner	Country base	Genre
MTV Arabia	2008	Arab Media Group – Dubai Holding	Dubai	Western hits and some Arabic hip hop
Nojoom	2004	Al-Abdool Audio and Artistic Group Studio – Suhail al-Abdool	Dubai	Gulf music
Rotana	2003	Rotana Holding Co. – Prince al-Waleed bin Talal	Egypt	Arabic hits
Mazzika	2003	'Alam El-Phan* – Muhsin Jaber	Egypt	Arabic and Western hits
Melody Hits	2002	Melody Entertainment Holding – Gamal Ashraf Marwan	Egypt	Arabic and Western hits
Music Now	1994	Part of Orbit, owned al-Mawarid Group – Prince Khalid bin Abdulrahman	Italy Bahrain	Western hits Mediterranean (Pay-TV)

*Though this is not the standard English transliteration of Arabic, this is how the company spells its name in English.

Studio musical performance in a variety programme

the musical capitals of the Arab world, Beirut and Cairo, where singing and audio-visual talent proliferated. In the 1970s, Lebanon's national broadcaster La Compagnie Libanaise de Télévision aired a talent show, *Studio al-Fann* (Art Studio), in which amateur singers competed weekly for national titles in various categories. In Egypt, national television treated audiences to live weekly concerts by the likes of Umm Kulthum and 'Abdelhalim Hafez. Another important Egyptian export was *Fawazir Ramadan* (The Riddles of Ramadan), a show that included extravagant singing and dancing episodes (to be discussed in detail in Chapter 5). In the early 1980s the Jordanian capital Amman hosted a new type of Arab regional musical exchange, when the second generation of the famed Rahbani musical family escaped Lebanon's Civil War to collaborate with Jordanian television on *Min Yawm-la-Yawm* (Day to Day), which included a number of musical videos. In addition, showbusiness personalities Ehsan Sadiq and Samira Baroudi hosted a musical show directed by Jordan's Hasib Yusef in which artists performed songs and which aired forerunners of music videos consisting of visual montage sequences with an audio track. In the satellite era, entertainment channels were the first to realise the importance of music in attracting audiences, specifically younger viewers. When it was still located in London, MBC's musical programming emphasised a pro-Western musical bias, one that was particularly evident in Lebanese starlet Razan Moghrabi's shows. Inspired by *Top of the Pops*, Moghrabi's show was named *Pops and Tops*, showcasing interviews, performances and music videos by Western artists intercepted with call-ins from Arab viewers. In the same period and under the direction of television director Simon Asmar, LBC had exclusive access to singers who were featured on a number of variety shows, such as *Layla Hazz* (Lucky Night) and *Iftah ya Simsim* (Open Sesame). The Lebanese channel also parlayed its access to Arab talent and its Western production values in its programmes' various musical performances.

Since 2005, specialised music channels have carved a distinct niche focused on producing and promoting music videos, along with 'peripheral' fare includ-

Razan Moghrabi and co-host Khaled al-Breeke on the set of *He Said She Said*

ing interviews, music news, chart shows, electronic press kits and the like. Music channels have developed synergies with a number of entertainment-related businesses including record producers, concert promoters and mobile-phone companies. Music channels are involved in conceiving and producing music videos, a strategy that allows them to maintain a steady supply of content while at the same time having access to exclusive programming material.

With their content clearly inspired by Western counterparts and with a transnational audience that spans Arab societies with various degrees of social liberalism and conservatism, music channels were from the beginning at the forefront of cultural translation between the global and the local. In 1993, Arab Radio and Television (ART) launched an Arabic music channel which later expanded into region-specific (i.e. ART America) or genre-specific (i.e. ART Tarab; tarab is the classical Arab song genre) channels. Under the umbrella of ART Music, these channels were involved in the production of music videos, organisation and taping of music festivals as well as a number of call-in and chart shows. The line-up on ART's five channels conformed to 'Islamic values'; owner Saleh Kamel insisted: 'I don't allow anything on ART that I wouldn't want my children to watch' (Ambah, 1995a). In 1994, another channel provider also based in Italy, Orbit Satellite Television and Radio Network, began transmitting a Western-themed music channel called Music Now. Staffed by veterans from MTV Asia, Music Now tried to use lessons to 'glocalise' Western music to Arab audiences. By presenting Arab- and English-speaking video jockeys (VJs), the channel was the first dedicated music channel of its kind to transmit to the Arab region in 1995. Under increased competition from free-to-air satellite music channels, Music Now rebranded itself as a world music channel by including more Arab and international music videos. Starting in 1996, Showtime Arabia, a subsidiary of Viacom, included MTV Europe and VH1 in its package of channels; the former included only one show produced for Arab audiences called *Mashawir* (Promenades) which originally featured no Arab music videos. Up until 2000, ART remained the main producer and broadcaster of Arab music videos, while Orbit and Showtime competed by scheduling Western music videos. Interestingly, ART and Orbit competed for Arab artists by covering concerts, holding festivals and producing specials. Simultaneously, entertainment channels like MBC and LBC-Sat featured segments or shows which included music videos as main components. Viewers from that time remember the rampant piracy of Western music videos on many satellite channels that cleverly – but not always successfully – tried to disguise the logos of European and American channels.

The Arab music television genre has witnessed dramatic transformations in the last decade. By the late 1990s, Arab music production had attracted many international labels such as Polydor and Universal, and thus initiated new practices in music-video production and promotion. Similarly, Arab television executives were attracted by the success of ART Music and the business models of MTV. Emerging private satellite television benefited from Egypt's newly liberalised media policies that allowed private ownership of satellite television channels and as a result saw in music an untapped niche market. In 2001, Egypt's music channel Dream TV drew in audiences disillusioned by ART's restrictive moral codes and fascinated by MTV's bold programmes. Many of Dream TV's shows were live and chatty, and mixed Western and Arabic music videos. Yet unable to keep up with the competition in televised music, Dream TV expanded to three channels dedicated to family, sports and movies. Another Egyptian music television group, Melody TV, launched in 2002 its flagship chan-

Billboard ad for Rotana music channels

nel, Melody Hits, which focused on Western music and then expanded into several niche channels (Arabic, games, movies) with various multiplatform services such as web and phone downloads. Melody Arabia competes with Mazzika TV, an outlet owned by the Egyptian music label 'Alam el-Phan and launched in 2003 as a video platform for promoting the label's artists. Another music producer, al-Khuyul production, established Nojoom TV in 2004, a four-channel music network based in Dubai. Mazzika TV took the MTV model a step further by featuring more graphics and animation and by introducing the message ticker, which eventually became a main feature of music channels in the Arab region. At the same time, Mazzika TV invested heavily in web-related activities such as ringtone downloads. By 2003, through a share swap between ART's chairman Saleh Kamel and Prince al-Waleed bin Talal, ART Music's five channels were transformed into the Rotana music channels. Building on ART's catalogue of music video and concerts, Rotana added its exclusive access to over a hundred artists signed to its music label. With its purchase of ART Music, Rotana became the third and largest music publisher to own television channels (Kraidy and Khalil, 2008). Since then, the competition has focused on securing content, particularly music videos, which intensified synergy between music publishers, promoters and television channels.

To this day, the growth of Arab music-television channels continues to capitalise on two main factors: value-added services and market segmentation. Value-added services opened new revenue streams while not impeding traditional advertising sources. They include, but are not restricted to, various interactive and multimedia gizmos such as text tickers, web and phone downloads, and pop-up advertising messages. After advanced technologies allowed music channels to be viable with only a few employees, small channels especially have relied on value-added services as their main source of revenue. At the same time, the music television market has been witnessing increased segmentation. Established channels as well as newcomers have been developing programming strategies that target specific demographic groups based on geographic location, cultural predilection, gender and age. Reflecting this trend, Melody TV and Rotana have created channels to cater for various musical styles and entertainment genres. For instance, Melody Arabia and Rotana Music mix current music videos with some variety shows, gossip and interviews. Newcomers like Emirati-owned Music Plus TV, 2004, gave viewers greater screen space to display their text messages, which particularly attracts younger viewers; while other Gulf-owned channels like Wannassa, operated by MBC, are dedicated to *khaliji* (Gulf-based) music and its fans in countries like Saudi Arabia, the United Arab Emirates, Kuwait and others.

Recent developments portend a growing integration of Arab satellite music channels into the global media industries. Since 2007, the Arab music-channel scene has attracted international players like the Canadian Much Music and the American Viacom. Much Music's Arab launch failed because the original company in Canada equivocated on whether to expand as a global franchise, finally deciding against that expansion and pushing interested Arab investors away. In contrast, MTV Arabia's venture into the region, first announced in late 2006 ('Launch of', 2006) has relied on the pioneering music channel's distinguished global image; however, MTV is entering a mature market that has been using the pioneering US music channel's programming models for years. According to MTV Arabia's manager, Samer al-Marzuqi, '[the channel is] targeting normal Arabs. We're not targeting educated, private school people. Those are Arab society's niche. They are not more than 10 percent of the population. We are trying to appeal to the masses' (el-Baltaji, 2008). However, this claim is undercut when one looks at the channel's youthful staff and its niche programmes like *Hip Hop Na* [Our Hip Hop], which focuses, in al-Marzuqi's words, on 'Arab rapping' (el-Baltaji, 2008), which is not exactly a mass musical genre in the Arab world. At the same time, the claim made by an MTV worldwide Vice-President that MTV Arabia's 'mix of Arabic and Western contents' will make it a distinct channel (al-Dossary, 2007) is ironically belied by the fact that many pan-Arab music channels follow precisely that formula.

In the future, it is likely that an increasing integration between pan-Arab television industries and global media conglomerates could fuel controversies in Arab societies over the depiction of women and gender roles in music videos. Talk shows on al-Jazeera, the Beirut-based National Broadcasting Network (NBN) and Heya TV, newspaper columns across the Arab world, cartoons and mosque sermons, have taken up the polemic surrounding Arab music videos, a debate that touches on gender roles and relations, sexuality and Western influence. At the heart of the controversy is the provocative depiction of women and gender relations on many locally made music videos. Featuring young, suggestively dressed, flirtatious female singer-performers, some music videos show bedroom scenes and lascivious dance numbers, with an overall atmosphere of sensuality and unbridled gender relations. Egyptian and Lebanese singers are known to be the most provocative in that regard; Lebanese pop diva Haifa Wehbi regularly triggers the ire of Arab politicians from Bahrain to Egypt, who use Wehbi's concerts in their countries as opportunities to score political points, bolster sagging political fortunes or simply to be the centre of media attention. These polemics can sometimes lead to frictions between executives and legislative government branches: to placate hostile members of Kuwait's parliament, an incoming Minister of Information created a committee of media personalities charged with 'monitoring music videos', a task akin to plugging a dike with a finger in the new transnational and commercial media environment in the Arab world, as the head of the committee, the Director of Kuwait Television's Channel 4, appeared implicitly to recognise during an interview with one of the authors (al-Sahly interview, 15 November 2005). Controversy was stoked by the ubiquity of music videos, which are not aired only on specialised outlets but also serve as 'fillers' between programming slots for general entertainment channels. Yet while clerics, critics and supporters have debated music channels' suggestive depictions of the female body and women's relations with men, several satellite channels have actively focused on the emerging Arab women's market, including an emerging industry segment of women's channels.

WOMEN'S CHANNELS

As the growing commercialisation of Arab television led to the establishment of niche markets, women were identified as a desirable demographic group that warranted investments beyond women's programmes on entertainment channels. As a result, channels exclusively dedicated to women have been established and have gained commercial and popular success. While these channels publicise women's issues and therefore can be said to provide a measure of empowerment to Arab women, in some cases their focus on traditional gender roles where women are depicted mostly as mothers, wives and shoppers (advertising oblige!) counteracts these channels' progressive potential. As we aim to show in the next few pages, there are multiple and contradictory opinions about the impact of women's programmes and channels on the actual lives of Arab women and on Arab societies at large, reflecting the wide spectrum of opinion on the Arab media sphere.

Historically, Arab women's programming has been available on free-to-air entertainment channels as well as on pay-TV. Like elsewhere in the world, daytime programming, mostly morning talk shows and daytime drama, is largely dedicated to women. Both genres are considered 'feminine' and address stay-at-home women with a mix of information and entertainment. Access primetime, the late afternoon and early evening programming time-frame leading into primetime, is also women-oriented, featuring social talk shows and dramas. For instance, LBC and MBC feature Egyptian and Syrian drama or dubbed *telenovelas* in the lead-up to their primetime. Similarly, pay-TV packages promote specific channels – such as ART's Arabic Movies or Arabic series on Showtime's *al-Shasha* (The Screen) – as 'women-oriented'. Increasingly, infomercials are produced to address women during these viewing periods. Showtime's pay-TV package even includes a shopping channel. Family and entertainment channels have identified women as an important niche; but their programme offerings are limited to entertainment and talk shows. Women are

Table 3.2 Women's Programmes on Arab Satellite Channels

Programme	Channel	Dates	Genre
Lil Nisa' Faqat	Al-Jazeera	2002–5	Social-political
Ra'edat	Al-Jazeera	2005	Historical
Kalam Nawa'em	MBC	2001–present	Social
Banat Hawwa	LBC	2007–9	Social
Ante	MBC	1998–2001	Social

offered light leisure, infotainment or infomercials, and few shows are dedicated to involving women beyond certain traditional roles, tastes and cultural modes.

Attempts by news channels to establish lively public fora for women to discuss their issues beyond traditional roles, like al-Jazeera's *Lil Nisa' Faqat* (For Women Only), have generally been short-lived. The show, which featured women-only groups of guests discussing wide-ranging issues like domestic violence, women's professional development, media representations of women, women and Islam, and sexuality and parenting issues, only lasted from 2002 to 2005. These important contributions notwithstanding, the show's real impact is contested among critics. One analyst saw in the show a platform for an Arab female counterpublic because it provided a space for women to discuss women's issues in a non-confrontational fashion and uninterrupted by men (Sakr, 2005), while another discerned a process of discussion 'where binary oppositions are consolidated; for example, women's position in Islam as opposed to women's position in human rights charters, veiled women as opposed to unveiled women …' (Abou al-Naga, 2004). From the latter perspective, al-Jazeera's treatment of women's issues focused on individual events at the expense of tackling the systematic workings of patriarchy (Abou al-Naga, 2004). The channel's commitment to women's issues was clearly strong because *Lil Nisa' Faqat* was to be replaced by a show about Arab female role models called *Ra'edat* (Pioneers). Al-Jazeera's management invoked a desire to integrate women's issues across the channel's grid, but the show was in all likelihood a victim of several factors. First, during our field research for this book, both of us heard insistent rumours in the industry, that male viewers, some of them influential, had complained that they were excluded from the show, which may explain why during the show's later years, especially when Luna al-Shebl hosted it, she repeatedly emphasised that men were welcome to call in and participate in the discussion. Second, the women-oriented television industry sector was growing rapidly and was characterised by high-production values and attractive presenters, with which *Lil Nisa' Faqat* was unable to compete. Third and most important, the show was most probably undermined by the Islamist faction in the channel, which can be traced back to how *Lil Nisa' Faqat* related to other al-Jazeera shows, especially *al-Shari'a wal Hayat* (Islamic Law and Life), whose semipermanent star, Sheikh Yusuf al-Qaradawi, holds conservative views on gender issues. As Dabbous-Sensenig (2006) argued, based on a textual analysis, the show

> is set up structurally and thematically in opposition to other talk shows on Al-Jazeera, in order to promote specific definitions of religious reality, at the expense of progressive or feminist definitions. As such, its aim seems to be less geared toward debating religion (and Islamic *shari'a*), than to promoting specific, mainly orthodox views on gender and Islam. (p. 78)

Al-Qaradawi's influence on discourse about gender issues via al-Jazeera was in clear view during an episode of *Lil Nisa' Faqat* discussing the *niqab*, or full facial covering, when the host cut off her female guests to 'end the discussion' via a recorded video featuring al-Qaradawi (Dabbous-Sensenig, 2006). As another Arab scholar succinctly put it, 'the tone of Sheikh al-Qaradawi is highly patronising towards women, lenient towards men, and accusative of the West' (Abou al-Naga, 2004). In this case, a fraught relationship between religious interpretation and gender roles helps explain why news channels like al-Jazeera have been unable to sustain programmes directed at women.

A small number of programmes have achieved popular success in primetime, many of them variations and adaptations of Barbara Walters's ABC morning talk show *The View*, but hosted by a multinational, pan-Arab group of women. These include LBC's *Banat Hawwa* (Daughters of Eve), hosted by 'Zahra from Bahrain, Hala from Egypt, Maha from Saudi Arabia, Sahar from Iraq, and Lama from Lebanon' (Haddad, 2008), thereby including national 'representatives' from countries that LBC considers its most important markets. Even the US government's al-Hurra launched a show called *Hunna* [They, (feminine)], with Lebanese, Egyptian, Saudi Arabian and Tunisian hosts. However, it is MBC1's *Kalam Nawa'em* which is the most well known among several Arabic-language television all-women-cast talk shows. *Kalam Nawa'em* followed a previous and

The hosts of *Kalam Nawa'em*

more educational MBC show called *Ante* [You (female)] which aired between 1998 and 2001. *Kalam Nawa'em* features four female hosts of various nationalities (Saudi Arabia, Lebanon, Egypt and Syria) debating and discussing issues of concern to women from all walks of life, often with studio guests, often male, drawn from showbusiness and social organisations: The show's cast has changed over the years, and has included Nashwa al-Ruwayni, formerly head of MBC's Cairo offices, Fawziyya Salama, editor-in-chief of *Sayyidati* (My Lady) magazine, Farah Bsayso, a Palestinian actress, Rania Barghout, a former Miss Lebanon and Muna Abuslayman, a Saudi English-literature professor who went on to head Prince al-Waleed bin Talal's Kingdom Foundation.

Since 2001, the show has featured various hot topics relating to women's role in society, religion, tradition and Western influence. *Kalam Nawa'em*'s approach, however, is softer than *Lil Nisa' Faqat*. In the former, each of the hostesses assumes an archetype of Arab women, from the liberal young professional, to the eloquent and intelligent woman who wears the veil, to the middle-aged, wizened mother-figure. Its studio is larger, more elaborate and more colourful than *Lil Nisa' Faqat*'s, and its production values more sophisticated than the al-Jazeera women's talk show. Whereas *Lil Nisa' Faqat* was cut from al-Jazeera's grid, *Kalam Nawa'em* remains one of MBC's signature programmes. This suggests that women's shows that have a 'soft' approach and an entertaining angle fare better than 'harder' and more journalistic programmes – a lesson that was learned quickly by entrepreneurs interested in investing in niche women's channels.

The appearance of channels dedicated to women signalled a heightened industry commitment to that niche market. Chief among these major institutional actors are the Lebanese-owned Heya TV (She TV) and Saudi-owned MBC4, commercial channels available on satellite across the region. Heya originated when Antenne Plus, a Lebanese terrestrial channel, was denied a licence during the 1996 restructuring of Lebanese television according to the 1994 Audio-Visual Media Law (see Chapter 6 for details). Relaunched as Heya TV in 2002, the self-proclaimed 'Arab Woman's Channel' started with a modest budget of US $3–4 million and was staffed predominantly (70 per cent) by women (Matar, 2007), especially for on-air roles, with veteran film-maker and director Nicolas Abu Samah as general manager. Heya TV's programming consists of talk shows, local serials, dubbed Latin American *telenovelas*, and infomercials, with the latter providing most of its revenue. The company has three flagship talk shows: *'al-Makshuf* (In the Open), *Jari' Jeddan* (Very Bold) and *Min Yawm la-Yawm* (Day to Day). Hosted by Mathilda Farjallah, a well-known and outspoken journalist (see al-Khoury, 2006; al-'Utaybi, 2006), *'al-Makshuf* has courted scandal by tackling controversial social and sexual issues important to

Arab women. *Jari' Jeddan* features daring interviews, often with female or male (though rarely) celebrities. *Min Yawm la-Yawm* integrates in-studio discussions with news reports about women's issues worldwide. Though these three shows reflect a feminist, sometimes activist sensibility (see Matar, 2007), others reflect Heya TV's commercial bedrock, which consists of fashion and shopping shows. For example, one primetime show, *Malikat* (Queens) is a recorded talk show which features beauty queens and models. Based on a textual analysis of Heya TV's talk shows and telephone interviews with some of the channel's leading figures, Matar argued that Heya TV's unique contribution is what she called 'its distinctly Arab feminist agenda' (2007, p. 320), which according to the author leads to 'the creation of an Arab feminist counterpublic … [by] bringing the private into the public but also through nurturing a feminist agenda that is played out in … discussions' (Matar, 2007, p. 524). This verdict, however, is not consensual. After all, Heya's main social contributions are limited to a couple of talk shows, albeit repeated on the schedule, amidst a profusion of consumerism. A male journalist (who used language that suggests a feminist sensibility) writing in the Lebanese daily *Assafir* criticised the channel for 'missing the fundamental issues' that face Arab women in the context of patriarchy (Nassar, 2006). According to the author, these include illiteracy, an endemic problem among Arab women, and 'momentous' political and social issues that animate many Arab conferences and symposia about women's issues and civil and political rights. Nassar (2006) also criticised the channel's unwillingness or inability to attract a top-level programme host from outside Lebanon, concluding with the harsh accusation that Heya TV merely focuses on 'jewellery, cosmetics … dieting and healthy cooking'. Nonetheless, since its 2002 launch, Heya TV has expanded its operations beyond Lebanon to Syria, Saudi Arabia, Jordan and the Maghreb, but most of their coverage seems to focus on Lebanon and the United Arab Emirates, and more specifically on Beirut and Dubai.

Because it caters to all women, old, young, rural and urban, Heya TV's programming lacks hipness, opening a wedge for competitors vying for the urban women's market. This niche is filled by MBC4, an urban, young and trendy channel relying almost exclusively on Western productions. MBC4, initially conceived as a hip, Western-content channel, was relaunched at the end of 2005 to focus on 'the modern Arabic woman' ('Reaching the', 2005). The latter is described by Muhammad al-Mulhem, former MBC Group's Director of Marketing, Public Relations and Commercials, as having achieved 'a level of intellectual and cultural sophistication that the media must cope with in terms of superior programming' ('Reaching the', 2005). This is part of MBC's strategy to segment the Arab market and reach each group (based on geography, gender, age or programme appeal) with a dedicated channel. The success of *The*

Oprah Winfrey Show (1986–) among young Saudi women has motivated Tim Riordan, Director of Channels at MBC to build MBC4's schedule around it ('Reaching the', 2005). Other Harpo productions like *Dr Phil* (2002) are a permanent fixture on MBC4, along with a number of mostly US reality shows, soaps and series (Kattan interview, 28 May 2008).

MBC4's push towards younger women, particularly in Saudi Arabia, has manifested itself in various promotional activities. Off screen, MBC4 initiated the *I Matter* road shows in Jeddah universities where discussion-based events explored topics ranging from confidence-building to healthy living and career success ('MBC Launches', 2006). These road shows were accompanied with a massive press and online campaign promoting a competition to select the best argument for why women matter in society. On screen, the channel's slogan, 'It's for you!', is emphasised in a series of promotional clips showing women – veiled *and* trendy – doing yoga, shopping, drinking cocktails or sending text messages. Until 2008, no Arabic programmes were broadcast on MBC4 but all content has had Arabic subtitles. Commercials, however, have been predominantly in Arabic. In an attempt to consolidate audience fragmentation, MBC transferred its highly successful Turkish series, *Nour* (or in Turkish *Gümüs*) from MBC1 to MBC4 with *The Oprah Winfrey Show* as a lead-in. *Nour*, which traces the story of a young executive who marries into her employer's family, is the third Turkish series to be broadcast on MBC and the first to use local Syrian dialect instead of classical Arabic, underscoring a trend towards a diversification of the Arabic spoken on Arab television. With *Nour*, MBC succeeded in three uncharted territories, first 'transferring' audiences from MBC1 to MBC4, partnering with Showtime Arabia to offer pay-per-view episodes of *Nour* through MBC Plus, and confirming that Arabs like drama that they feel is socially and culturally proximate regardless of its national origin (Turkey) and the Arabic dialect in which it is dubbed (Syrian). Like Heya TV, nevertheless, MBC4 has received its share of criticism. Writing in the Beirut- and London-based, Saudi-owned, pan-Arab daily newspaper *al-Hayat*, the female journalist Baysan al-Sheikh (2006) argued that MBC4 represents the ills of women's programmes on Arab satellite television, by focusing

> on the latest fashion fads, clothing and make-up, in addition to cooking and shopping advice, and protocols of social etiquette. In some sense, these programmes bring Arab women back to the cage of the harem but in a modern guise, exactly like the veiled women on MBC4 who remained subjected to the old tradition of the *hijab*, but in an inventive way, making it look like a big rose. (al-Sheikh, 2006)

Programming oriented towards women is now widely available on Arab television. The competition between free-to-air satellite and pay-TV channels has resulted in the growth of a variety of programming genres – movies, series, shopping and fashion, in addition to traditional daytime talk shows and soaps. The continued presence of several channels dedicated to Arab women is a sign that the industry recognises the long-term viability of the women's market. At the same time, this risks isolating women's issues from broader social, economic and political issues, a sort of ghettoisation, though some scholars believe, as we have already seen, that women-only shows such as *Lil Nisa' Faqat* and dedicated channels like Heya TV provide a platform for a women's counterpublic that gives women's issues more exposure to the broader pan-Arab television audience. Driven by commercial calculations and social concerns – which are not necessarily mutually exclusive – Arab women's television in the future will have to contend with the tensions stemming from the socially and religiously contested status of Arab women. As they seek more and more narrowly defined niche markets, the television industries are likely to spawn diverse programmes for women, some 'forward-looking', featuring relatively more socially liberal women's roles, others pushing in the other direction to reassert prevailing gender norms. In the latter category, religious channels, to which we turn in the next section of this chapter, play an increasingly important role, at once re-traditionalising and modernising religious ideas and practices.

RELIGIOUS CHANNELS

Religious programming, part of state television channels in several Arab countries decades before the satellite era took off in the 1990s, has enjoyed a renewed popularity in the satellite era. It is worth recalling that Christian broadcasting exists in the Arab world, both terrestrial and satellite and until recently mostly based in Beirut, and that there are currently Christian satellite channels in Egypt, Iraq and Lebanon. These channels, however, are outside the mainstream of the Arab satellite television industries, which is why in this book we focus on the more widely watched and more socially impactful Islamic religious channels. Friday prayers and sermons were transmitted live as well as other forms of religious festivities. In Saudi Arabia, after initial controversies over the introduction of television (see Kraidy, 2006d), clerics were empowered to shape television policy and content, which enabled them to influence the growth of the national television sector in ensuing decades. As a result, religious programming has figured predominantly on state television, including prayer five times a day. Saudi television featured the first televised religious show in the 1960s and 1970s, featuring Sheikh 'Ali Tantawi (Boyd, 1999), probably the first Arab tele-cleric (see also Chapter 5). In the 1980s, more than 25 per cent of programmes were religious (Boyd, 1999). By the late 1990s, around 50 per cent of programmes on Saudi Television Channel One were religious (Al-Saleh, 2006). In Egypt, religious programming grew after the country's defeat in the 1967 war with Israel, an event which rejuvenated Islamism in Egypt and beyond. In Saudi Arabia, Egypt, and most other Arab countries, state television increases religious programmes during the holy month of Ramadan.

Privately owned Islamic satellite channels first appeared in the late 1990s. ART established Iqra' (Read) in 1998 as a channel appealing to women and youth worldwide. According to the launching press release, Iqra' 'aimed to counter the dominance of Western TV programmes in the Persian Gulf' (Ambah, 1998). Sheikh Saleh Kamel, the owner of ART and a prominent figure in Islamic banking, was instrumental in establishing this channel and shaping its identity. Though programming was initially not restricted to religion, within a few years, Iqra''s Islamic identity was solidified, taking over as the Islamic 'channel of record' from state-owned Saudi Channel One. Iqra''s religious programmes emulate entertainment television, featuring several charismatic male and female 'born-again' preachers and live interaction with audiences. Iqra''s popularity is highest in Egypt and Saudi Arabia where it produces most of its programmes. Since March 2008, Kamel himself even presents a show, *al-Souq* (The Market), in which he shares his experiences with young people – combining motivational speech with the reality-TV premise of *The Apprentice* (2004–).

The trend set by Iqra' was followed by al-Majd (The Glory) and al-Resalah (The Message). The first grew in 2002 out of an Islamic publishing house owned by the (Saudi) al-Shmaimri brothers called al-Majd, to include multiple outlets: al-Majd satellite channel, a Koran channel, a science channel, a history channel, a news channel, a documentary channel, four children's channels, a production house and a marketing company (al-Khareef, 2007). Unlike its competitors, al-Majd aimed to provide a full line-up of Islamic-compliant (no sex, no alcohol, no

Table 3.3 Leading Islamic Channels

Channel	Owner	Country base	Genre	Access
Iqra'	Arab Radio and Television – Sheikh Saleh Kamel	Saudi Arabia-Egypt-Jordan	Saudi-Wahhabi and Egyptian al-Azhar	Free-to-air on pay-TV platform
Al-Majd Holy Koran Channel	Al-Majd Satellite Broadcasting Limited, al-Shmaimri brothers and associates	Saudi Arabia-Dubai-Egypt	Saudi-Wahhabi	Free-to-air on a pay-TV platform
Al-Resalah	Kingdom Holding – Prince al-Waleed bin Talal	Kuwait	Moderate Saudi	Free-to-air

The headquarters of al-Majd
channel in Amman, Jordan

singing, no dancing, religious content, etc) channels that could only be received
via an exclusive set-top box. In less than two years, al-Majd secured a strong subscriber base and opened production centres in Dubai, Amman, Cairo, Mecca and
Riyadh (al-Khareef, 2007). On al-Majd's channels, only certain sounds and
human chants are permitted, following conservative doctrinal interpretations that
prohibit or severely restrict the use of songs, music videos and the appearance of
women as presenters or without proper Islamic veil (al-Abdallah, 2007).

Iqra' and al-Majd can be described as traditional Islamic channels, stern and
preachy even when the channels feature charismatic hosts and strong production
values. In contrast, al-Resalah was launched as an unabashedly hip Islamic alternative. Al-Resalah was established in 2006 by Kingdom Holding, owner of
Rotana ('al-Resalah (The Message)', 2006). It has a slick screen appearance and
features a mix of prayer, talk shows and music. It also features cartoons and animated films infused with moral messages. In a press release, Tariq al-Suwaidan,
the channel's general manager, said that 40 per cent of the programmes would
be youth-oriented, 30 per cent would target women and families, and 10 per cent
would focus on children. Cartoons are produced in Turkey, Egypt and Jordan ('al-
Resalah (The Message),' 2006). The channel is owned by Prince al-Waleed bin
Talal who made its priority to present 'Arab heritage through a modern medium'
and to counteract the misconceptions of Islam in other societies ('al-Resalah (The
Message)', 2006). Like some of Rotana's other programmes that we discussed
elsewhere (Kraidy and Khalil, 2008), al-Resalah is positioned as a bridge between
East and West (see 'Interview with', 2006; also Echchaibi, 2007). As such, it fit
al-Waleed bin Talal's agenda to help bring about a hipper and 'moderate' Islam
(for more on al-Waleed's involvement in Arab media, see Chapter 3 of Kraidy,
2009). Other niche channels, such as al-Baraka TV, were shut down by Egyptian
authorities over transmission technicalities in February 2008. To counter the rising influence of the Muslim Brotherhood in Egypt, the Mubarak government

allowed Salafi Islamist channels al-Rahma, founded in 2006, and al-Nass, launched in 2007, to transmit from Cairo (Field and Hamam, 2009).

There is a discernible trend to establish Arab-based Islamic channels that broadcast in English (not to be confused with English-speaking Islamic channels like the British Islamic Satellite Channel better known as 'Islam Channel'). The motivation behind these channels is to reach non-Arabic-speaking but English-speaking Muslims living in Europe and Asia. For example, Cairo-based al-Huda [The Right Path] is a free-to-air satellite channel with a religiously moderate message. Made possible by a US $13.3 million initial budget, the channel's programmes include Koranic teachings and reciting, direct *fatwas* and talk shows. It draws its anchors from the variety of ethnic and racial backgrounds represented in Islam with the objective of highlighting the 'universality of Islam' (Sheikh Hamad, 2005). Such channels clearly address a pan-Islamic rather than a pan-Arab audience, and their use of English renders them non-influential players in the Arab television industries.

Arabic-language religious channels helped create two types of television stars: the *tele-sheikh* (tele-cleric) and the *tele-da'ia* (tele-preacher). Starring in his al-Jazeera show titled *al-Shari'a wal Hayat* (Islamic Law and Life), the Egyptian cleric Yusuf al-Qaradawi issues religious opinions known as *fatwas* and discusses general social and political issues. In contrast to clerics, who typically base their authority on formal theological training at recognised institutions, *da'ias* tend to be charismatic, born-again Muslims who dedicate their lives to religious preaching. Satellite television gave *da'ias* like the Egyptian 'Amr Khaled superstar status. Khaled's charisma, trendy clothing and 'modernist' Islamic discourse focusing on youth has led to over-the-air skirmishes between him and more established religious leaders like al-Qaradawi (see Echchaibi, 2007). For example, in the aftermath of the Danish cartoons controversy, al-Qaradawi in March 2006 criticised Khaled for participating in a high-profile inter-faith dialogue in Denmark, claiming that Khaled was not qualified to represent Muslims in such a dialogue (see 'Al-Qaradawi: Preachers', 2006; al-Shafi'i, 2006). In addition, prominent clerics and preachers have fraught relationships with Arab governments. On the one hand, Arab regimes consider mainstream (and therefore relatively moderate) Islamic media as an antidote to radical political Islamism, so they give personalities like al-Qaradawi and Khaled a considerable margin for manoeuvre. At the same time, since many Arab regimes lack popular legitimacy, they feel threatened by charismatic television personalities whose religious message enjoys a considerable popular following, and attempt to control them via a combination of coercion and co-optation.

THE RISE OF HYBRID TELEVISION GENRES

During the last decade, thematic mixing of gender, music, youth and religion in shows that can be described as hybrid genres, has gained prominence on pan-Arab television. Mixing some of these categories is not new, especially with music and religion. During Ramadan, general channels used to compile videos of natural and religious sites to songs like Fayza Kamel's 'Allahi Laysa Li Ilak 'Awna' (No Help for Me but You, My God), Asmahan's 'alayk Salat Allah Wa Salamu (God's Peace Be upon You). More recently, channels like Rotana have interrupted their broadcasts to remind their mostly young viewers of prayer times (see Kraidy and Khalil, 2008). Other channels have produced or promoted artists who perform Islamic songs, what has been labelled as 'Islamic Pop' (Kraidy, 2006b) or 'New Age Islam' (Echchaibi, 2007). In spite of some criticism, the music videos were well received and are heavily rotated during Ramadan. The most famous Islamic music video artist is Sami Yusuf, a British singer of Azeri origin whose 'al-Mu'allim' (The Teacher) music video remains one of the most popular hits since its launch during Ramadan 2004 (see Pond, 2006). The following year, an Egyptian boy band released 'Kan Nifsi' (I Wish I Could), and a string of hits followed including a commentary on the Danish cartoon controversy, 'Ella Ibn 'Abdallah' (Except for the Son of Abdallah), featuring an all-female band in a protest song. In Saudi Arabia, two local companies, Full Stop Advertising and Silvergrey, teamed up to produce Ahmad Bou Khater's 'La Sawfa A'ud ya Ummi' (O Mother, I Will Come Back). Even established non-religious singers like the Syrian Asala wore a veil in 'Khaliha 'Ala Allah' (Leave the Matter to God), a song about having faith in God. While some critics took offence at the juxtaposition of Arabic pop and Islamic prayer, others welcomed this *al-fann al-hadef* (purposeful art) as symptomatic of a modern Islam. Since then, Islamic music videos have achieved relatively widespread acceptance among pious Muslims.

Though far more controversial, the story of Arab reality television seems to follow a similar trend involving the increased hybridity of genres. As we saw in Chapter 2, pan-Arab, format-adapted reality shows MBC's *al-Ra'is* (Big Brother), and especially LBC's *Star Academy*, caused heated controversies from 2003 to 2008. Reality television embodies a new business model based on interactivity among new media in the form of voting via mobile telephones and the Internet, and has contributed to new production practices in the industry. Though close interactions between males and females on stage and in shared living quarters have attracted record youth audiences, they have triggered the ire of clerical and social leaders over gender roles and relations (Kraidy, 2006a and d; 2007). Because most of these shows feature singing competitions, they operate as a pipeline of new talent for the Arab recording industries, spawning synergies that include CDs, music videos, ringtones and concert tours managed by conglomerates like Rotana (Khalil, 2006a). Like music videos, however, reality television has been appropriated in locally acceptable ways, as visible in reality shows that feature teams competing to perform good deeds Islamic-style or individuals competing in Koranic recitation (see Kraidy, 2009, for a full treatment of the Arab reality-television controversies). Some networks have satellite channels that are periodically dedicated to individual reality shows, like LBC's Nagham, which is a music-video channel for approximately half of each year, and dedicated to *Star Academy* and at other times to other LBC reality shows. Such channels are substitutes for the web-streaming that is part of some reality shows in the West, because limited Internet availability and weak connections pre-empt successful web-streaming in most Arab countries. Nonetheless, it is noteworthy that as of this writing there are no niche channels permanently dedicated to the reality genre.

CONCLUSION

In this chapter we have explored the emergence and growth of specialised niche channels since the early days of the Arab satellite television era. In those initial stages, these channels attempted to develop a pay-TV model, a business model they are still struggling to establish. As the television industry grew increasingly commercial, satellite channels pursued niche markets with renewed enthusiasm. Youth, women and religious people emerged as key demographic target groups for these channels. Young people, especially wealthy denizens of the Gulf, are attractive to the advertising industry because of their diverse consumption preferences ranging from clothing and fashion accessories, through soft drinks to mobile devices. Women, seen as primary deciders in household consumption choices, are targeted by advertisers of fashion, jewellery, beauty products and services, in addition to household items ranging from shampoo to cooking oil. Religious people also represent a lifestyle community that eats *halal*, dresses differently from the mainstream Arab population and purchases religious books, cassettes and DVDs, in addition to specially tailored gizmos like Islamic mobile phones that ring at prayer times and have a compass pointing to Mecca, the direction that Muslims must face when praying.

These desirable demographic communities based on age, gender and religion that have become the feverishly pursued targets of advertisers are at the same time sensitive social categories in Arab countries. As a result of these overlapping market imperatives and social tensions, music, Islamic and women-focused satellite channels have been commercially successful, socially at the vanguard, and occasionally controversial. Though shows and channels dedicated to women have a mixed record as far as promoting meaningful change for Arab women, Arab media workers are actively setting new standards and shaping norms.

Women are challenging conservative norms, for example, in war reporting, especially during the 2006 war between Israel and Lebanon, when several women
correspondents distinguished themselves with their professionalism (for example see al-Fardan, 2006) and became the subject of admiring social conversation
(as witnessed by both authors of this book, who were on the ground in Lebanon
during the summer 2006 war); or through writing screenplays for television
drama, where women are gaining prominence (see Yasin, 2006). This increasing
specialisation and competition is beginning to change the generally conservative
line that religious channels have taken on women's issues. For example, al-
Resalah is clearly more progressive on gender roles than Iqra'. As mentioned in
Chapter 1, the Egyptian channel al-Mehwar features a show in which a veiled
woman psychologist dispenses advice and guidance on sexual issues to callers,
males and females.

   Although religion, gender and age are important markers of market niches,
this chapter has hopefully accomplished the task of explaining that, like the
demographic groups they target, niche channels are not monolithic; rather they
are diverse, fluid, contested and, most importantly, dynamically related to each
other. They show that there are many ways to be a woman, to be young and to
be pious in the Arab world, a fundamentally important matter that television
industries looking for new audiences appear to have recognised before other
social and political institutions. As a result, niche channels play an important role
in differentiating various Arab audiences from each other, a role all the more
important when we consider the broad, mass-audience strategies and therefore
homogenising tendencies of the leading pan-Arab news channels, to which we
turn in the next chapter.

4

Pan-Arab News Channels

Before the satellite era, the evening news bulletin on the state-owned television channel was the only audio-visual source of information in any given Arab country. Those seeking other electronic sources of news listened to foreign radio broadcasters like the BBC and the French-owned Radio Monte-Carlo Middle East, a trend that was boosted significantly by the poor performance of Arab government broadcasting during the 1967 war with Israel. This inaugurated a major pattern in the Arab television industries, especially when it came to television news: war and conflict have for four decades been major drivers of ✭ institutional development. In the 1980s, warring militias in Lebanon established *war* illegal radio and television stations, undermining the state's sovereignty over broadcasting (Kraidy, 1998b). A decade later, when Saudi authorities imposed a news blackout on the 1990 Iraqi invasion of Kuwait, viewers turned to foreign channels like CNN, which was available on satellite. At the same time, as we saw in Chapter 1, conflict and repression pushed dissident politicians and businessmen to establish satellite channels in Europe. More recently, al-Jazeera established its reputation during the Anglo-American invasion of Afghanistan in 2001 and al-Arabiya made its entrance on the satellite scene with intensive coverage of the beginning of the Iraq war in 2003.

Though war has been an auspicious opportunity for a satellite channel to enter the competitive field of Arab satellite television news, conflict provides no guarantee for continued institutional success: while al-Jazeera and al-Arabiya have continued to grow, Abu Dhabi TV, whose extensive and hard-hitting coverage of the 2003 Anglo-American invasion of Iraq led some observers to believe that al-Jazeera and al-Arabiya had met their match, failed to sustain its coverage, lost many viewers, receded to the status of a second-tier channel, and restructured itself into a general entertainment channel (Khalil, 2004). In 2002, LBC-Sat merged its satellite news operations with Saudi-owned newspaper *al-Hayat*, combining the former's technical expertise and transmission capacity with the latter's international network of correspondents. Despite the merger and the war in Iraq, shackled by LBC's reputation as an entertainment channel, the LBC–*al-Hayat* joint venture was unable to establish itself as a leading pan-Arab source of news. Conflict has also given rise to local Iraqi and Palestinian channels covering the news from the viewpoints of various local actors. Clearly, some channels were better than others at exploiting the news opportunities presented by recurrent conflicts in the Middle East.

Viewership of news channels like al-Jazeera and al-Arabiya tends to peak during times of crisis, a pattern consistent with international viewership trends. While the Israeli–Palestinian conflict has been a constant theme in Arab reporting, the war in Iraq, conflicts in Lebanon and Sudan have also increased the Arab television news audience, often at the expense of entertainment channels. The need for crisis reporting has increased the strain on entertainment channels to allocate, sometimes for extended periods, resources for continuous news coverage. These channels tend to expand their news departments in times of crises, provide extensive news coverage and offer more current affairs, documentaries and talk shows related to the conflict; simultaneously, they reduce their entertainment programmes, as MBC did during the first Intifada in 2000 (Khalil, 2006b). These costs are justified to maintain a channel's visibility and to ward off the spectre of permanent audience loss to news channels. This strategy aiming at keeping entertainment channels relevant in times of war appears to be working. In January 2009 during the Israeli campaign on Gaza the viewership of news channels was 13.4 per cent compared to 33.4 per cent for general entertainment channels (*TV Trend*, 2009).

In a second developmental pattern related to conflict, inter-Arab political rivalries have driven the growth of satellite news channels. After initial attempts to control access to information and restore state sovereignty over the airwaves by banning satellite dishes and restricting the import of satellite decoders into the mid-1990s, Arab governments expanded state television to include satellite broadcasts. The competition between these two major channels – al-Jazeera and al-Arabiya – mirrored a broader geopolitical conflict between the two channels' sponsors, respectively the rulers of Qatar and Saudi Arabia. These two countries' immense financial resources, deriving from natural gas in the case of the former and oil in the case of the latter, were crucial in establishing a satellite news sector because the sponsors could ignore costs – television news, unlike entertainment, is rarely profitable – as they sought political influence. Other states involved in rhetorical wars have used a mixture of threats, inducements and direct investments in satellite channels to gain or increase access to the airwaves. In the last decade, governments in Egypt, Jordan and Syria have allowed the establishment of privately owned, government-friendly satellite channels, but most of these have failed to endure or to establish a reasonable following. As we show in this chapter, some non-state actors like Hamas or Hezbollah, have launched satellite channels that, in a region bedevilled with chronic crises in which these movements have high stakes or direct involvement, have become important news sources even if their programming is not exclusively dedicated to news and public affairs.

The consolidation of Arab television news channels into multichannel networks, akin to the entertainment channels discussed in Chapter 2, is a third important pattern shaping the development of television news. Both al-Jazeera and al-Arabiya are now part of what industry insiders call multiplatform conglomerates. Our in-depth analysis of al-Jazeera and al-Arabiya will clarify the implications of the twin processes of consolidation (of the industry at large) and specialisation (within conglomerates).

A fourth noteworthy pattern is the advent of business channels. Breaking with a long-standing tradition that Arab news is political or crisis news, the growth of this sector in the 2000s has been stoked by a drastic increase in demand for economic information, itself boosted by the high energy prices' financial windfall in the Gulf petro-monarchies, real-estate speculation throughout the region led by the growth of Dubai, foreign direct investment from the Gulf countries in real estate throughout the Arab region, the tide of Iraqi refugees which has inflated housing prices in Amman and Damascus, and the flight of Arab money from the West in the post-9/11 environment of stricter monitoring of global financial flows aimed at choking sources and flows of terrorism funding. As we explain later in this chapter, the television business news sector has undergone a process of specialisation.

As a result of war, inter-Arab rivalries, the agendas of radical non-state actors and demand for business news, the contemporary Arab television news industry is vibrant, diverse and increasingly specialised. As shown in Table 4.1, besides the news coverage available on general entertainment channels which is usually

Table 4.1 Arabic-language Pan-Arab Television News

News sources	News and public-affairs content	Examples
Entertainment channels	Newscasts and political talk shows (primarily local focus)	LBC-Sat, MBC, al-Iraqiya
News networks	Continuous news, current affairs, documentaries and talk shows	Al-Jazeera, al-Arabiya
Business channels	General business news; sector-specialised business news (i.e. real estate, tourism, financial markets)	CNBC Arabiya, al-'Aqariya
Foreign Arabic-language news channels (see Table 6.1. for details)	News, current affairs, talk shows	Al-'Alam, al-Hurra, France 24, Rusya al-Yawm
Radical channels	'Militant' news integrated in a general news and entertainment channel format	Al-Manar; al-Aqsa

limited but which expands in times of crises, Arab viewers have access to a number of pan-Arab twenty-four-hour news channels, in addition to a number of specialised news channels and foreign news and current-affairs networks. Also, foreign government-owned or affiliated channels broadcasting in Arabic (discussed in detail in Chapter 1) target Arabs with the agendas of their sponsors – these channels have generally had dismal ratings. In this chapter we nonetheless focus on al-Jazeera and al-Arabiya because they are the industry's dominant news players. We will also see in our detailed analysis of Hezbollah's Beirut-based al-Manar that radical channels provide an intriguing alternative model to al-Jazeera and al-Arabiya: transnational, militant, non-state-owned, supported by a mix of advertising and subsidies, and mission-oriented.

AL-JAZEERA: THE MAVERICK

Al-Jazeera, the Arabic-language news and current affairs channel based in Doha, Qatar, that challenged Western hegemony over global news, was born out of a series of fortuitous circumstances. When Sheikh Hamad bin Khalifa al-Thani overthrew his father on 27 June 1995 and replaced him at the helm of the Emirate of Qatar, he launched a series of initiatives designed to put Qatar on the map and move it from under the sway of Saudi Arabia, the neighbour and big brother with whom the Emir's father was close but whose influence the Emir and his entourage resented. For more than a century, Qatar was a British protectorate. After it earned independence in 1971, Qatar faced major security dilemmas as a minuscule country of 4500 square miles located between regional rival heavyweights Saudi Arabia and Iran.

In 1994, then-Prince Hamad bin Khalifa proposed plans to expand Qatar television's programmes and begin satellite broadcasting. When he became head of state in 1996, creating a Qatar-based, pan-Arab satellite television channel became a central part of his plan. The new Emir had the means to bankroll his plans to increase Qatar's regional power because the tiny Persian Gulf state he rules sits on a trillion cubic feet of natural gas, a national reserve that is exceeded only by Russia's and Iran's. Following the failure of BBC Arabic, the Emir of Qatar issued a decree in January 1996 establishing al-Jazeera (The Island) satellite channel with a start-up grant of US $137 million. With 120 former employees of BBC Arabic, al-Jazeera went on air in late 1996, and in January 1997 expanded satcasting hours from six to eight per day. The channel was part of a trend of media liberalisation in Qatar, whose authorities abolished the Ministry of Information in 1998, making the Qatar Radio and Television Corporation and the Department of Printing and Publications stand-alone state institutions; yet al-Jazeera maintains to this day close ties with the Qatari Ministry of Foreign Affairs and terrestrial broadcasting remained government-owned.

Al-Jazeera ID logo

ALJAZEERA

In a pan-Arab environment of government-owned television channels whose news bulletins consisted mostly of 'protocol' news, detailing the ruler's schedule, al-Jazeera's blend of hard-nosed reporting, unbridled talk-show debates and investigative ethos took the Arab world – viewers and rulers alike – by storm. The channel hosted Israeli officials, Islamist Egyptian clerics, Saudi dissidents, exiled Arab intellectuals, feminist activists and Arab government ministers. Its flagship programme *al-Ittijah al-Mu'akis* (The Opposite Direction) became a *cause célèbre* first in the Arab world and then globally, and its Syrian host Faysal al-Qasim had a rare gift for eliciting heartfelt, no-holds-barred debates on the air. On *al-Shari'a wal Hayat* (Islamic Law and Life), superstar Egyptian preacher Yusuf al-Qaradawi dispensed advice on topics ranging from women working outside the home to the appropriateness of fellatio (which he found acceptable between two consenting married adults). At the same time, *Hewar Maftouh* (Open Dialogue) brought two or three studio guests and allowed a dozen viewers to participate on the telephone. *Minbar al-Jazeera* (The al-Jazeera Pulpit) took public participation one step further by simply moderating a flow of incoming viewers' calls, faxes and email messages on a specific topic introduced by the host.

Al-Jazeera's editorial slant combines Arab nationalism, Islamism and Third-Worldism. In addition to dogged coverage of the plight of the Palestinian and Iraqi peoples under occupation, which is highly critical of Israeli and US actions and policies, the channel is also scolding of pro-US Arab states like Egypt, Jordan and Saudi Arabia, and supportive of radical movements like the Palestinian Hamas and the Lebanese Hezbollah. Newscasts, talk shows and documentaries reflect a fondness for the Muslim Brotherhood, and occasionally talk shows feature guests who express sympathy for Osama bin Laden. But the channel's airing of videotaped messages by bin Laden was perhaps in the eyes of its Western audiences al-Jazeera's gravest mistake. As a result, al-Jazeera quickly became the *bête noire* of the Bush administration and Arab governments. In a region where Saudi princes and their political and business associates dominated satellite media, al-Jazeera provoked the ire of Saudi and other rulers. One by one, on and off, most Arab regimes banned the channel from reporting from their territories. The deference with which Arab rulers had become used to being treated by their media was swept to the wind. By early 2004, the government of Qatar had received more than 500 complaints from Arab governments focusing on al-Jazeera (Lamloum, 2004).

In the US, though the channel initially received rave reviews from government officials and the media as a beacon of freedom in a desert of repression, the tune changed after the attacks of 11 September 2001, when high-ranking officials in the George W. Bush administration harshly criticised al-Jazeera for airing videos featuring al-Qaeda leader Osama bin Laden. US criticism of al-Jazeera grew with the channel's coverage of the Afghanistan and Iraq wars, which was often critical of US policies and strategies and showcased these wars' civilian victims who were often neglected by the US media. The strain between al-Jazeera and the United States had bloody consequences, a development that was perhaps inevitable due to the channel's unique scoop coverage of the Afghanistan and Iraq invasions, respectively in 2001 and 2003. On 13 November 2001, al-Jazeera's Kabul office was hit by a US missile at a time when the building was empty (Malik, 2001). Al-Jazeera's Baghdad correspondent Tariq Ayoub was not as lucky; he was killed on 8 April 2003, when US planes bombed the channel's office in Baghdad ('US Warplanes', 2003). Hostility to al-Jazeera in the United States grew to the extent that US staffers for al-Jazeera English's Washington, DC office reportedly encountered discrimination when applying for rental apartments and three years after its launch the channel is incapable of acquiring US commercials or cable distribution (Levine, 2006).

Several factors explain al-Jazeera's uniqueness. Its success is premised on a combination of factors, such as flexibility and the promotion of employee initiative, independent thinking and self-growth, in addition to the prestige of its status as a maverick channel (Zayani and Sahraoui, 2007). Al-Jazeera's core values have been described as '... a combination of the precision of the BBC and the speed of CNN' (2007, p. 61). This does not mean that there are no problems within the channel. In fact, there is tension between the news and programme areas. Whereas the former relies on largely anonymous teamwork, the latter has promoted a star system whereby certain programme hosts become guardians of fiefdoms that have direct connections to the Qatari political elite, and therefore are not accountable to the institution itself. Repeated pressures – mainly from the Bush administration – on the channel to rein in its editorial line have also had their effect, and 'the very perception of the network as a beacon of free speech is starting to succumb to a reality check' (p. 105). Most importantly, the 2007 *rapprochement* between Saudi Arabia and Qatar meant a decline in the channel's aggressive coverage of Saudi affairs and a concomitant loss of cachet with its audience. There has also been friction between members of al-Jazeera's editorial board and staff members, many of whom feel their margin of independence has been shrinking (Zayani and Sahraoui, 2007). In addition, there are long-standing internecine struggles in al-Jazeera, between the religiously oriented wing close to the Muslim Brotherhood and secular Arabists. Some of the channel's programmes have aired episodes that were stridently propagandist in favour of the Muslim Brotherhood, and there have been a few particularly unsavoury programmes, such as a documentary favourably comparing Osama bin Laden to Marxist guerrilla leader Che Guevara.

In recent years, al-Jazeera made a conscious strategic move to be a 'network' with thematic channels covering sports, current affairs, documentary, demographic channels oriented to toddlers and children, in addition to news portals. This comes at a price. Though the English-language channel had been trumpeted for months as 'al-Jazeera International', it was re-labelled 'al-Jazeera English' at the last minute before its launch on 15 November 2006, keeping Waddah Khanfar, al-Jazeera's General Manager, firmly in charge (Kraidy, 2008d). This reflects the fact that al-Jazeera remains an Arab media conglomerate whose mothership is a hard-hitting, Arabic-language news channel (see Table 4.2).

Table 4.2 Al-Jazeera Network

Channel	Date established	Ownership and/or allegiance
Al-Jazeera	1997	Operates under the Qatari Ministry of Foreign Affairs
Al-Jazeera Sports	2003	Operates one free-to-air service and since 2004, manages five pay-TV channels
Al-Jazeera Children's Channel (JCC)	2005	Owned by the Qatar Foundation for Education Science and Community Development; nonetheless uses al-Jazeera's infrastructure
Al-Jazeera Mubasher (Al-Jazeera Live)	2004	Live broadcasts of major conferences, speeches and meetings of political or general interest
Al-Jazeera English	2006	The first world English channel based in the Middle East with major studios in Kuala Lumpur, Doha, London and Washington, DC.
Al-Jazeera al-Watha'eqiyya Jazeera Documentary)	2007	Featuring documentaries produced by in-house or commissioned regionally, also acquires international (al-documentary programmes
Bara'em (Buds)	2009	Owned by the Qatar Foundation for Education Science and Community Development; nonetheless uses al-Jazeera's infrastructure

Targets of al-Jazeera's editorial slant took several years to mount their riposte: led by Saudi moguls with contributions from Kuwaiti and Lebanese investors, al-Arabiya (The Arabic One) went on air on 3 March 2003, as a new Arabic-language satellite news channel tasked with countering al-Jazeera's worldview with coverage amenable to the Saudi-led Arab status quo. As already mentioned, the competition between al-Jazeera and al-Arabiya has mirrored the geopolitical feud opposing the al-Thani and al-Sa'ud, the two countries' ruling families. Nonetheless, the two channels appear to vie for two distinct audiences: whereas al-Jazeera clearly caters to Arabists and Islamists joined by their opposition to Western imperialism and US support of both Israel and the Gulf monarchies, al-Arabiya ostensibly addresses a 'liberal' audience whose members are less hostile to the West and to the Arab status quo. These two core groups of viewers that the two channels seek to attract notwithstanding, it is clear that al-Jazeera and al-Arabiya are locked in a battle royale over the imagined pan-Arab audience. In this regard, the speed and efficacy with which al-Arabiya succeeded to rise to the level of challenger to al-Jazeera is a story that has not been told amidst scholars and journalists' obsession with al-Jazeera. The following section seeks to remedy, however briefly, that gap in the literature.

AL-ARABIYA: THE CHALLENGER

Al-Arabiya is the news channel of the MBC Group, one of the Arab world's leading media conglomerates, owned by well-connected Saudi businessman Sheikh Walid al-Ibrahim, based in Dubai Media City (See Chapter 2 for a detailed discussion of MBC Group). Lebanon's Hariri Group in addition to Kuwaiti, Jordanian and other Arabian Gulf interests contributed to the initial investment of US $300 million (Khalil, 2006b). These investors were close to the Saudi establishment and shared its hostility towards al-Jazeera. Until then, the Saudis had resorted to largely indirect defensive measures, such as organising a pan-Arab commercial boycott of al-Jazeera and coordinating with allied Arab countries like Egypt and Jordan to expel al-Jazeera's correspondents. The creation of al-Arabiya signalled a new phase in a Saudi plan to counter al-Jazeera, which MBC Group owner Sheikh Walid al-Ibrahim described to an American journalist as 'the CNN to al-Jazeera's Fox News' (Shapiro, 2005).

Al-Arabiya's visual appearance contrasted sharply with al-Jazeera's. Al-Arabiya's open newsroom studio located on the fourth floor of the MBC building in Dubai Media City, has a futuristic feel; it is a circular and large set, three-dimensional in appearance. Silver and glass dominate, giving it an airy and transparent look, made more appealing by elements of blue and red. Al-Arabiya's logo consists of the word al-Arabiya written in white in a modified, squared 'modern'-looking Arabic font (interviews with al-Hage, 29 June 2005; and Costandi, 3 June 2004; Kraidy, 2009).

The lobby at al-Arabiya channel at Dubai Media City

The message that the channel seeks to convey visually is one of transparency and an ostensible 'modernity'. This design has become trendy in the region after al-Arabiya's production team replicated it for Bahrain TV and Saudi news channel al-Ekhbariya (Khalil, 2006b).

The timing of al-Arabiya's launch was propitious. Just as the invasion of Afghanistan by US and allied forces had given al-Jazeera the opportunity to establish itself as a leading regional and global news player, the Anglo-American invasion of Iraq in 2003 would be al-Arabiya's golden opportunity. The channel's strategy to compete with al-Jazeera, in addition to twenty-four-hour coverage of the entire Arab region, rested on two pillars: first, the focus would be on building audience share within Saudi Arabia, taking advantage of the channel's Saudi ownership as a home-turf advantage; second, as the channel's General Manager and Chief Editor told one of the authors, al-Arabiya would patiently build audience share in one Arab country after another, taking advantage of important events, especially elections, to go in and air intensive coverage with the goal of eclipsing its competitors (mainly al-Jazeera) and then try to retain the audience it gained in specific countries afterwards (al-Rashed interview, 27 June 2005; Khatib interview, 29 June 2005). The channel also benefited from high-profile appearances by US officials, most famously US President Obama's first television interview in January 2009. This strategy has been largely successful, though al-Arabiya has had to contend with being second place after al-Jazeera in most Arab countries – with Iraq and Saudi Arabia as notable exceptions – as reflected in several surveys of the Arab audience (see Table 4.3).

Table 4.3 Ratings in Saudi Arabia for News Channels[1]

Channel	Channel ratings for total population month of January		
	2008	2007	2006
Al-Arabiya	23.95%	22.2%	24.29%
Al-Jazeera	12.83%	17.3%	19.78%

Source: IPSOS-Stat.

Al-Arabiya reflects the Saudi way of doing business. Its editorial policy is aligned with Saudi and US policies in the Arab world. It eschews controversy to the largest extent possible, and when its reporting or talk-show questioning turns aggressive, it is usually in the opposite direction – i.e. pro-US, pro-Saudi – to al-Jazeera. That objective affects the kinds of programmes the channel airs, most of which feature no live debates, no live telephone calls from viewers, nor opinionated guests – its forays into interactivity consist of occasional, highly managed town-hall meetings and call-in programmes. In spite of this political conservatism, the channel espouses the views of the Saudi liberals and bills itself as a balanced Arab voice. 'We are trying to redefine the news', said al-Arabiya's Executive Editor, Nabil Khatib by which he meant forgoing big pan-Arab issues like Iraq and Palestine and focusing on issues Arabs care about like 'health, education, livelihoods' in addition to more human-interest stories (Shadid, 2006, A01; interview with Khatib, 29 June 2005).

Though it does not challenge the Arab political status quo, al-Arabiya has had its share of trouble. Early on, the channel attracted the moniker (including from a Hezbollah official) al-'Ebriya (The Hebrew One) for what some perceive as relatively sympathetic coverage of Israel (Francis, 2007). In August 2003, high-ranking US government officials criticised al-Arabiya for airing footage of armed men threatening to shoot members of the Iraqi Governing Council. Later that year, in October, a poll commissioned in Iraq by the US Department of State found good news for al-Arabiya: 37 per cent of those polled said they used it as their main source of news, compared to 26 per cent who said the same about al-Jazeera (Iraq Television, 2003). The fact that al-Arabiya was gaining market share in Iraq made it a target. On 16 November 2003, the Iraqi Governing Council banned al-Arabiya correspondents from Iraq because the channel, undoubtedly in an attempt to lure Iraqis, especially Sunnis, and to deflect accusations it was partisan towards Iraqi self-claimed secular Shi'i politician Iyad Allawi, had broadcast an audio taped message from Saddam Hussein. Also, after the assassination of Lebanese former Prime Minister Rafiq al-Hariri in February 2005, al-Arabiya engaged in a protracted media war with the Syrian regime of Bashar al-Asad ('Al-Arabiya Finds', 2005), airing a widely covered interview with exiled former Syrian Vice-President 'Abdulhalim Khaddam in which he accused the Syrian regime of various crimes including the assassination of al-Hariri (al-Arabiya's coverage of Syria's regime shifted for a period in 2009 after the Saudi and Syrian leaders 'reconciled'). Though less controversial than al-Jazeera, the channel suffered a series of attacks, including the September 2004 killing of reporter Mazen al-Tumayzi by the US military, the 22 February 2006 abduction and murder of reporter Atwar Bahjat in Iraq, and an explosion at al-Arabiya's Gaza City office in January 2007 (Shadid, 2006, A01). According to the Committee to Protect Journalists, al-Arabiya lost six journalists and five support staffers between March 2003 and January 2009 ('Journalists Killed', 2008). The rivalry with al-Jazeera continues to be one of al-Arabiya's central preoccupations. In the summer of 2005, a little over two years since it went on air, al-Arabiya launched a promotional campaign with the theme 'Closer to the Truth', perhaps a subtle reminder that the channel considered itself more truthful and professional than al-Jazeera. Two years later, in late summer 2007, the channel shifted to a new slogan 'So You Know More' (Habib, 2006), setting al-Arabiya's putative rationality and appeal to viewers' minds against al-Jazeera's postulated sensationalism.

In an attempt to appeal to groups who are relatively under-served by Arabic-language news channels like youth and women, al-Arabiya introduced two new programme genres that have since their appearance been imitated by other channels, including al-Jazeera. First, the Saudi-owned, Dubai-based channel launched *Sabah al-'Arabiya* (The Morning of al-Arabiya), a soft-news morning programme, in the tradition of *Good Morning America*. Shot in the glass lobby of the MBC building with an artificial lake and palm trees in the background, the programme features a male and a female host whose informal demeanour includes their relaxed dress style and conversational tone. White and orange are the show's colours, which set it apart from the channel hard-news segment where white, blue and red dominate (see Kraidy, 2009, Chapter 1). Second, al-Arabiya in the summer of 2005 expanded its financial and business news to cater to increased interest in stocks and real estate in the Arabian Gulf countries, especially Saudi Arabia and Kuwait. Al-Arabiya now competed directly, especially during the morning hours, with business channels like CNBC Arabiya, located in a more modest building on the edge of the Dubai Media City, from which it lured several business writers and programme hosts. Al-Arabiya has since then moved into cyberspace, developing not only al-Arabiya's Arabic- and English-language websites, but also new platforms for audio-visual content akin to an Arabic YouTube (Al-Bakkar interview, 4 December 2007). Whether the channel can shed the image that it is friendly to Saudi and US policies is uncertain; what is beyond dispute is that within a few years of its launch, al-Arabiya has managed to grab a significant audience share and has become a major player in the pan-Arab media market as a whole. As one of two leading pan-Arab news channels, al-Arabiya is a successful counterbalance to al-Jazeera.

AL-MANAR: THE RADICAL ALTERNATIVE

Hezbollah's al-Manar satellite channel emerged as a model for a distinctive type of radical and religiously grounded but nonetheless general (news and entertainment) channels that appeared in Lebanon, Palestine and Iraq. These are *de facto* atypical news channels because they do not follow the genres of entertainment channels nor do they provide twenty-four-hour news programmes. Instead, these are 'militant' institutions with clearly defined and unabashedly ideological missions that they pursue through a mix of news and carefully selected entertainment, education and religious programmes. These channels are extensions of groups who consider media as a weapon in their struggle. As the Iraqis celebrated the fall of Saddam's regime, Sunni and Shi'i groups were rushing to establish television channels to support their militias (see Chapter 1). In Palestine, Hamas established its own television channel al-Aqsa TV (in reference to a historically and symbolically important Jerusalem mosque) in 2006. For these channels, the role model remains Hezbollah's al-Manar channel. Established in Lebanon, al-Manar combines paramilitary propaganda with mainstream television genres, nationally in Lebanon and transnationally in the Arab world. In the next section we examine al-Manar's history, organisation and programming.

Al-Manar is dedicated primarily to the Party of God's struggle against the state of Israel. Al-Manar, Arabic for 'The Beacon' or 'The Lighthouse', is the flagship of Hezbollah's communication apparatus, which also includes al-Nour [The Light] radio station, *al-'Ahd* [The Era] newspaper, which was launched on 13 June 1984, and various minor radio stations and publications (Jaber, 1997). Like the other media outlets operated by the Party of God, al-Manar is integrated in Hezbollah's Information Unit, headed by Sheikh Hasan 'Ezeddin. Hezbollah launched the channel on 3 June 1991, more than six years after the founding of the Party of God in the aftermath of Israel's 1982 invasion of Lebanon and ensuing occupation of the southern part of the country. At first, the channel offered a 'muscular mixture of revolution and religion' expressed in newscasts, talk shows and propaganda clips, in addition to 'clips of resistance activities shot on site by al-Manar's intrepid flak-jacketed, camouflaged cameramen' (Hamzeh, 2004, p. 59), a mishmash of cinéma-vérité editing and point-of-view shooting that could perhaps be described as the first foray into reality television in the Arab world.

Al-Manar expanded its operations in anticipation of or in response to major crises and events in the Middle East. In 1996, the channel began broadcasting propaganda clips in Hebrew, confirming that one of al-Manar's functions was to wage psychological warfare against Israeli soldiers who at the time occupied South Lebanon. The channel had by that time established a Hebrew Observation Department whose staff monitored Israeli broadcasts and passed along clips and information to al-Manar's bosses and Hezbollah's leaders (Blanford, 2001). In the following years, al-Manar intensified its psychological warfare with a series of propaganda clips called 'Who's Next?', featuring the pictures of captured Israeli soldiers followed by a white screen with a big question mark, connoting that more kidnappings of Israeli soldiers were forthcoming (Hamzeh, 2004). Hezbollah also used the channel to reach members of the South Lebanon Army (SLA), a pro-Israeli militia that started as a splinter of the Lebanese military, prodding them to switch sides and repent (Jaber, 1997). Al-Manar officials have continuously mentioned plans for full broadcasts in Hebrew, and in 1998 they advocated the creation of a Hebrew-language satellite television channel (Yehia, 1998). However, al-Manar's main expansion has continued to be in its Arabic-language broadcasts.

Following the withdrawal of Israeli troops from South Lebanon in May 2000, for which Hezbollah took credit in light of the party's relentless resistance to the Israeli occupier, and the eruption of the second Palestinian Intifada in September 2000, al-Manar inaugurated its satellite transmissions, signalling a strategic shift 'from being the channel of the resistance into ... being the channel of Arabs and Muslims' (Hamzeh, 2004, p. 60). To that end, the channel expanded its satcasts from four hours, which it had started on the eve of the 24 May 2000 (Israeli withdrawal) (Yehia, 2000), to eighteen per day as the Intifada broke out in September 2000, then to twenty-four hours per day in January 2001 (Blanford, 2001; Hamzeh, 2004). By that time, 70 per cent of the channel's programmes were self-produced and its budget had grown tenfold to an estimated US $10 million (Blanford, 2001). In spite of the expansion, the focus remained on the channel's core mission of countering Israel ideologically and psychologically. In December 2001, al-Manar's former chief Nayef Krayem stated that 'al-Manar is an important weapon for us ... It's a political weapon, social weapon, and cultural weapon' (Blanford, 2001). Five months later, in an interview published in the Francophone Lebanese daily *L'Orient-Le Jour*, Sheikh Hasan 'Ezeddin, head of Hezbollah's Information Unit, spoke of the importance of achieving a 'balance of terror' with Israel (Haddad, 2002). This would become a central component of Hezbollah's anti-Israel strategy and one in which al-Manar would play an important psychological-warfare role.

Al-Manar's programming also includes *tarfih hadef* ('purposeful' entertainment) that contributes to the channel's central mission of combating Israel. This led the channel to broadcast *al-Shatat* (The Diaspora), a Syrian dramatic production of the Protocols of the Elders of Zion, the European anti-Semitic tract,

A press conference during the
July war as seen on various
screens

which led to a ban on al-Manar's broadcasts in France and the United States.
On 13 December 2004, the French Council of State ordered the satellite oper-
ator Eutelsat to stop relaying al-Manar's broadcasts to France within forty-eight
hours, on the basis that its programming had 'a militant perspective with anti-
Semitic connotations'; it also cited the need to preserve public order; al-Manar
voluntarily stopped beaming via Eutelsat's satellite after being notified, but
complained that its right to freedom of speech was being infringed ('With a',
2004) – nonetheless, al-Manar's leadership admitted later that airing the show
had been a mistake (Deloire and Berretta, 2004). First in France and later in
most of Europe, al-Manar could not guarantee to the European legislatures that
it would refrain from airing anti-Semitic programmes. On 17 December 2004,
the US State Department added al-Manar to its Terrorism Exclusion List (TEL)
with specific resolutions concerning the channel's satellite transmission to the
US, its broadcasts around the world via the Internet, and to block all and any
transactions with al-Manar affiliated persons (Boucher, 2004). In the US, al-
Manar was accused of violating the Patriot Act and the satellite carrier Intelsat
was asked to cease the channel's broadcast. However, viewers in both Europe
and North America can watch al-Manar's programmes – uncut and uncensored
– through various webcasts.

Though al-Manar remained focused on combating Israel ideologically, in addition to criticising and attacking US policies in the Middle East, the channel's
programmes have appealed primarily to Lebanon's Shi'i community, and secon-
darily al-Manar has served to underscore Hezbollah's putative openness to other
communities in Lebanon. In that context, for example, al-Manar broadcast an
Iranian-produced drama series about the life of the Virgin Mary, featuring a story
which combined Koranic and Biblical storylines which was made available in
stores as a DVD by al-Manar's parent company, the Lebanese Media Group. It
also changed its image, upgrading its studios and 'softening' its logo by rounding

its edges. Al-Manar's psychological-warfare and propaganda functions resurged during the July and August 2006 war between Hezbollah and Israel. During that conflict, al-Manar's programmes consisted of hourly news bulletins, followed by 'open microphone' call-in shows, followed by a series of propaganda clips. These propaganda clips were effective in explaining and illustrating Hezbollah's view, expressed by its leader Hassan Nasrallah in one of his televised speeches, that this was a US war fought through the proxy of Israel. These views were repeated in news bulletins and live conversations with callers and studio guests. But the propaganda clips were more effective in that they synthesised this idea and expressed it in its simplest, crudest versions possible. Al-Manar also renewed its psy-ops campaign, in Arabic and Hebrew, taunting Israeli soldiers with Hezbollah's battleground achievements and warning them of surprises Hezbollah's fighters had in store for them. By the third day of bombings, 16 July 2006, the Israeli air force had destroyed al-Manar's headquarters, but the channel resumed broadcasts within two minutes from a secret back-up studio (Shams, 2007), with satellite transmission taking over when terrestrial broadcasts were forcibly shut down by Israeli bombs. Despite physical destruction, the war brought good news for al-Manar, as the channel shot from number eighty-nine to number ten in pan-Arab television rankings during the conflict ('Dramatic Changes', 2006). As both authors witnessed during their presence in Lebanon during the summer 2006 war, al-Manar was widely followed across sectarian lines, not least because the channel was the voice of one of the conflict's leading protagonists.

Over the years, al-Manar's terrestrial channel, focused on Lebanon, and satellite channel, addressing Arab viewers, especially Palestinians, and diasporic audiences, have not differed much. Both broadcasts begin at 6.00 am, Beirut time, with a recitation from the Holy Koran, which lasts for a full hour on the satellite channel but for only a half hour on the terrestrial channel. A sample of programming looks as follows: a morning newscast at 7.30 am, followed by *Sabah al-Manar* (al-Manar's Morning) at 8.30, and a current-events talk show *Ma'a al-Hadath* (Following Events), then a brief news bulletin from 11.30 to 12 noon. The afternoon begins with infomercials, then a news bulletin at 3.30 pm, followed by a political programme such as *al-Rabe'a* (4 o'Clock), an afternoon political show hosted by a man and a woman, then an entertainment programme like *al-Manar as-Saghir* (The Little Manar), a children's programme and a militant programme such as *Woujouh al-Intisar* (Faces of Victory), which chronicles heroic deeds by Hezbollah fighters during the summer 2006 war with Israel. The evening programme carries political talk shows such as *Mazha Ba'd?* (What Next?), hosted by Egyptian journalist 'Amru Nasif, or *Bi 'Uyunehem* (In Their Eyes), in English with Arabic translation, between several news bulletins. Sometimes there will be a drama series in the afternoon, most likely with a historical theme, for example the rise and conquests of Mongolian leader Ghengis Khan. There are also French- and English-language newscasts and irregularly scheduled programmes that follow specific events. Al-Manar produces no less than ten live shows, including the news bulletin, and eight non-live shows. The programming grid is interspersed with commercials, mainly for consumer items, public-service announcements for various Shi'i charities and social organisations affiliated with the Party of God, and promotional clips publicising Hezbollah's actions and undermining its Lebanese political rival, US policies and Israel.

Al-Manar clearly constitutes an alternative model for satellite television news in the Arab world. Unlike al-Jazeera and al-Arabiya, al-Manar is not sponsored by a nation-state, but by a militant movement. The channel has several revenue streams, ranging from a diverse advertising base to reported Iranian funding. Unlike al-Jazeera and al-Arabiya, who speak two 'mainstream' political discourses, al-Manar follows an unabashedly radical editorial line, one focused on Hezbollah's mission of combating Israel militarily, psychologically and ideologically, in addition to focusing on the Shi'i community in Lebanon, the Party of God's main constituency. Al-Manar has thrived on the recurring crises hitting the Arab region, especially those in which Hezbollah was a principal actor. Al-Manar's model has inspired several imitators, including al-Aqsa, the satellite channel of Hamas, and various Iraqi insurgent channels. For as long as protracted crises continue to rock and polarise Arab societies, it is likely that these channels will continue to attract sizeable audiences.

PAN-ARAB BUSINESS CHANNELS

Radical channels are not the only alternative to al-Jazeera and al-Arabiya. In addition to the music, women's and religious channels discussed in Chapter 3, business channels have since the early 2000s been one of the fastest-growing niches in the Arab television industries. At the origin of the interest in business news is the expansion of Arab stock markets due to repatriation of Arab investments from Europe and North America after 9/11, ensuing growth in inter-Arab investment and surging oil revenues. In 1998, Dubai TV launched Dubai Business Channel to focus on business, finance and real estate in Dubai, but this channel did not survive the restructuring of Dubai TV (Hammad interview, 25 April 2009). This opened the door for a pan-Arab franchise of the US cable channel CNBC, CNBC Arabiya, which attracted a growing viewership. Seeing the initial success of CNBC Arabiya and the increased interest in Gulf financial markets, al-Arabiya decided to increase its business coverage in the winter of 2005. Building on a small group of former CNBC Arabiya staff, al-Arabiya expanded coverage of Arab business and stock markets, resulting in a significant increase in al-Arabiya's daytime ratings, which for a while matched its primetime viewership (al-Hajj interview, 25 May 2008).

The logo of the CNBC Arabic franchise, CNBC Arabiya

Since 2005, Arab business television has become increasingly segmented into specialised coverage of industry sectors, such as finance, real estate or tourism. Specialised business channels have become a fixture of the pan-Arab media and business landscape (see Table 4.4). Their success is driven by the elevation of business news to the level of importance of political news by big players like al-Arabiya, eager to build up its ratings among the growing number of Saudis and other Gulf countries' residents with investments in the fast-growing stock markets of the Gulf Cooperation Council countries. Since these channels' viability is linked to economic performance, business news faces an uncertain future as the global economic crisis that began in autumn 2008 may drive some of these channels to shut down or encourage consolidation of this sector.

Stimulated by unprecedented market activities, financial speculation and oil

Table 4.4 Business and Business-sector Channels

Channel	Year started/ relaunched	Location	Type
Dubai Business Channel	1998– 2004	Dubai	General business
CNBC Arabiya	2003	Dubai	General business and stock market
Al-'Aqariyya (Real Estate TV)	2004	Dubai	Also provides two other channels in Arabic: al-'Aqariyya TV 2 and English-language Real Estate TV
Arab Business Channel (ABC)	2005	Egypt	Focus on Egyptian stock market and general business news
Al-Eqtisadiya TV (Economy TV)	2006	Dubai and Riyadh	Gulf stock market
Asia Business TV	2006	Dubai	Arab and Asian business news in Arabic and English
i2 TV	2006	Dubai	Telecommunications
Aviation Satellite Channel	2006	Jordan	Aviation
Atlas Travel	2007	Bahrain	Travel and tourism and Culture TV
Sharm TV	2007	Egypt	Focuses on Egyptian tourism

revenues since 2001, the growth of business channels has recently slowed down due to diminishing advertising revenues and the global economic crisis that began in autumn 2008, which increases the likelihood of shutdowns, mergers and acquisitions in that sector. The fate of business news channels is key to understanding future trends in the increasingly commercial Arab television industries, because business news is more closely connected to market forces than the bigger, political-influence-oriented channels like al-Jazeera, al-Arabiya and al-Manar, and because business channels have carried market segmentation and the search for niche audiences to a level beyond the women's, music and religious channels discussed in Chapter 3.

TRENDS IN PAN-ARAB TELEVISION NEWS

Technological, institutional and economic factors have changed how news channels gather, package and disseminate news in the Arab world. This can be seen, first, in the changing nature of electronic newsgathering. Arab news channels were initially dependent on news agencies to cover international stories, but eventually established bureaux and trained stringers to handle newsgathering and production. Reliance on the Associated Press, Reuters and Agence France Presse continues when it comes to news from areas inaccessible to these channels, like Israel – with the exception of al-Jazeera and al-Arabiya, both of which have bureaux in Israel and the Palestinian territories. But the growing number of news channels encouraged the establishment of regional or country-specific newsgathering services such as Ramattan in the Palestinian territories, Video Cairo Sat in Egypt and Baghdad and Video Beirut in Lebanon. Some channels like al-Arabiya have established their own newsgathering service, Middle East News (MEN); others like al-Jazeera have established news-sharing agreements with local channels in the region, such as New TV in Lebanon. As a consequence, today news sources are more numerous and more diverse than they were a decade earlier.

A second major trend concerns the expansion of television channels across multiple platforms, including the Internet and mobile phones, under the mantra of digital interactivity. Even before migrating to the Internet, pan-Arab satellite news channels offered a level of interactivity unmatched by state channels. During the 1990s, live call-in programmes bridged the distance between Arab viewers and news channels located in Europe. Additionally, two-way satellite communication was used to relay comments between reporters, guests and sometimes the general public. Since then, talk-show guests or news talking heads in Beirut, Cairo or Riyadh have been able to interact with a pan-Arab and diasporic audience. Another level of interactivity depended on fax, telephone and the Internet to connect with anchors and studio guests. Unlike their US counterparts, Arab producers do not always apply a seven-second delay when

airing a phone call. Instead, depending on the sensitivity of the topic, Arab producers probe callers off air before they decide to put them on air: a customary
practice consists in taking a caller's number and calling back at the channel's
expense, thus double checking the identity of the caller.

News channels have devoted considerable resources to establish themselves
on the Internet, through a variety of websites and news portals. Business channels like CNBC Arabiya have opted for a website that displays programming
schedules and channel information and allows for a certain level of interactivity. However, larger news channels like al-Arabiya and al-Jazeera have developed
news portals that achieve a level of synergy with their on-air presence. While this
is not a study of news portals, it is important to highlight certain important features. First, these portals are not reserved exclusively to items generated by these
channels; they also include wire and newspaper stories – in the original Arabic
or translated. Second, video and audio segments are widely available on portals.
For a while, al-Arabiya offered a webcast of its live feed for free, but since 2006,
this became a paid service offered through a third party. In comparison, al-
Jazeera offers an audio version of its main newscast as well as a video selection
of its reports. Third, these news portals are highly interactive, experimental and
quickly integrating within convergent media platforms. Al-Jazeera pioneered
with web votes, comments on stories and programmes, and al-Arabiya featured
web-based contests. More recently, al-Arabiya expanded to feature videos sup-
plied by its viewers – inspired by CNN's iReport. A study by the Arab Advisors
Group on Arab news portals concluded that

> [A]nalyzing the demographic breakdowns of the web portals' visitors, it appears that
> most users in the Arab world are in Saudi Arabia, while many Arabic-speaking users
> from outside the region live in the United States. Additionally, males consistently
> outnumber females as viewers of Arabic news on the web. (*Arabic Online*, 2006)

Shot of various screens

The report reaffirmed the importance of both the Saudi market and diasporic viewers to the growth of Arab satellite news channels on the Internet.

A third noteworthy pattern concerns language use, news-presentation style and news values. Unlike entertainment television's reliance on Lebanese and Egyptian dialects, Arab television news has historically relied on Modern Standard Arabic to reflect seriousness. With the introduction of satellite news channels, a trend developed towards a simplified version of Modern Standard Arabic, which evolved from combining classical Arabic with some local dialects. While still formal and standardised, this 'new' dialect eliminates some of the more idiosyncratic localised idioms, enabling easier communication between journalists, reporters, talk-show hosts and expert guests. This does not mean that the language of news has become strictly standardised; there are differences between channels: al-Jazeera's anchors tend to be ostensibly serious while al-Arabiya's adopt a demeanour of managed informality. On al-Arabiya, it is not unusual to see news anchors ad-lib in their local accents, rare on al-Jazeera. Al-Manar uses Modern Standard Arabic in news and channel promotions, but its talk shows often feature the spoken Lebanese dialect.

Leading Arab satellite television news channels have adopted distinctive sartorial styles. At al-Jazeera male and female anchors tend to dress conservatively and they are allowed to follow Islamic codes if this is their preference; thus it is not unusual for male anchors to grow beards or not wear ties. Star female anchor Khadeeja bin Qanna wears the veil on air, and a few co-workers have followed her example. At al-Manar, all female anchors abide by Hezbollah's dress code, which consists of a long overcoat with a veil showing only the face, with no make-up. In contrast, al-Arabiya's institutional policy prohibits its female anchors from wearing the veil and encourages a Western look for men and women, including Saudi anchors, who tend to be young and hip. Al-Arabiya was the first channel to have a non-veiled woman anchoring live from the Saudi capital Riyadh, during the Jeddah Economic Forum in 2005.

Different language uses and clothing styles reflect deeper divergences between channels that often have to do with sharply distinct news values reflecting the various editorial lines. For instance, al-Jazeera tends to focus on hard news, while al-Arabiya emphasises soft news with 'positive' story angles; light 'kicker' stories are a constant feature of al-Arabiya's newscasts whereas they are virtually absent from al-Jazeera's news coverage. It is not uncommon for al-Arabiya to feature a story about a concert in Dubai, the birth of a panda in a California zoo or a breakthrough in facial cosmetic treatments. The two leading channels do not conceal their political inclinations. In their use of language, selection of guests and choice of topics, Arab channels have rival viewpoints on the conflicts in Palestine, Lebanon, the situation in Darfur and other issues. Take for example the case of a Palestinian attack in Israel that Western television channels would call 'suicide bombing': al-Jazeera and al-Manar refer to the bomber as a 'martyr'; al-Arabiya anchors would say that the bomber 'blew himself up'. The situation gets further complicated when describing attacks on US forces in Iraq: for al-Jazeera and al-Manar, the descriptor is 'resistance', for al-Arabiya it is 'terrorism'. Al-Jazeera does not refer to the self-awarded religious title of the Saudi King, *Khadem al-Haramayn al-Sharifayn* (Custodians of the Two Holy Shrines), whereas al-Arabiya never mentions his name without the title.

CONCLUSION

In this chapter we discussed al-Jazeera and al-Arabiya, the most influential Arab satellite news channels that constitute the main source of information for Arab viewers, in addition to examining a radical alternative like al-Manar, which has served as a model for revolutionary or insurgent channels in Iraq and Palestine. We have also discussed established and emerging trends in Arab and pan-Arab satellite television news. These include a continuing rivalry between al-Jazeera and al-Arabiya that reveals stark differences between the two channels' editorial slant, language use, visual style and news selection, and extends to Internet and interactive content. Technological and institutional developments have also transformed the dynamics of newsgathering, production and dissemination in the Arab region. Another important trend consists of the rise of a business-news sector that is growing increasingly specialised, with channels focusing on financial markets, real estate or tourism.

In reviewing Qatar-based al-Jazeera and Dubai-based al-Arabiya, we focused on their history, organisation and their impact on the television industry, suggesting that satellite television has curbed Arab governments' control over news content but allowed an 'anywhere-but-here' phenomenon. Channels like al-Jazeera would refrain from criticising or even negatively reporting on its funding state while al-Arabiya would strive to defend and deflect criticism against Saudi Arabia. It is important to note that while commercially driven, the advertising revenues alone rarely cover the large expenses associated with satellite links, bureaux, journalists and high-value news production. Consequently, private news channels have to resort to the deep pockets of political patrons.

We also noted that in spite of being jolted into reform by their loss of airwave sovereignty to privately owned, rival-government-friendly channels like al-Jazeera, al-Arabiya and al-Manar, government-owned channels are still confined to a dull and stale newscast presentation. Through al-Jazeera and al-Arabiya respectively, Qatar and Saudi Arabia have opted to project political influence transnationally without directly owning and operating satellite channels. Most other Arab governments, however, simply attempted to revive and expand the

reach of their state-owned channels, an endeavour that has met very limited success. Indeed, grandiose restructuring plans announced by state services like
Bahrain TV, Syria TV and Libya TV have for the most part amounted to the
introduction of new faces and the use of technological gimmicks. Their content
and presentation is stuck in the age of 'protocol' news and parading regime
achievements. Even as they realise that they are losing national audiences to
transnational television actors, many Arab states have been unable to relinquish
control of their broadcasting operations.

Radical non-state or (in the case of Hamas) semi-state actors have also established relatively sophisticated satellite channels to mobilise their constituencies
and promote their cause to the broader Arab public. Ownership of satellite television channels by political/military groups like Hezbollah, Hamas and various
insurgent groups in Iraq further underscores the demise of state control over
Arab and pan-Arab television, and lays the foundation for rhetorical wars
between radical groups and their opponents, whether these are states or rival
formations. At the time of this writing, tensions simmering between Hezbollah
and the Egyptian government since the 2008–9 Israeli offensive on Gaza, have
erupted in a war of words after the Egyptian government arrested a Hezbollah
operative who admitted to smuggling weapons for Hamas. Though radical news
channels do not enjoy high ratings most of the time, in times of crisis their viewership tends to spike, posing a real challenge to governments and their policies,
and constituting real competition to top news channels like al-Jazeera and al-
Arabiya.

The importance of news channels for Arab and pan-Arab politics aside, in the
Arab world and elsewhere news channels incur higher costs than entertainment
channels. Unlike news, drama, comedy and talk shows do not require foreign
bureaux, international correspondents and intricate logistical operations. In the
Arab world, not only do these entertainment genres tend to cost less than news;
they also attract more advertising. As Chapter 5 explains, the convergence of
entertainment production and advertising, which is the commercial engine of
the Arab television industries, culminates in the holy month of Ramadan, a
thirty-day period that perhaps better than any other season captures the essence
of contemporary Arab television.

NOTE

1. When considering these figures, keep in mind that Saudi viewers tend to under-
   report viewing al-Jazeera because of its criticism of the Saudi royal family. As we
   will see later, these figures are not stable, changing during Ramadan and conflict.

5

Ramadan: Drama, Comedy and Religious Shows in the Arab Sweeps

This chapter focuses on Ramadan, the ninth month in the Islamic lunar calendar, at once a period of religious devotion and the most important season for Arab television when the industry shows its very best productions, viewership soars, advertising rates peak and television programmes become topics of daily conversation. During this holy month, the Prophet Mohammed is believed to have received his first revelations of the Koran. Muslims have for a long time considered Ramadan a time to renew one's faith through prayer, fasting and charity work. Typically, Muslims refrain from food and drink from dawn until dusk, when they break the fast with the meal of *iftar*. But observance of Ramadan has increasingly involved consumption rituals including elaborate gatherings, shopping vacations and elaborate television viewing that begins with the period of *iftar* and extends into the early hours of the morning – for an overwhelming majority of Arab Muslims, television is *the* central leisure activity. The holy month ends with a major Muslim holiday, *'Eid al-Fitr*. Scholars have probed the cultural and audience rituals around Ramadan (Armbrust, 2002 and 2005; Salamandra, 2008) but not the political economy of Ramadan television.

From the television industry's standpoint, Ramadan is a do-or-die television season that shapes production, programming and acquisition trends for the entire year. During this high-stakes month, Arab television channels make unusual efforts to sustain existing audiences and attract new viewers, culminating in

'Eid al-Fitr celebrations

special programmes celebrating *'Eid al-Fitr* (in the US this is comparable to special programming broadcast during the sweeps periods or at year-end for Christmas and New Year). Television executives air their very best programmes during Ramadan. Many advertisers spend the lion's share of their yearly budgets during this month (though others are beginning to question the effectiveness of Ramadan television advertising due to the proliferation of ads): according to many industry insiders we interviewed, the number of commercial spots tends to increase by 15–30 per cent and product-placement packages range from US $200,000 to 1.5 million for a month-long programme. Reputations – of writers, directors, actors, even channels – are made, remade or unmade during this month-long television marathon. Programmes that prove successful during this crucial thirty-day period are rerun for the entire year and inspire novel production and programming trends. State-owned channels use Ramadan to regain, however temporarily, their eroding national audiences, with local community-oriented programmes. Clerics use religious programmes to mobilise believers to renew their faith. This chapter shows that the articulation of television industry practices, advertising strategies, political and religious agendas, viewership patterns and broader social impact makes Ramadan television a particularly rich locus for understanding the manifold processes of localisation and regionalisation shaping Arab television.

RITUALS OF RAMADAN TELEVISION
Ramadan introduces key lifestyle changes – in socialising, eating and sleeping – that affect viewership patterns. Because many Muslims fast from dawn to dusk, governments and companies reduce working hours to adjust to employees' reduced energy levels. All social activities are scheduled for after *iftar*, when television primetime begins and stretches late into the night. Television schedulers take two aspects into consideration: the exact start and end of the month of Ramadan and the timing of *iftar*. Because of the vagaries of the lunar calendar, television executives get official notification of Ramadan's beginning and end a few days before the start and end of the holy month. As a result, schedules are implemented at the last minute and sometimes viewers miss launching episodes of special programmes. Determining the timing of the *iftar* is imperative to separate daytime from primetime programmes. Because the Arab world is spread over five time zones, this task is complicated by the fact that *iftar*'s timing is determined by the movement of the sun, determination of which is an approximation. Given the importance of the Saudi market, pan-Arab channels tend to follow the timing adopted in Saudi Arabia for determining both the beginning of Ramadan and the timing of *iftar*. In fact, channels reserve their best programming for after al-Maghreb's (Dusk) prayer, between 6.00 and 11.00 pm

Greenwich Mean Time, depending on the time zone (Saudi Ramadan primetime can extend until 2.00 am local time).

During Ramadan, viewers tend to favour local (national) terrestrial channels
during primetime and shift back to satellite channels during the late evening. As
families tend to spend time together after *iftar*, national television channels air programmes that appeal to a sense of community. National television channels in
Egypt and Saudi Arabia have historically been instrumental in setting these trends,
and these two countries continue to be important benchmarks for Ramadan television. Egypt has the largest single-country population (approximately 80 million),
and therefore cannot be ignored by advertisers. Saudi Arabia is more important:
its national advertising market constitutes 10–15 per cent of total advertising
expenditure in the region. This, with advertising expenditure on pan-Arab, i.e. not
national, at 40 per cent of total (national and pan-Arab) advertising expenditure,
and taking into account that much of pan-Arab advertising targets Saudi viewers,
puts advertising expenditure directed at Saudi Arabia at approximately 50 per cent
of the total for the region (Hamadeh, 2008; Neimat, 2007; *Emerging Dubai*, 2006;
al-Hamamsy, 2005). An examination of the development of Ramadan-specific
television genres in Egypt and Saudi Arabia paves the way for examining the current importance of Ramadan for Arab television at large.

In the 1970s and 1980s, Egypt's Ramadan television menu consisted primarily of traditional musical performances, comedies and drama serials. *Fawazir
Ramadan* (The Riddles of Ramadan), a musical riddle staged like mini-Broad-
way scenes, were broadcast roughly one hour after *iftar*. Every night, Egyptians
were treated to memorable riddles, with performers like Nelly and Sherihan,
that viewers had to solve to win prizes at the end of the month. Although sold
to most Arab national channels, the *Fawazir* lost its appeal with the introduction
of satellite television and mounting criticism from conservatives who objected
to the dancing and sensuality of the programme. Another Ramadan fixture is *al-
Camera al-Khafeyya* (Candid Camera), which replaced the Fawazir during the
1990s as the post-*iftar* programme of choice in Egypt. Initially introduced in the
1980s by Tarek Nour Communications (TNC), *al-Camera al-Khafeyya* became
an instant popular and commercial success. Other Ramadan favourite television
genres included comedic plays, and more importantly *musalsalat* that draw on
stories of everyday Egyptian life, particularly inspired by Nobel Prize-winning
novelist Naguib Mahfouz. Broadcast nightly during primetime and rerun during the day, Ramadan *musalsalat* are also an occasion for Egyptians to see their
favourite movie stars on television, performing a crucial cross-over function
between the Egyptian cinema and television industries.

In comparison, Saudi TV's programmes during Ramadan historically consisted of religious shows, fewer serials (than in Egypt), game shows and

children's programmes. In the mid-1970s, classic religious shows like *Ma'edat al-Iftar* (The Table of Iftar) and *Nour Wa Hedaya* (Light and Guidance) featured the famous cleric Sheikh Ali al-Tantawi combining social remarks, religious advice and witty commentary. Al-Tantawi was an inspiration for generations of clerics who found in television an ideal vehicle for propagating the faith. (Up to this day, Saudi TV and al-Majd, discussed in Chapter 3, rerun al-Tantawi's on-air comments a few minutes before the *iftar*; many of these videos have found their way onto the Internet). Game shows combined religious and cultural knowledge with some light entertainment, exemplified in *Huruf* (Letters), a show broadcast between 1986 and 1996. In addition to cartoons, Saudi TV dedicated segments for children and youth including various shows featuring the character of Baba Farhan (Papa Farhan), especially his show *Mawaheb wa Afkar* (Talents and Ideas), and a children's version of *Fawazir* with riddles related to the Koran and Islam invited viewers to send in their answers by mail at the end of Ramadan (al-Saleh, 2005).

PRODUCTION AND PROGRAMMING

The contemporary Ramadan television season is marked by high-quality production, family-oriented themes and a plethora of new, Ramadan-specific programmes. In practice, scandalous social talk shows, music videos and Western movies take a backseat to drama, comedy and religious shows. In the satellite era, executives at pan-Arab channels like MBC, LBC and Dubai TV work eleven months to create programmes for the thirty days of Ramadan; they re-infuse popular light entertainment and religious genres with Ramadan themes and compete to acquire top *musalsalat* from independent production companies. Competition has led channels increasingly to promote their Ramadan fare in the preceding month to lock in viewers and lure advertisers, in spite of potential delays in production deliveries, fear of censorship and timing issues peculiar to the lunar calendar. Three scenarios govern the way free-to-air channels in particular acquire Ramadan programmes. Channels like MBC finance specific programmes and outsource production to companies across the region. Others like LBC-Sat and most pay-TV channels, acquire exclusive first-runs of serials from private production houses. Other channels with limited resources resort to reruns of *musalsalat*, in-house interactive game shows or low-cost religious programmes. More generally, production crews and on-air talent adhere to strict guidelines including conservative looks, guarded behaviour and restricted use of music, tempering commercial excess to bring programmes in tune with the general atmosphere of piety (see Kraidy and Khalil, 2007). Though mindful of the important Saudi market, channels target 'all Arab countries and all the Arab viewers everywhere' (al-Dowsari, 2006). At the end of Ramadan, *'Eid al-Fitr* is celebrated over three days when final episodes of *musalsalat* are shown, game-show competition results are announced and one-time special variety shows and concerts are aired ('Ramadan Kareem', 2006).

THE HISTORICAL EVOLUTION OF RAMADAN DRAMA AND COMEDY

Early (1970s) television drama featured actors from the theatre, radio and film. Egypt's lead in the film industry boosted drama production there while adaptations of Arab or European literature, like the works of Umru' al-Qais and Victor Hugo, flourished in Beirut; Egyptian actors used their local accent, Lebanese drama featured classical Arabic. In contrast to drama, comedy production was limited and its local focus prevented all but a few comedians from achieving pan-Arab fame, which they usually accomplished – the Syrian Durayd Lahham being a case in point – through film rather than television. In the 1970s and 1980s, the Lebanese war and the Arab boycott of Egyptian products (after Egypt signed a unilateral peace agreement with Israel) forced the industry to develop regional productions. Foreshadowing current trends, these productions were filmed in Amman, Athens or Dubai, and employed multinational Arab casts and crews.

The introduction of satellite television in the early 1990s boosted demand and expanded the geographical bases of drama production. During the 2004 Ramadan season, free-to-air channels aired twenty-one serials while pay-TV channels broadcast nineteen (*Ramadan's Drama*, 2004), in addition to many *musalsalat* shown on state channels. Saudi Arabia and Kuwait now have small drama and comedy sectors, while Syria and Jordan specialise in historical and social dramas. Lebanon contributes with sketch comedy and dubbed *telenovelas* while Egypt introduced multi-year drama sequels that run over several Ramadan seasons. Beginning in 2000, *musalsalat* have followed cyclical trends, with specific subgenres – historical, thematic (terrorism), biopic – dominating the market each year. Producers have experimented with new subgenres such as epics, sitcoms, hospital drama and adult cartoons.

THE *MUSALSALAT*: ARAB DRAMA SERIALS

As one of Arab television's most common programme genres, the *musalsal* (singular) typically includes approximately thirty episodes lasting about forty-five minutes each, and covers a broad range of subjects and narrative styles. *Musalsalat* (plural) are characterised by a continuing storyline with characters moving closer to a dénouement at the end of the last episode. Many serials depict the universal theme of a protagonist struggling for recognition and inclusion in society. Settings for *musalsalat* range from past periods of pan-Islamic rule to modern urban centres, and characters range from historical figures to contemporary public servants and ordinary people.

Egypt produces a large number of social serials that dramatically document aspects of urban and rural Egyptian life. These serials tend to have a distinct moralistic objective like *Qadeyat Ra'i 'Am* (A Case of Public Opinion), which dealt with and strongly condemned rape. In addition to its sociological aspect, Egyptian drama played a significant role in strengthening law and order, and nationalistic sentiment in the face of growing Islamisation, as in *Dumu' fi 'Uyun Waqiha* (Tears in Insolent Eyes), with movie star Adel Imam as a counter-espionage agent, or in *Ra'fat al-Haggan*, where Mahmoud Abdelaziz plays an intelligence officer planted in Israel. While Egyptian serials focus on domestic settings and issues, they resonate in the Arab world because of shared cultural experience, as in *Lan A'ish fi Gilbab Abi* (I Will Not Live in My Father's Robes), where a rural mayor tries to maintain his dynasty and protect his extended family. Since the liberalisation of the media production sector in the 1990s, a generation of Soviet-trained film and theatre directors has re-energised Syrian *musalsalat* with bold themes and innovative techniques, particularly in epic and historical serials (Kraidy, 2006c; Salamandra, 2005). Some, like *Ayyam Shameya* (Damascene Days), portray the city's politics at the beginning of the twentieth century; others, like *Zanubia*, the queen warrior, depict Syria's Arab-Islamic heritage; another subgenre, epic serials like *al-Mawt al-Qadem Ela-l-Sharq* (Death That's Coming to the East), the story of a peaceful town taken over by a rene-

Desktop wallpaper featuring the lead character in *Bab al-Hara* (note how the show is sponsored by Nakheel, a real-estate developer)

gade group, resonates with Syria's contemporary geopolitical concerns. Kuwaiti *musalsalat* are socially oriented and carry direct moral and educational lessons; they usually describe the encroachment of modern values and lifestyles on traditional society. Kuwaiti series like *Mahzhuzha wa Mabruka* (Lucky and Blessed) or *al-Embarator* (The Emperor) were marketed across the region, and were popular in the Gulf.

Since 2005, the increased transnational flow of capital and people has encouraged satellite channels to diversify production sites, invest in multinational serials and experiment with new subgenres. Building on the commercial success of some Egyptian drama sequels of the 1980s and 1990s, television executives and production companies are encouraged to schedule sequels (see Table 5.1). Because sequels allow for better production, promotion and media sales, they have become a reliable strategy to yield high viewership while keeping production costs under control. As a result, they have emerged as a central weapon in television executives' Ramadan arsenal. The recent success of the Syrian *musalsal Bab al-Hara* (The Neighbourhood's Gate) is often cited as an industry model. Set in the early twentieth century, *Bab al-Hara* is a nostalgic look at the traditions and social relations in a Damascus neighbourhood. The series invokes tensions around the demise of social bonds, traditional family life and the changing role of women. Broadcast on MBC since 2006, the series has entered public discourse signalling major competition between Syrian and Egyptian drama. To promote the second season, MBC organised a competition that allowed the winner to visit the set and crew; and the agreement on a third instalment was announced as breaking news on al-Arabiya, underscoring how news channels serve to promote entertainment channels within multichannel television conglomerates like the MBC Group.

The increasingly competitive drama sector involves growing investment in cinematography, set and costume design, and special effects. Given the tight time-frame of the Ramadan season, programmes can simply not accrue audi-

Table 5.1 Multi-year (sequel) *Musalsalat*, 1989–2009

Seasons	Country of production	Title	Genre
2006–9	Syria	*Bab al-Hara*	Historical/social
2007–8	Egypt	*Al-Masrawiya*	Historical/social
2007–8	Egypt	*Al-Dali*	Social
2000–3	Egypt	*Al-Rejal 'Adat*	Social
1999–2000	Egypt	*Zenzenia*	Historical/social
1994–9	Syria	*Hamman al-Quishani*	Historical/social
1994–9	Egypt	*Yawmiyat Wanis*	Social
1991–5	Egypt	*Layali al-Hilmiyya*	Historical/social
1989–1	Egypt	*Ra'fat al-Haggan*	Espionage/historical

ences over time, so *musalsalat* must attract viewers immediately; hence the popularity in recent years of biographical serials exploring the lives of famous singers or politicians, which can be presold to television channels because their subjects guarantee publicity and audience interest. These have included chronicles of famous singers, like *al-'Andalib* (The Nightingale), about the life of 'Abdelhalim Hafez, dramatisations of significant moments in history represented by *Salaheddin* (Salaheddin reconquered Jerusalem from the Crusaders) and semi-hagiographic experiences like *Akher al-Fursan* (Last of the Knights), based on poetry by the ruler of Dubai and featuring Lebanese lead actors, Syrian director and crew, and filmed in more than ten Asian and African countries (Abu Sheeba, 2005; Omar, 2008; Omran, 2006).

These developments reflect an industry trend that has moved away from worrying about national sensitivities in casting and towards recruiting transnational casts and crews – a clear indication that the industry continues to regionalise. Jordanians pioneered the regional promotion of national productions via a pan-Arab cast and Jordanian–Syrian co-productions. There have been a couple of notable Syrian–Moroccan collaborations on historical serials like *Saqr Quraysh* (The Eagle of Quraysh) and *Rabi' Qurduba* (The Spring of Cordoba). Today it is common to see an established Syrian writer, a capable Egyptian director and star actors from Jordan, Lebanon and Morocco collaborate on a *musalsal*. This makes good business sense: multinational casts enable access to multinational markets. This also helps drama tackle topics of broad pan-Arab significance like extremism in the *al-Tariq ela Kabul* (The Road to Kabul) or the Palestinian conflict in *al-Taghriba al-Filistiniyya* (The Palestinian Estrangement) (Hazeen, 2005). In all this, the long-dominant Egyptian drama industry is sharing the stage with Syrian and Gulf producers in an increasingly regionalised industry.

TELEVISION COMEDY

Historically, Arab comedies have been 'humorous' melodramas emphasising gender and class stereotypes, with physical and slapstick twists. For instance, common themes involved acrobatic situations with fat/slim people or a submissive husband with an assertive wife. As with most television genres when satellite television was introduced, the humour repertoire has been expanded and transformed by their fusion with other performance traditions, various national humour heritages and Western comedy formats. Today, pan-Arab television comedy encompasses two distinctive subgenres, both going back to Western, English-language comedic tradition: on the one hand, situation comedy inspired by popular American sitcoms from the 1990s like *Friends* (1994–2004) and *Everybody Loves Raymond* (1996–2005); on the other hand, slapstick comedy harking back to the British tradition represented by

The Benny Hill Show (1969).

Since 2005, half-hour sitcom-inspired serials have gained popular appeal among both young and adult viewers. These shows started to appear on channels in Egypt, Kuwait, Lebanon and Morocco; but with local exposure, limited budgets and modest writing. Promoted as a youthful genre and a relatively inexpensive alternative to Ramadan serials, sitcoms entered regional distribution through the same company that introduced *Candid Camera* to Egypt: Tarek Nour Communications (TNC) which, in 2006, collaborated with film director Sherif Arafa and with Samir Amro Atef, head writer on *'Alam Simsim*, the Egyptian (licensed) version of *Sesame Street* (1969–). Often compared to the US sitcom *Dharma and Greg* (1997), the sitcom *Tamer wa Shaw'iya* (Tamer and Shaw'iya) is built around class differences between husband and wife: Tamer, a wealthy lawyer, and his wife Shaw'iya, a working-class schoolteacher. The scenarios developed and written by Atef and his 'writers' workshop' are unique glimpses into the quirks and foibles of young couples experiencing globalisation in post-*infitah* (economic opening or liberalisation) Egypt, and the challenges of modern lifestyles. A second successful comedy, also supervised by Atef, *Rajul wa Sitt Sittat* (A Man and Six Ladies) is the story of a lead male character and six women including his sister, wife and her sister, daughter, his mother and scrooge mother-in-law, all sharing the same house. Adopted from US work practices, Atef's 'writers' workshop' is a recent innovation in Arab scriptwriting which allows a number of writers to collaborate on plots, dialogues and final scripts (Nour interview, 8 March 2008; Atef interview, 28 April 2008).

Situation comedies have become a fixture of Ramadan television, on both terrestrial and satellite channels; nonetheless, when compared to state-owned channels, commercial satellite channels have featured more exciting content and slicker production values. The appeal of the sitcom format extends beyond the Ramadan cluttered season to reruns because of its advertising-friendly half-hour format and the absence of a central plot, which enables frequent reruns of individual episodes with no narrative necessity to air them in sequence. Per our observation of programming grids, by Ramadan 2008, a couple of sitcoms from Egypt and Lebanon aired on regional channels and half a dozen were on the air in 2009. Other popular comedy forms include multicast, reality-based comedies like Kuwait's celebrity-style candid camera *Sadun* (Hunted), where famous Arab people are 'punked'. Several channels initiated comedy shows similar to *Second City Television* or *Saturday Night Live*, with mostly pre-recorded comedy sequences, fictional characters and satirical imitations of politicians or celebrities.

An example of this trend is the LBC show *Bas Mat Watan*, whose *double-entendre* name means both 'Smiles of a Nation' and 'When a Nation Died'. This has been the most watched show in its category in Lebanon, where the political satire genre has been highly popular for more than thirteen years. As one of the longest-running shows broadcast on LBC-Sat, during Ramadan *Bas Mat Watan* adds new sequences and is broadcast daily instead of weekly. Drawing on forms of street theatre, the show's multitalented cast performs a number of skits, parodies and songs. Focusing on political satire and social commentary, *Bas Mat Watan* has a crude comedic style that often raises eyebrows even in a relatively liberal country like Lebanon; in some instances, it has stirred controversy. As a traditional feature of the show, a comedian imitates a public figure and is interviewed as a special guest commenting on the various political issues of the week. The 1 June 2006 episode featured an imitiation of Sheikh Hasan Nasrallah, Hezbollah's charismatic leader. A few minutes after the show ended, hundreds of Hezbollah supporters, mobilised by text messages and phone calls, descended on Beirut streets to voice their anger at the show and demand an immediate apology. Television channels competed to broadcast calls for calm by Nasrallah himself, but even that and a hurried apology by the show's producer failed to calm the demonstrators. Hezbollah leaders and security forces took over the street to restore order. Other small demonstrations erupted in support of Hezbollah in various parts of the Arab world (Haugbolle, 2007; Yassine, 2007).

Saudi Arabian comedy has also moved to a prominent place on Ramadan television schedules. Since its beginning, Saudi TV encouraged dramatic and comedic productions but the lack of theatrical traditions impacted the ability to write, produce and find actors ('Assere interview, 1 March 2008). This changed in the satellite era as talent became increasingly regionalised. Since 1993, *Tash Ma Tash* (Hit or Miss/Fizz or No Fizz), a half-hour collection of comedic sketches, has been the most watched Ramadan programme in Saudi Arabia. Originally broadcast exclusively on Saudi TV 1 (aka Channel 1), *Tash Ma Tash* moved to MBC in 2006 in a five-year, US $17 million deal. The primary character, Fuad al-Hijazi (the name connotes the Hijaz, the traditional and conservative heart of Saudi Arabia), champions traditional ways. Over the years, the show has adapted to specific changes within Saudi society commenting on social, political and economic issues, addressing the position of women, the status of education and the problems of the public sector. In one sketch, the producers addressed the religiously sanctioned Saudi driving ban on women, with female characters asking whether they should be allowed to ride donkeys, and if so whether the animals would have to be female as well. *Tash Ma Tash* was not immune from hostile *fatwas*, political complaints from Saudi ministers, censorship by Saudi television and even death threats to its creators and cast members. To protect itself from excessive or unwarranted violations, the Saudi producing company, al-Hadaf (The Target), established an internal religious advisory committee comprising paid and volunteer members to monitor both scripts and video production.

As an adaptable television genre, comedy serves multiple, often contradictory, functions: a symbol of freedom and openness, a central focus for national awareness of multifarious issues, a barometer of changing social and cultural practices, and as an instrument to diffuse resentment and suppress opposition. In 2002, Bashar al-Asad succeeded his father as the President of Syria and promised political reforms and increased freedoms. Promoted as part of a new era in media freedoms, the Ramadan sketch comedy *Buq'at Daw'* (Spotlight) started by featuring themes about state corruption and abuse of power but soon became unable to escape censorship.

While shows like *Bas Mat Watan* and *Tash Ma Tash* are located respectively in Beirut and Riyadh, popular reactions to these satirical shows are rarely predictable given new transnational forms of media dissemination. In fact, censored sketches find their way to the Internet and circulate as viral videos on YouTube and equivalent media – one 2006 *Tash Ma Tash* sketch that skewered the Saudi religious police spread like wildfire on the Internet for weeks before it was officially banned from appearing on television by Saudi censors. Such implicitly or explicitly socio-politically charged programmes also raise the problem of regional/national acceptance. To what extent are local Lebanese politics of interest to a Saudi, an Emirati or an Egyptian? How accepting are Syrian or Saudi politicians of being ridiculed, imitated on regional television? Pan-Arab channels now recognise the need to produce more regionally relevant comedies, yet fail to produce successful hits. Using the sitcom format, LBC offered *9/11*, which traced Kuwaiti exchange students during the period of 9/11 and was produced in Lebanon with Kuwaiti actors and a Lebanese crew and director. Building on the celebrity status of former participants in the popular reality show *Star Academy*, LBC-Sat 'recycled' them as the pan-Arab cast of *Jeran* (Neighbours), a sitcom featuring two groups of males and females as next-door neighbours – clearly inspired by the NBC sitcom *Friends*. When MBC realised the regional appeal of US adult cartoons, its television executives pitched an Arabic version of the popular American animated sitcom, *The Simpsons* called *al-Shamshun*. Dubbed using the Egyptian dialect and featuring Egyptian superstars, *The Simpsons* lost much of its original bite and humour as translators tried to respect the spirit of Ramadan. Successful regional comedies are hard to produce, so it remains to be seen whether sitcoms can meet with pan-Arab success ('Who Wins', 2005; al-Hakeem, 2009).

RELIGIOUS PROGRAMMES

During Ramadan, religious programmes increase on local and free-to-air channels but remain virtually absent from pay-TV, with the exception of the religious channel al-Majd (see Chapter 3). Used interchangeably with Islamic, the term 'religious' refers to the overarching approach for a range of talk shows, call-ins and drama serials. The success of Islamic channels has forced both local and general entertainment channels to qualitatively and quantitatively develop religious programmes – especially during Ramadan. As a result, channels like MBC resort to charismatic clerics and team them with experienced anchors in simple talk shows like *al-'Ifta'* (The Edict), which provides on-air counselling after Friday prayer.

The long and monotonous sermons of yesteryears have receded in favour of programmes featuring influential sheikhs (clerics), *da'iya* (preachers) and inspirational speakers. Some tele-Islamists have created multimedia empires with books, CDs, DVDs, websites and, most centrally, television. For example, Saudi Sheikh Salman al-'Audah presents his talk show *Hajar al-Zawiya* (The Cornerstone) and provides additional material on the Internet. The Kuwaiti General Manager of Saudi-owned religious channel al-Resalah, Tariq Suwaidan, draws lessons from the life of the Prophet Mohammed; his programme *al-Rasul al-Ensan* (The Messenger as Human) was followed by a series of books. Perhaps the most successful is 'Amr Khaled, the charismatic Egyptian preacher who every year revamps his daily show during Ramadan to focus on themes related to the holy month and to feature live viewer participation. His programmes are broadcast on both religious and general channels and are followed by a number of ancillary activities including personal appearances at conventions and gatherings (Sa'ud, 2005; 'Religious Programmes', 2007; 'Ramadan Sheikhs', 2008).

Many clerics and preachers consider Ramadan an auspicious opportunity to promote religious conformity. Inspirational speakers and religiously committed young celebrities appear in programmes or extended public-service announcements encouraging young people to practise their religion and to cope with the temptations of modern life. In this context, *Yalla Shabab* started as a Saudi show, produced in Egypt by MBC and featuring a group of young Arab male and female presenters, and later evolved into a social institution (producing DVDs, running a coffee shop, etc) that reconciles a modern lifestyle with Islamic preaching. The *Yalla Shabab* group is available on the Internet and through youth centres throughout the year but reconvenes as a television programme throughout Ramadan. One of its founders, Ahmad al-Shughayri developed a spin-off programme under the name *Khawater* (Thoughts), a series of inspirational talks about contemporary challenges. Religious shows are often interspersed with public-service announcements and short social-marketing skits that encourage young people to pray ('Ramadan Sheikhs', 2008).

During Ramadan, religious channels broadcast *musalsalat* with directly religious themes. Veiled actresses who become inspirational talk-show hosts often return to star in religious or historical *musalsalat* that respect these actresses' commitment to wearing the *hijab* (the veil). Retired actresses have returned to star in socially redeeming stories while wearing the *hijab*, like Huda Sultan in *Arabesque* (2007) and Sabrine in *al-Fanar* (2008). Ultimately, though, what is most interesting about religious programming during Ramadan is the momentary competition between general and religious channels to capture the spirit of the holy month and increase the size of their audience ('Azour, 2006).

THE GLOBAL, REGIONAL AND LOCAL ON RAMADAN TELEVISION

Ramadan television is a microcosm of the entire Arab television industries, revealing the entanglement of religion with history, social resonance, creativity, advertising and commercial competition. Arab media, reflecting Arab societies, are undergoing twin processes of (pan-Arab) regionalisation and localisation in the context of media and cultural globalisation. Capital and talent now move between nation-states, but audiences are drawn to locally themed stories, themselves sometimes adapted from global formats. During Ramadan there is an emphasis on local Arabic-language programmes as opposed to imported Western shows. As a result, channels like Dubai-based and -owned 'One TV, dedicated to Western programmes, schedule reruns because of perceived loss of audience. While Arab music channels try to accommodate the spirit of the month with religious songs, softer music and fewer sensual images, MTV Arabia decided against playing music during Ramadan 2008 (Kattan interview, 28 May 2008). Consequently, as mentioned above, the real competition during Ramadan is between two locally made kinds of programmes, nostalgic community-oriented shows aired by national channels, and bedazzling high-quality productions on satellite entertainment channels.

Different socio-cultural and political requirements in regional and local production contribute to a double censorship of television serials. Local censorship dictates what can be written, what can be filmed and what can go on the air. During the editing stage, programmes often undergo additional censorship to conform to the conditions of the buying channel. Excessive censorship, or lack thereof, has often been at the core of many controversies surrounding Arab television serials. During the past five years, controversies have resulted from themes such as prostitution and addiction in *Khalf al-Qudban* (Behind Bars); or state corruption and abuse of power like *Ghizlan fi Ghabat al-Dhi'ab* (Gazelles in Wolves' Forest). A historical revisionist approach is also controversial especially surrounding public figures, like the life and suicide of actress Su'ad Husni in *Cinderella* or political events such as *Zaman al-Khawf* (Time of Fear) which follows a public servant during the insecure period between the 1982 Israeli invasion of Lebanon to the 1991 Gulf War or *Rasa'il al-Hubb wal-Harb* (Letters of Love and War) which recounts events in Lebanon, Syria and Jordan over the last thirty years. The use of historical settings with true or fictionalised characters is a common approach to avoid censorship.

Some controversies result from political opposition to television productions like *Nasser*, a *musalsal* on the life of former President Nasser, which Egyptian state television refused to broadcast. Nasser's importance in the birth of republican Egypt inspired many Egyptians brought up in a different era to follow the serial in spite, or perhaps because of, the regime's disapproval. Similarly, serials can be banned on local terrestrial channels because of stringent and sometimes outdated censorship laws; the 2004 Ramadan serials in Kuwait became controversial after the Directorate of Censorship at the Kuwaiti Ministry of Information banned works containing offensive scenes like unsanctioned relationships, alcohol drinking and drugs (Nyouf, 2004). Censorship rules are relaxed, however, when regimes want to relay specific messages or even endorse specific themes like combating extremism and raising awareness against terrorism. In fact, the Ramadan season of 2005 had no less than ten series with anti-terrorist messages from Saudi Arabia, Syria, Jordan and Egypt.

Recent works by Syrian director Najdat Anzour reflect the extent to which the contemporary satellite television industries treat topics that a few years ago were considered off limits. A self-claimed proponent of anti-extremism, Anzour earned himself a number of death threats after questioning the extremist beliefs that seventy-two virgins will be waiting for the would-be bomber in *al-Hour al-'Ayn* (The Pure and the Beautiful). This heavily publicised serial taking place in al-Muhaya compound (a gated community for foreigners, mostly Westerners, in the capital Riyadh) in Saudi Arabia, traced various socio-political issues in Saudi society including the physical attack on the female Saudi television presenter Rania al-Baz. During the 2005 season, threats from extremist organisations had stopped broadcasts of the *musalsal al-Tariq ela Kabul* (The Road to Kabul). Fearing a similar backlash, *al-Hour al-'Ayn*, though its script was supervised by renowned anti-extremist Saudi writer Abdullah bin Bejad, eschewed addressing the rhetoric of the al-Sahwa al-Islamiya (The Islamic Awakening), a radical Saudi Islamist movement that challenges the Saudi religious establishment from the ideological right. Even before it aired, extremists had begun attacking the show and pressuring sheikhs to issue *fatwas* banning its broadcast. In the follow-up, *al-Mariqun* (The Renegades), Anzour provides real-life emotional and vivid accounts of terrorist attacks in Damascus, Cairo, Baghdad and London. One plot follows a middle-class young Syrian man who is recruited by fanatical Islamists (al-Jaza'iri, 2005). Covered heavily by the media, controversial *musalsalat* reflect interconnections between capital, states, audiences and creative media work, on a regional rather than simply national scale.

The regionalisation of production has complicated local and inter-Arab media politics. Though the television production sector was liberalised in Egypt and Syria throughout the 1980s and 1990s, allowing the establishment of private production companies, in practice the state retains considerable influence: logistically through controlling production facilities, studios and shooting locations; financially through transnational collaboration or co-production that the state can block; and organically as many producers are part of state media bureaucracies or close to leading politicians. Because it co-produces many serials, the Egyptian government retains control over distribution and can therefore prevent the distribution of critical programmes. The power to influence production also resides in non-state actors: Gulf-based satellite channels finance and acquire the majority of Syrian *musalsalat*, giving them considerable leverage over an important sector of the Syrian economy. In the past, Egyptian television production suffered from the Arab boycott after its peace treaty with Israel, while Saudi productions in Syria slowed dramatically after a war of words erupted between the two countries in 2006 over Lebanese and regional politics. Public sectors in Egypt, Syria and Jordan have tried to support better production practices in collaboration with the various media-industry unions. Jordan in particular has emphasised various forms of co-productions to encourage its local industries through financing, casting or technical crew development. This policy has helped controversial serials such as *al-Tariq al-Wa'er* (Rough Road) and *al-Taghriba al-Filistiniyya* (The Palestinian Estrangement), both Syrian–Jordanian co-productions, to enter regional markets. At the same time, commercial pan-Arab channels like MBC have been encouraging multinational productions (sometimes going against states' protectionist impulses, especially in Egypt): the hit serial *al-Malek Faruq* (King Faruq) was produced in Egypt with a Syrian director, a Syrian actor and an Iranian special-effects crew and produced by a Saudi company ('Assere, interview with author, 1 March 2008).

A popular trend is to recruit major stars to sustain individual programmes with high ratings. In the absence of a strong film industry, television stars increase their fees at the detriment of the overall production costs, forcing producers to invest less in overall production quality because budgets are swallowed by inflated star fees. Television executives and media buyers also influence the choice of lead actors and actresses. Tariq al-Ganayni, one of Egypt's top producers, complained that more than one-third of the production budget is commonly spent on star salaries and perks (al-Ganayni interview, 28 April 2008).

For instance, *An al-Awan* (The Time Has Come) cost US $2.3 million, US $700,000 of which went to the actress and singer Warda. In order to agree to direct a television show for the first time, film director Sherif Arafa received US $540,000 out of a US $2.7 million budget for *Lahazat Hareja* (Critical Moment, the Dubai TV version of US hospital drama *E.R.*, 1994–2009) ('Ramadan Productions', 2006). In order to fight these excesses, television executives have increased pressure on producers either through direct supervision of the development and production processes or by establishing specific quality-control checks on production. Channels are concerned because many high-budget serials fail to achieve the predicted popular success because of clutter, bad scheduling, competition or weak promotion. The high risks involved in production and programming and the compressed thirty-day time-frame for success, have given rise to various levels of veto powers by producers, television executives and advertisers, and have compelled television executives to think of alternative revenue streams through scheduling reruns of Ramadan serials in different time periods, selling them to pay-TV channels and releasing them on DVD.

Growing commercial risk has encouraged the industry to rethink some of its established practices. Producers and television executives we interviewed said that rather than restricting the first run of *musalsalat* to Ramadan, then rerunning them throughout the year, new *musalsalat* should become a stronger, year-long presence. To that end, reliable industry research should foster long-term planning, establish quality control and track audience habits, with the focus remaining on oil-rich and population-rich Saudi Arabia. A marketing trade magazine concluded that 60 per cent of Saudi residents are fervent TV viewers: 'Most of these, 75% are urban, 80% are Saudi locals and 20% are Arab expatriates. The vast majority, 80% are between 15–45 years old' ('Ramadan Kareem', 2006). In Egypt, it is estimated that 55 million out of 70 million watch television during primetime – 72 per cent of the total population – (Malik, 2006); in 2005 they watched a daily average of five hours and thirty-eight minutes ('TNS Ratings', 2005). Audience ratings suggest that specific genres, particularly drama and comedy, are the most popular Ramadan programmes. Excluding local Saudi TV, MBC has been the most-watched television channel in Saudi Arabia with the top five programmes (See Table 5.2). The latter are all television serials, including the highest rated *Tash Ma Tash*, in addition to various *musalsalat* from Saudi, Egypt and Syria. In other words, an estimated 53.4 per cent and 44.4 per cent of Saudis watched *Tash Ma Tash* during Ramadan 2006 and 2007, respectively. Audiences across all age groups favour entertainment channels: MBC, Dubai TV and LBC were ranked respectively first, second

Table 5.2 Top Programmes in Saudi Arabia during Ramadan

Programme	Channel	Rating	Programme	Channel	Rating
1 Tash Ma Tash	MBC 1	53.4	1 Tash Ma Tash	MBC 1	44.4
2 Khaled Bin al-Waleed	MBC 1	22.1	2 Bayni Wou Baynak	MBC 1	35.6
3 Ghashamsham	MBC 1	20.8	3 Mazna and Family	MBC 1	29.4
4 Sahibat al-Emtiyaz	MBC 1	17.4	4 Bab al-Hara II	MBC 1	28.7
5 Hadayiq al-Shaytan	MBC 1	13.8	5 Lahzat Du'f	MBC 1	15.1

Ramadan 2006 Stat-IPSOS   *Ramadan 2007 Stat-IPSOS*

Table 5.3 Television Ratings in Saudi Arabia [excluding Saudi TV (terrestrial)

Channel	Rating	Channel	Rating
1 MBC 1	44.9	1 MBC 1	43.1
2 Dubai TV	25.8	2 Al-Arabiya	22.8
3 Al-Jazeera	14.6	3 MBC 2	17.6
4 Al-Arabiya	13.7	4 Al-Jazeera	11.2
5 LBC Sat	11.9	5 LBC Sat	10.6

Ramadan 2005 Stat-IPSOS   *January 2008 Stat-IPSOS*

and fifth during Ramadan 2005 (news channels al-Jazeera and al-Arabiya ranked third and fourth respectively in terms of the percentage of viewers who tuned to these channels during Ramadan), underscoring the appeal of entertainment over news (see Table 5.3).

Ramadan's massive audiences, large budgets and intense competition have pushed Arab television industries to make a qualitative leap, raising standards in production, market research and audience measurement. At the centre of this transition is the tightening relationship between the television and advertising industries. Until the mid-1990s, media planning and buying were based on a combination of insider information, previous channel performance and personal experience. Since then, the growth of the Arab advertising industry has enabled partnerships between local companies and global agencies like Leo Burnett, Draft-FCB and Saatchi and Saatchi. The market-research industry still struggles to provide reliable daily tracking data that would enable media buyers to adapt their plans to viewers' tastes – an ability at no time more crucial than during Ramadan. The development and current state of Arab advertising and audience research is therefore an important element of the Ramadan season on Arab television (and to a lesser extent of television programming during the other eleven months of the year). To understand this important aspect of the industry, the following section addresses these questions:

- How do advertising practices hinder and/or promote growth in the Arab television industries?
- What insights does audience research contribute to understanding viewership patterns, programming preferences and audience profile?

ADVERTISING AND AUDIENCE RESEARCH

During Ramadan, the number of television commercials rises by 25 per cent compared to the rest of the year, in tandem with increases in viewership by around 30 per cent during the holy month (the advertising inventory is still kept at about twelve minutes per hour, but extended viewing hours explain the increase in the number of commercials). Estimated pre-discounted figures from 2005 suggest that during Ramadan general entertainment channels like MBC grossed over US $68 million compared to just US $6 million for religious channel Iqra' (*Pan-Arab*, 2005). In the Gulf Cooperation Council countries (Bahrain, Kuwait, Oman, Qatar, Saudi Arabia, United Arab Emirates), advertising spending doubles during Ramadan (from a monthly average of 8 per cent during eleven months of the year to 15 per cent of the yearly budget during Ramadan alone) and has been increasing on average by 30 per cent per year (Hamadeh, 2008). Though primetime is extended and advertising opportunities increase, there are two different views among media buyers. One group consists of firm believers of heavy advertising during Ramadan because products can increase market share; another group cites advertising clutter, high cost and ferocious competition as arguments against placing commercials during Ramadan. For Karim Nour, Director of Business Development at TNC, Ramadan commercials represent 'a form of entertainment', and the Arab audience admires them just like Americans follow National Football League ads (Nour interview, 8 March 2008). This view reflects the television industry's reality, with Ramadan remaining the most important period of the year for television advertising.

The relationship between television and the advertising sector has changed drastically in the satellite era. In the 1980s, the Europe-based Arab press (which anticipated the offshore television channels discussed in Chapter 1) spawned a media-sales sector whose representatives aimed to consolidate sales efforts and attract regular advertisers for Arabic-language publications based in Paris and London. Advertising was allowed on very few state-owned channels, and was subject to various restrictions including the duration and content of commercial breaks. Since the 1990s, advertising-sales representatives work as intermediaries between television channels and advertising companies. Media-sales representatives guarantee channels a minimum monthly income, a pre-set yearly budget or a percentage of revenue from

advertising. The system has clear advantages. As private specialised companies with expertise and daily contact with the advertising market, media
representatives have regional networks of offices whose staff coordinates
sales in countries that are sometimes inaccessible to a television channel. But
there are also problems with this arrangement. For instance a channel's revenues are rarely affected by the negative or positive performance of its
programmes. In some instances, there is a mismatch regarding content and
sales opportunities within a television channel between the programming
department and the sales department. Most importantly, sales representatives
sometimes resort to aggressive tactics such as massive volume rebates that
might have deleterious long-term effects on television channels' advertising
rates.

   Outsourcing of media sales expanded with the continuing commercialisation
and regionalisation of the Arab television industries. A leading media-sales company is the Dubai-based Choueiri Group, which is often accused of
monopolising the field because it controls eight of the most-watched pan-Arab
channels, including LBC-Sat until 2008, MBC and Dubai TV (Addington,
2005b). Choueiri Group's share of the market is estimated at 20 per cent of a
US $2.4 billion (Toutounji, 2007). The founder Antoine Choueiri began his
career with offshore Arab publications, and his success is associated with the
rise of LBC from a local Lebanese station in the mid-1980s to a leading pan-
Arab channel in the mid-1990s (see Chapter 2). The Choueiri Group was briefly
in charge of the media sales for al-Jazeera and did not renew the contract for
'political reasons' (Addington, 2005b) – Saudi Arabia's boycott of al-Jazeera
because of the feud between the Saudi and Qatari royal families meant that
Choueiri could not collect revenues from the Saudi market, an untenable situation for a savvy businessperson. Advertising in the region is politicised, as a
channel's political stand more often supersedes its ratings among politically conscious advertisers. Even as al-Jazeera became the most-watched pan-Arab news
channel, advertisers avoided it for fear of alienating Saudi authorities and losing access to the lucrative Saudi market.

   Market saturation has pushed many in the industry to search for alternatives
to traditional commercial breaks. One trend is to provide a certain level of synergy between the channel's investors and the media vehicle. The television
channel then guarantees minimum revenue by advertising the investors' businesses. This is particularly true in the case of Dream TV in Egypt: the channel's
name and much of its commercials are dedicated to promoting its owner Ahmad
Bahgat's Dream real-estate businesses. In many cases (Dubai's Infinity
TV, Lebanon's New TV and Future TV, Kuwait's Rai TV), business interests are

Two hosts of Future TV's
Superstar: Egyptian Wael
Mansour and Lebanese
Mageda Khattar

coupled with political aspirations. Another trend is to utilise the new wave of interactive tools to enhance the channel's revenue. This may include a range of value-added services in the form of SMS2TV (Short Messaging System to Television), MMS (Multimedia Messaging System), ringtones, websites etc. This is a risk-free, low-budget operation usually outsourced to specialised companies in return for a share of revenues (Dalati, 2005). One of the most cited examples is Beirut-based Future TV's *Superstar*'s first season finale in 2003. SMS revenues were estimated at US $4 million for a two-hour show, an enormous amount by regional standards (the voting itself was carried over a week) (Battah, 2006a, 2006b). Currently, there are various niche channels that are almost exclusively driven by value-added services, primarily entertainment music channels. One such channel, the Beirut-based al-Jaras TV, tied up to a gossip magazine with the same title, has initiated the concept of a VIP SMS: instead of having text messages appear on the screen to be read, an anchor/video jockey reads these messages aloud for an additional charge. During an April 2009 visit to Jordan Media City in Amman, Jordan, both authors 'toured' a number of channels that consisted of a small booth in which a single operator checks text messages before feeding them on air.

Until recently, programme sponsorships were limited to verbal or credit mentions in addition to promotions or spot ads. Given the growth in the number of advertisements and the ensuing clutter, product placement has gained in popularity among advertisers and is increasingly visible in reality shows, drama and comedy serials. For instance, *Star Academy* had product placements for a number of regional or international brands such as Lebanon's Diet Centre, and the soft drink Pepsi. Since the early 1990s, the Saudi hit comedy show *Tash Ma Tash* has relied mostly on product placements to finance its production. Furniture stores and fast-food chains were featured on the show, either via product use or

The toolkit (computer, television monitor) required for feeding mobile-phone text messages to television screens

verbal mention ('placement' involves the product being visible for extended periods of time; 'use' entails occasional appearance; 'verbal mention' describes occasional references to the product in conversation). Until the programme moved to MBC, an average sponsor spent no less than US $80,000 per show per season (Abbas, 2006).

The increased commercialisation of the pan-Arab television industries, the booming advertising sector, the advent of product placement and the growth of advertising budgets have not been matched by reliable audience measurement. Companies involved in conducting audience research can be divided into two broad categories: television audience research and marketing/consumer-research companies. Some of these companies are international affiliates like Egypt-based Taylor Nelson Sofres (TNS), Beirut-based STAT-Ipsos and Dubai-based Pan-Arab Research Centre (PARC). Consumer-research companies who are occasionally involved in audience research include UK-based YouGovSiraj and Chicago-based Synovate, both focusing primarily on Gulf consumers out of offices in Dubai and Saudi Arabia. The methods used are diaries, computer-assisted telephone interviewing (CATI), surveys and focus groups. The frequency of research is irregular with a few exceptions like in Egypt, Saudi Arabia, Lebanon and Dubai (see Table 5.4)

Table 5.4 Audience, Consumer and Television Research Companies

Activity	Research company	Headquarters
Television audience	Pan-Arab Research Centre (PARC)	Dubai, UAE
	STAT-Ipsos	Beirut, Lebanon
	Taylor Nelson Sofres (TNS)	Cairo, Egypt
Marketing/	YouGovSiraj	London and Dubai
consumer research	Synovate	Chicago and Jeddah
Content analysis	COMTRAX	Beirut
Major research methods	Diaries, computer-assisted telephone interviewing (CATI), surveys and focus groups	
Regular research frequency	Egypt, Saudi Arabia, Lebanon and United Arab Emirates	

Television executives, media planners and media sales use several audience-measurement tools to monitor the Egyptian and Saudi markets. In Egypt, PARC relies on a number of techniques including 'day after' interviews that focus on recall and CATI surveys to evaluate specific programmes or commercials. PARC's comprehensive media-habits research is conducted yearly and is based on face-to-face interviews with an average weighted sample of 6000 participants. This research includes television ratings in addition to radio, Internet and cinema. Since October 2004, TNS has measured and analysed data from a weekly TV Diary panel of 1050 Egyptian homes. Participants are asked to keep a diary of their terrestrial and satellite viewings and fill in data at fifteen-minute increments (*TNS–Egypt*, 2008). In Saudi Arabia, STAT-Ipsos offers weekly CATI-based television ratings with an average sample of 5000 respondents. In 1997, an alliance of agencies and television channels initiated a pilot people-meter in Saudi Arabia with 600 participants. The experiment failed because of issues related to the privacy of participants and representativeness of the sample (Eapen interview, 7 April 2008). There is also little marketing knowledge to rely on: ESOMAR, a leading market-research association, estimates that per capita research spending in Egypt is US \$0.15, compared to US \$22.88 in the US (Richter and El Senussi, 2005).

One of the biggest challenges has been the attempt to implement people-meters, so far fully operational only in Lebanon and Dubai. The majority of the stakeholders are interested in extending the use of people-meters to the pan-Arab region, but cultural, political and economic constraints have hindered the process (Allison, 2008). Arguments against the introduction of people-meters centre on questions about the privacy of families and individuals; this is further complicated when governments have questioned the security measures related to the process. The potential financial losses for some of the media-buying units and the broadcasters have resulted in a dire situation: people-meters are welcomed but no one is willing to pay for them. At the same time, the Choueiri Group and others have suggested that marketers are not paying enough per capita for advertising, and that, as a result, advertising rates should continue to increase for those channels with the largest market share unless clients and governments are convinced by people-meters.

Pan-Arab audience research remains woefully underdeveloped when compared to the satellite television industry. The situation is compounded by the explosion of new multimedia and networked devices through which people can consume media. Corporate clients, advertising agencies and satcasters have raised pressing concerns about the methods and the ethical conduct of audience-research companies (Malik, 2006). Worries about the ability of existing models to produce long-term insights into audience viewing habits are fuelled by widely held beliefs that market and audience-research companies fudge results to favour companies with which they have business links.

CONCLUSION

By bringing the largest audience of the year and viewers who spend many hours every night of the month watching television, Ramadan is a crucially important season for producers, directors, actors, advertisers and viewers. Once a year, state-owned television officials are given a thirty-day opportunity to compete head-on with satellite channels to attract viewers. Through a combination of appeals to national identity and nostalgia to the community life of yesteryears, national terrestrial channels manage to regain sizeable national audiences for brief periods during Ramadan. During extended primetime hours, terrestrial and satellite channels treat viewers to an ever-increasing range of programme genres, including historical *musalsalat*, situation comedies, and religiously themed programmes. Ramadan reflects the transformation of key industry practices and the set of future trends in production and programming.

As the most popular television viewing period of the year, Ramadan is a good lens through which to examine the interplay of national and regional forces whose interaction shapes the Arab television industries. Capital and talent are increasingly transnational but stories remain anchored in historically identifiable (or imaginary) Arab locations. In general, *musalsalat* have become the dominant Ramadan programming genre in spite of censorship. In contrast, comedy has for the most part stayed local as humour's ability to travel between Arab countries is hindered by local cultural and political sensitivities. Religious programming tells a different story about a society trying to maintain its Islamic socio-cultural traditions in the face of impinging modern global lifestyles. The adoption of Western visual aesthetics, production values and presentational styles aims primarily to win an eroding youthful audience.

By capturing massive television viewership, production and advertising budgets, with high-quality drama, comedy and religious programmes, Ramadan has increasingly shaped the Arab television industries at large. Realising the opportunities to be had by extending television *musalsalat* beyond the thirty-day Ramadan season, television executives have restructured their *modus operandi* to develop, produce and broadcast new serials throughout the year (while still saving the best for Ramadan). Simultaneously, advertising executives are re-organising their sales structures to limit 'rate card' volume discounts and present more reliable audience research to encourage advertising investments outside Ramadan. This deregulated, commercial, pan-Arab television industry has thrived for two decades as Arab governments attempt to find ways to regulate it. Today's transnational, commercial and multimedia-connected television industries pose great challenges to Arab policy-makers and regulators. The next chapter describes and analyses national experiences with television policy and regulation in the Arab world, proceeding to explore how various models of media–state relations and country-specific regulatory frameworks have shaped an emerging television-policy regime.

Television Policy and Regulation in the Arab World

National media policies in the Arab world have traditionally reflected a handful of concerns. First of all is regime survival. In a region with few rulers who enjoy popular legitimacy, kings and presidents have long regarded media institutions as a key instrument to hold on to power. Royal families, ruling parties and political dynasties have since the late 1950s monopolised television broadcasting, banning critical coverage of themselves, the armed forces and other components of the apparatus of power. Second, putative moral values and socio-cultural concerns motivate many Arab media policies. Television is especially susceptible to censorship based on concerns about its impact on national and cultural identity, relations between men and women, young people, and prevailing moral values. These concerns are permeated by religious discourse, whether by governments seeking to justify policies through religion, or Islamist opposition decrying governments' lack of legitimacy. In this realm the West figures often as the source of a 'cultural conquest' and opponents of Westernised television content act as moral guardians. Third, as newly independent Arab states struggled to solidify national unity and foment socio-economic development, television policies in many Arab countries focused on promoting socio-economic development while preventing coverage of financial and economic issues in ways that may undermine national economic health. Fourth and more recently, there is a trend in which media policy is shaped as much by national or subnational economic policy as it is by customary power politics and foreign policy (of course, these realms of governance are separate only for analytical purposes). This is manifest in the case of Dubai, but is growing in other countries and regions as well, where economic factors sometimes compete with political considerations in shaping media policy. This chapter subsequently shows how the emergent pan-Arab policy regime is animated by a volatile relationship between politics and economics.

Recently, new challenges have arisen, compounding customary policy concerns focused on the political, socio-cultural and economic issues. Three of them are particularly relevant to us. The first is the decline of state broadcasters combined with the rise of a transnational pan-Arab media space. Consequently, many states have embarked on a process of liberalisation – understood in the narrow sense of allowing privately owned satellite channels to operate within strict political constraints – with the twin goals of reaching their own national

Table 6.1 Foreign-owned Arabic Satellite Television Channels (Launched since 2001)

Channel	Sponsor	Launch date	Headquarters
Deutsche Welle World TV	Deutsche Welle – includes Arabic news and current affairs	2002	Berlin, Germany
Al-'Alam	Iranian government managed by Islamic Republic of Iran Broadcasting	2003	Tehran, Iran and Beirut, Lebanon
Al-Hurra	Funded by US Congress reporting to the Broadcasting Board of Governors (BBG)	2004	Springfield, VA, US
France 24	French government, co-managed by private TF1 Group and public channel A2	2006	Paris, France
Russia Today	State-owned Russian News Agency RIA-Novosti	2007	Moscow, Russia
BBC Arabic	BBC World funded by the British Foreign Office	2008	London, UK
France 24	French government, co-managed by private TF1 Group and public channel A2	2006	Paris, France
CCTV Arabic	Chinese government	2009	Beijing, China

viewers and projecting transnational influence. This has included establishing 'media cities' (Egypt, UAE, Jordan, Syria) with relatively favourable financial and political terms and enacting laws permitting privately owned satellite stations to transmit from their territories. Attempts to directly privatise state television assets, for example in the cases of Channel 3 in Jordan and Télé-Liban in Lebanon, have had mixed results. In both cases, the state was ultimately compelled to retain ownership.

The second is the advent of more aggressive opposition movements, whose local and transnational activities make excellent use of the new pan-Arab media and especially the television environment. Whether Saudi dissidents speaking on al-Jazeera from London, bloggers affiliated with the Muslim Brotherhood in Egypt posting videos of police abuse that end up on satellite television, or a defecting Vice-President of Syria ('Abdelhalim Khaddam) appearing on a Saudi-owned channel (al-Arabiya) to attack the regime of which he had still been a part two weeks earlier. In the 1960s and early 1970s, Beirut hosted Arab dissidents – exiled politicians, fiery intellectuals and threatened journalists – who spoke and wrote critically. Nowadays London, Paris and various Arab capitals host dissenters against other Arab regimes and orchestrate television wars, which have occurred first between Qatar and Saudi Arabia, waged through al-Jazeera and al-Arabiya; then between Lebanon and Syria, a particularly lopsided struggle since LBC and Future TV reportedly are popular among Syrian viewers while few if any Lebanese watch Syrian television; third between Saudi Arabia and Syria caused by differences on Lebanon, Iran and Iraq; fourth between Hezbollah and Egypt during Israel's war on Gaza in late 2008; in addition to rival geostrategic alignments in the struggle between the United States and Iran for dominance over the Middle East.

The third development is the onslaught of Arabic-language television channels operated by non-Arab states including al-Hurra [The Free One], funded by the US Congress, Rusya al-Yawm [Russia Today], bankrolled by the Kremlin, al-'Alam [The World], owned by the Iranian state, the resuscitated BBC Arabic, Deutsche Welle World TV, France 24, a French channel broadcasting in various languages, including Arabic and CCTV Arabic, launched by the Chinese government in 2009. These channels reflect post-9/11 anxieties in the capitals of great and regional powers, and the resurgence of the Arab world as a geopolitical flashpoint. Though remarkable in itself, the presence of these channels should not be confused with influence. None of these propaganda outlets has been consequential to Arab public discourse, and their ratings remain dismal, which is why in this book we do not give them systematic consideration. The fact that Arab viewers have largely spurned these channels reflects the vibrancy of the indigenous satellite industry.

These developments bring to the fore a combination of political, economic and socio-cultural challenges that Arab states have scrambled to address through media policies that are developed reactively and often haphazardly. In this chapter, we aim to give a broad picture of national policy regimes in the context of an increasingly regional (pan-Arab) television industry. Instead of dwelling on specifics that are subject to change at any time, or aiming for a geographically representative but analytically superficial approach, we attempt to identify broad themes, distinguish emerging patterns and analyse overlaps and connections between national policies and the pan-Arab media environment. To do so, we have selected four Arab countries, some regionally influential, others that represent key patterns in national media policy. Our analytical approach uses the cases of Saudi Arabia, Lebanon, Syria and the UAE to articulate the national–transnational, internal–external dynamics that link established policy regimes with emerging modes of governance in the region.

Though national Arab regulatory frameworks exhibit similarities and overlaps, they also reflect the fact that each Arab country developed media regulations and policies to meet challenges distinct to that country, whether social, political or in some cases economic. Media policies in most Arab countries have the overarching objective of safeguarding the political power structure by excluding from the airwaves anything exhibiting dissent that could threaten the status quo, typically by the ubiquitous catch-all prohibition of media material susceptible of harming a country's 'national reputation'. Once we step beyond regime survival and monopoly over power, however, we can discern diverging priorities among Arab states. National experiences with media policy and regulation that we discuss in this chapter represent influential models of policy grounded in distinct yet overlapping social, political and economic contexts. Saudi Arabia, which we discuss next, represents a policy model geared at internal control and external projection of influence, in which the state retains full control of television internally while making use of Saudi media tycoons as proxies to do its bidding transnationally.

TELEVISION POLICY IN SAUDI ARABIA: INTERNAL CONTROL AND EXTERNAL INFLUENCE

As discussed in Chapter 1, Saudi Arabia occupies a special position in the world of Arab media. With its petrodollars, large and relatively wealthy population and limited entertainment opportunities, Saudi Arabia constitutes an important target for pan-Arab advertising and as a result for Arab media programmers and producers. Saudi Arabia's uniqueness in the Arab television industries resides also in the kingdom's particular philosophy on the role of television in society, and attendant media structure, policies and regulations. To understand television policy in Saudi Arabia, it is first necessary to grasp the threefold relationship between the House of al-Saʻud, the clerical establishment and the Saudi tycoons that shapes the television industry in the country (see Kraidy, 2007).

Like many other rulers in the developing world in the middle of the twentieth century, the royal family of Saudi Arabia launched a television service in the 1960s to promote national unity and move forward with a modernisation plan. Even today, promoting national cohesion is a primary objective of Saudi media policy (Saʻate, 1992). With a surface of nearly 2.2 million square kilometres (approximately 830,000 square miles), Saudi Arabia has a large national terri-

Table 6.2 Saudi Television-Policy Milestones

Date	Event
1962	Ministry of Culture and Information established
1963	Saudi television launched
1965	Militants march on television building
1979	Saudi authorities use TV effectively during siege of Mecca
1981	Saudi Higher Media Council moves under Interior Minister
1991	MBC launched with royal family blessing
2003	Al-Arabiya launched to counter al-Jazeera
2004	Al-Ekhbariya launched as an all-news national channel
2009	Saudi Ministry of Culture and Information contracts Florida-based Harris Corporation to modernise radio and television infrastructure

tory and is the world's fourteenth-largest nation-state. Its population of 27 million people (including between 5–6 million foreign residents) dwarfs the number of residents of other Gulf petromonarchies. In terms of population density, however, Saudi Arabia ranks 205th worldwide at eleven inhabitants per square kilometre (or twenty-nine per square mile). In such a sparsely populated expanse, in which the population retains strong local, tribal and sectarian identities, television plays a crucial role in sustaining feelings of national belonging, what the historian Benedict Anderson called the 'imagined community' of the nation. For the al-Sa'ud clan, television was a vital instrument to bolster its legitimacy as ruler of the realm.

Saudi history is full of controversies triggered by the introduction of 'new' media (Kraidy, 2006d). A long-standing alliance between the al-Sa'ud and the al-Sheikh families gives the former supremacy in politics while awarding the latter leadership in the domains of religion, education and culture. This means that establishment Wahhabiya, dominated by clerics associated with the al-Sheikh family, holds sway over Saudi media policies. As a result, throughout the last half-century, clerics had a major influence over television content in the kingdom. For example, after crises such as the storming of the Grand Mosque of Mecca by armed militants in 1973, clerics pressured the Minister of the Interior, who in turn pressured the Minister of Culture and Information, to prohibit the presence of Saudi women as newscasters on television. But as Saudi media space grew more integrated into the larger, pan-Arab media space, clerics lost some of the power to determine what Saudi viewers watched. This has also led to an increase in public pronouncements and religious rulings about television that are made outside the purview of state institutions that are explicitly tasked with media regulation like the Ministry of Information. Nonetheless, as reflected in Table 6.2, the ruling family has engaged in a systematic development of its media apparatus.

The Saudi Ministry of Culture and Information was established in 1962 (Rugh, 1980), shortly before King Faisal announced a plan to launch a national television service by 1963. According to Boyd (1999), the decision was motivated by several factors. First, television was a vital instrument of modernisation and there was a need for it in order to cater to a growing Saudi professional class that experienced television in Egypt and Lebanon. Second was the need to counter hostile propaganda from Egypt, mostly reaching Saudis through radio. Third, television was an educational and developmental tool. Finally, television would foster national unity. Nonetheless, in 1965 militants marched on the Saudi television building to shut it down because they deemed it to be un-Islamic. Trying to control the demonstrations, Saudi police shot dead a prince whose brother took revenge ten years later when he assassinated King Faisal in

1975 (Boyd, 1999). Nonetheless, television served the royal family well in December 1979, by demonstrating, after days of conflicting accounts, that armed militants who had stormed the Grand Mosque were in the custody of Saudi security services (Trofimov, 2007). To tighten control on the media, a July 1981 royal decree reshuffled the Saudi Higher Media Council and placed the Interior Minister and royal Prince Nayef at the head of a new media committee that controlled information policy in the kingdom (for more details, see Chapter 3 in Kraidy, 2009).

During the following years Saudi princes and business moguls expanded their stakes in pan-Arab television industries, beginning with MBC in 1991, followed by ART and Orbit and continuing with Prince al-Waleed bin Talal embarking in 1993 on an ambitious series of media acquisitions and joint ventures, including his Rotana conglomerates and a majority stake in LBC-Sat (as discussed in previous chapters; see also Kraidy and Khalil, 2007). In 2003, a Saudi-dominated consortium of investors launched al-Arabiya (discussed in Chapter 4), the agenda of which has been to counter al-Jazeera's editorial line and reflect Saudi interests.

The external expansion of privately owned Saudi satellite channels notwithstanding, the Saudi government still owns and operates all terrestrial and satellite television channels based on Saudi territory. The state-run Broadcasting Service of the Kingdom of Saudi Arabia (BSKSA) is in charge of all television activities and private television channels are prohibited from satcasting from Saudi soil (as of spring 2009, however, MBC was working on establishing a terrestrial, Saudi-oriented channel in Jeddah). Saudi TV now has four channels, in addition to al-Ekhbariya, which was launched in 2004 as an all-news channel run by the Ministry of Culture and Information from the capital Riyadh in the wake of terrorist attacks in the kingdom. As in the 1980s, changes in television policy reflected the government's desire to be able to provide coverage at a time of crisis. Al-Ekhbariya was launched as part of wide-ranging television reforms that included revamping Channels 1 and 2, and launching a sports channel, all designed to attract Saudi viewers back to state television in the wake of their migration to al-Jazeera and al-Arabiya. A 2004 survey published in the trade magazine *Arab Ad* indicated that these efforts were partly successful, revealing that 82 per cent of Saudi households watched al-Jazeera, compared to 75 per cent for al-Arabiya and 33 per cent for al-Ekhbariya ('Saudi Arabia', 2004). As of January 2009, al-Jazeera remains the most-watched news channel in Saudi Arabia, though al-Arabiya and Saudi TV 1 are gaining audience share (*TV Trend*, 2009).

Basic censorship guidelines have remained consistent since the 1960s, prohibiting any sexually arousing scenes, women with revealing clothing, women dancing or scenes which 'show overt acts of love', drinking alcohol, betting and gambling, attacks on any of the 'heavenly religions', criticism or mockery of other countries and their rulers, criticism of the House of Sa'ud, and references to Zionism and excessive violence (Shobaili, 1971, quoted in Boyd, 1999, p. 164). These guidelines are implemented with slight variations. In the case of Egyptian movies shown on Saudi television, unmarried actors acting as a married couple are prohibited from sitting on the same bed at the same time and in the same room with the door closed; no women should appear on the screen during Ramadan, and parents cannot be seen kissing their children of the other sex (Index on Censorship, 1992, quoted in Boyd, 1999, p. 165). There are occasional periods when media policy is tightened or relaxed, because, as Boyd put it, '[T]elevision always reflects what the Ministry of Information believes to be the mood of the country' (Boyd, 1999, p. 163).

The Ministry of Culture and Information is not, however, the only institution where television policy is discussed. When they feel side-stepped by the royal family on matters of media policy, Saudi clerics feel empowered to make consequential public statements about the television industry. In September 2008, during Ramadan, several Saudi clerics were vocally critical of television programmes, especially of a Turkish series dubbed in Arabic featuring an egalitarian romantic relationship of a young married couple. The series, called *Nour* [Light] in Arabic, had caused a commotion in Saudi Arabia, with reports of women neglecting their professional or familial duties to watch the show, and others warning of the danger that the show posed to the numerous Saudi viewers who were enthralled by it. One of the main problems was that MBC, a recognisably Saudi institution, aired the show. The first official pronouncement came when Saudi Arabia's Grand Mufti issued a religious edict condemning *Nour* as 'un-Islamic'. Though accusations against media moguls of corrupting society are not new in Saudi Arabia, clerical attacks were particularly harsh during Ramadan 2008. In mid-September 2008, Sheikh Saleh al-Luhaydan, head of Saudi Arabia's highest juridical authority, stated on a radio programme that the owners of television channels airing programmes considered to be immoral or debauched may legitimately be killed. After King Abdallah reshuffled his cabinet in early 2009, a group of thirty-five clerics in late March 2009 issued a call to the new Culture and Information Minister to ban the appearance of women on Saudi television and in the press ('Saudi 'Ulemas', 2009).

TELEVISION POLICY IN LEBANON: INTERNAL STABILITY AND EXTERNAL IMAGE

If in Saudi Arabia television reflects the mood of the society because of deliberate media policy, in Lebanon the same thing occurs in spite of media policies.

As Browne (1975) wrote in one of the earliest academic articles on Lebanese television, during civil strife television officials were instructed *not* to reflect what was occurring on the ground. But that was a time when the government still held monopoly power over news on Lebanese television, a situation that changed radically during the 1975–90 war. Nearly thirty years after television's 1956 launch in the country, the Civil War unleashed chaos on the airwaves when the Lebanese Forces, a Christian-Nationalist militia, launched LBC in 1985, followed by myriad other unlicensed stations (Boyd, 1991; Kraidy, 1998b). The reassertion of post-war state authority in the early 1990s led to the 1994 Audio-Visual Media Law (AVML), through which several stations (owned by politicians and representing the country's dominant sectarian groups) were licensed (Kraidy, 1998b).

Lebanon's 1994 AVML was the first Arab legislation that integrated privately owned radio and television. The 1989 Taef Agreement – the official accord that ended the war, signed in the eponymous Saudi resort city – called for the regulation of the country's unlicensed media. These radio and television stations were a symbol of wartime anarchy and tarnished the prestige of a re-emerging state. The AVML was passed in October 1994. It revoked Télé-Liban's exclusive broadcasting rights, therefore legalising private broadcasting. It reaffirmed that media freedom was guaranteed by the constitution, and gave the Council of Ministers the authority to issue licences. The law also created the National Council of Audio-Visual Media (NCAVM) and charged it with setting technical standards, monitoring media performance and recommending sanctions. The powers of the Minister of Information were enhanced to include the right of auditing all financial records, since the law prohibited stations from operating in deficit for a protracted period. The NCAVM reported to the Minister of Information in a purely advisory role. The law affirmed core prohibitions against stirring sectarian conflict, insulting the head of state and those of friendly countries, and endangering public order and national security (Kraidy, 1998b).

نيسان2005 استقلال لبنان   MTV billboard advertisement

On 2 February 1996, the Council of Ministers awarded licences to four television channels and rejected several dozen applicants. All four licensed stations had close connections to leading politicians including the Prime Minister and the President of the Council of Deputies. Licensing also fell in line with Lebanon's political tradition of division of resources along confessional lines. Though the law stipulated multisectarian channel boards, in practice LBC was the Maronite station; Future TV the Sunni broadcaster; MTV the Greek Orthodox station; and NBN the Shi'i channel. By licensing only a few privately owned television stations and establishing a regulatory framework, the 1994 AVML set the ground for commercial competition to operate in tandem with political calculations and sectarian considerations (Kraidy, 1998b). In the first few years thereafter the government used direct and indirect media-control mechanisms (Kraidy, 1999b) and there have been several major political crises over media policy. The last two of these crises, the closure of Murr Television (MTV) on 4 September 2002, and the forced disconnection of New TV in December 2002, reveal political instrumentalisation and overlapping jurisdictions in media-policy formulation and implementation, in addition to the customary twin concerns of Lebanese media policy – preserving stability internally and projecting a positive national image externally.

The decision to close MTV and the raid by security forces that shut the channel down, stunned the country, raised troublesome questions and publicised contradictions in policy. First and foremost was the strong condemnation of the raid by Ghazi Aridi, Minister of Information in the then-al-Hariri-headed cabinet. In a public statement given from outside the MTV building, Aridi condemned the shutdown as 'purely political' and affirmed his lack of knowledge of the decision, raising questions about who – it obviously was not the Information Minister – was running media policy in the country. Second, the way in which the Beirut Court of Publications reached a verdict without giving an opportunity for the station to appeal, raised questions about legal due process and overlapping jurisdictions. This is an important issue because under the 1994 AVML the Minister of the Interior is charged with monitoring and sanctioning the media. Third, the way the action was carried out smacked of repression, with security forces pushing, beating and hurling obscenities at the station's employees and others who worked in the building. Finally, the shutdown set an alarming precedent as it was the first time in Lebanon's history that a television station was permanently shut down by the authorities (Kraidy, 2003, unpublished manuscript). After fundamental changes in the Lebanese political landscape that began in 2005 when Syrian troops withdrew from Lebanon, MTV re-opened in April 2009.

The Beirut Court of Publications ordered the closure under the provision of

Article 68 of the Election Law, which prohibits radio and television stations from airing electoral advertising. This law was initially passed before the 1992 elections, Lebanon's first post-war elections, in order to prevent Lebanon's then-unregulated and anarchic, sixty-station television sector from becoming a propaganda nightmare. The law called for the 'complete suspension of violators', without right of appeal before the order is executed. When MTV was shut down, appeals with various courts revealed that the government had interpreted 'complete' to mean 'permanent'. The other troubling issue is that the 1992 Election Law was superseded by the 1994 AVML, which charges the Information Minister (in consultation with the National Council for Audio-Visual Media) with the task of ordering sanctions against television stations (Kraidy, 1998b). The shutdown of MTV exposed more than any other incident the convoluted regulatory environment in Lebanon, which is prone to overlapping jurisdictions and crippling political interference.

While technically, MTV did violate the law by airing political communication during the 2000 legislative elections, so did virtually every other television station, including Future TV and Télé-Liban. MTV, however, had become the voice of the anti-regime, anti-Syrian, predominantly Christian opposition. As information revealed after the 2005 Syrian withdrawal made clear, MTV was shut down by orders from Syrian military intelligence. Because of the politicisation of media regulations and the seemingly overlapping jurisdictions, the year 2002 ended with calls to revise and update media laws in the country, in addition to renewed calls for reforming the judiciary and granting it more independence. However, under Syria's suffocating control of public affairs in Lebanon, these calls went unheeded, and some observers worried that the traditionally vibrant Lebanese media sector was forcibly driven to increasingly resemble Syrian television, to which we turn next (the situation changed radically after Syrian troops withdrew from Lebanon in spring 2005 and, as a result, the Syrian regime lost its ability directly to control Lebanese media institutions). As it returned to the airwaves in April 2009, MTV has to contend with a more commercially competitive media environment than when it was shut down, which raises questions about the channel's ability to become a top player once more.

TELEVISION POLICY IN SYRIA: CONTROLLING NEWS, LEVERAGING ENTERTAINMENT

Created during the brief union with Egypt under the United Arab Republic in the late 1950s and early 1960s, Syrian television has long operated under a propaganda paradigm dedicated to the leader's cult of personality, endorsing the values of Arabism, and finally promoting national socio-economic development. Under the reign of Hafiz al-Asad, Syrian television was for the most part geared to preserving Asad's cult of personality through broadcasting visual spectacles acclaiming the leader (see Wedeen, 1999) in addition to protocol news focused on Asad's speeches, meetings and statements. In the early years of Bashar al-Asad's rule, a brief period of relaxed censorship and repression known as the Damascus Spring, which lasted from summer 2000 to autumn 2001, was followed by a brutal reassertion of state power through arrests and media closures. In ensuing years, as other Arab countries revamped their national channels and launched or allowed privately owned satellite companies to operate from their territory, Syria's satellite television channel lagged behind, prompting demands for reform by Syrian journalists and critics writing for the most part in offshore, pan-Arab newspapers.

Syrian news and political programmes have been stuck in a protracted crisis created by a combination of bureaucratic inertia, indecisive policy formulation and a hostile geopolitical context, and perhaps most significantly, a perception that Syrian television is out of touch with the population, which has deserted it *en masse* in the last decade (Na'ameh, 2007). External challenges and loss of audience have driven Syrian media-reform attempts, focusing on issues ranging from regulating the structure of the industry to the design, colour schemes and wardrobe choices that control the appearance of Syrian television.

In recent years, as they faced media onslaughts from Lebanon and Saudi Arabia, Syrian authorities have enacted small but historically significant reforms, which included, first, allowing a privately owned Syrian satellite television channel to open. Production is in Syria and transmission is out of Dubai, ostensibly to counter the 'negative image' of Syria on Arabic satellite channels ('al-Sham Satellite', 2005) and purporting to 'confront suicidal thought [i.e. terrorism] without video clips' (Hamidi, 2005). Second, the regime allowed the first privately owned Syrian FM radio stations, ostensibly to provide Syrian listeners with an alternative to the trendy Lebanese radio stations, which is increasingly important in light of Syria's humiliating withdrawal from Lebanon in 2005 (Azmashli, 2005). Third, a media city was launched in the outskirts of Damascus ostensibly to attract non-Syrian companies but also to allow selected local companies a higher degree of autonomy. Things have stalled on that end because of government interference and bureaucratic hassles. Fourth, reform includes appointing an increasing number of women in television broadcasting, to add to its attractiveness, soften the image of Syrian broadcasting and expand the audience of Syrian television newscasts (Badr, 2005). Most visibly, a woman was appointed Director of Syrian Television, and promptly declared: 'Why don't we make the (television) screen a bridge between citizens and the state?' (Hajj Abdi, 2005). Previous Minister of Information Mehdi Dakhlallah, widely seen as a reformer and a former journalist himself, announced that Syrian media are in a transition from 'dirigiste media' to 'media with a purpose' ('Information Minister', 2005). In addition to a commitment to a new political parties law, the final resolution of the summer 2005 Baath party congress included an official call for a new legal framework for the media. Concrete follow-up steps are yet to be observed, and Dakhlallah's zeal to reform Syrian media led to a lengthy prison sentence.

A recurring story in the media and culture pages of the Arab press concerns the stunning artistic and commercial success of Syrian television drama in the Arab world. Starting in the early 1990s, the Syrian state apparatus offered its facilities and equipment to private producers and directors, requesting rights of first broadcast of their production in return. After a few initial successes, film-makers and drama and fiction writers were drawn to the television industry, with the result that the image and plots of Syrian drama greatly improved. The next stage was the rush of Gulf television channels, terrestrial and satellite, to purchase Syrian drama for broadcasting during the holy Muslim month of Ramadan (see Chapter 5), the Arab world's peak of the television season. Increased profits and recognition have led to a quantitative growth of Syrian television production, in addition to a qualitative evolution, in that the largely historical themes of the 1990s have given way to bolder sociological treatments of contemporary issues such as terrorism and AIDS. A substory of the success of Syrian television drama is the rising anxiety in the Egyptian television drama industry because of the inroads made by Syrian television drama in recent years. There are frequent reports of verbal hostilities between Syrian and Egyptian television artists and managers at Arab and international professional gatherings or festivals. However, perhaps the ultimate recognition of the quality of Syrian television drama is the growing number of Egyptian–Syrian co-productions.

The Syrian case shows a schizophrenic media policy through which the regime maintains its control of the news and political programmes that it considers instrumental to its power, while relinquishing direct control over drama production, enabling relatives and associates of pillars of the regime to make significant financial profit (Kraidy, 2006c). The economic model of Syrian drama production, which has still not been adequately researched, relies heavily on investments and audiences from the Gulf, where Dubai has emerged as the centre of gravity of the pan-Arab television industry, a story we analyse in the following section.

TELEVISION POLICY IN THE UAE: DUBAI AS A DIGITAL HUB

The United Emirates policy environment is important because it embodies what we call remote-controlled *laissez-faire*, most clearly illustrated in Dubai Media City's undisputed leadership in the trend of media cities that includes Egypt,

The entrance to Dubai Media City and its slogan 'Freedom to Create'

Jordan and Syria. Kuwait, Qatar, Hamas and the Maronite Church in Lebanon have also announced plans to open media cities (for the latter see Noun, 2009). Since its launch, Dubai Media City (DMC) has developed into a regional and global hub for seven media activities: marketing, broadcasting, new media, publishing, music, film and events services. Spawned by Dubai's economic transition to a service economy, DMC reflects the growing importance of economic policy as a shaper of media policy in the other Arab world.

Dubai has scarce natural resources. Consequently, it aimed to become a major commercial hub between South East Asia and Europe. Since 1979, Dubai has adopted an economic policy that depends less on natural resources than on its geographic location with the establishment of free zones such as the Jebel Ali Port. In a short time, Dubai has managed to compete with Beirut's status as a banking centre, Egypt's media production capacity and North Africa's tourist attractions. In January 2001 DMC was officially operational with a setup cost estimated to be over US $800 million (*Media Cities*, 2004). In retrospect, DMC was strategically positioned to benefit from its unique geopolitical situation. By creating investment opportunities like DMC, Dubai benefited from the repatriation of Arab money from the West after the events of 9/11 and also from Iranian and Saudi oil revenues. With its motto 'Freedom to Create', DMC has also provided an ostensibly 'safe' but in fact highly self-censored haven for creative talent escaping dire security or working conditions in countries like Lebanon, Egypt, Palestine, Iraq and Syria whose citizens make up the core media labour force.

Since its launch, the number of users of DMC has increased from 880 in 2004 to over 1200 in 2008 (*Dubai Media*, 2009). DMC's main clients are local, regional and international companies and freelance individuals in various media activities including publishing and printing, broadcasting, advertising and marketing services, music, leisure and entertainment, and information agencies. In 2005 alone twenty new television channels were introduced and by 2009, DMC was home to over sixty satcasters operating some 150 channels. This rapid growth, coupled with market demand and scarcity of space, has paved the way for a number of connected projects. Over US $110 million were spent in building Dubai Studio City (DSC) with the intention to increase film and television production in the Emirates. The trade magazine *Arab Ad* estimated that only 20 per cent of Arab television output is produced in Dubai ('Arab Satellite', 2005). Also, DMC has sponsored two festivals to encourage and promote production activities. The Dubai International Film Festival has become a gathering for Arab, Hollywood and Bollywood producers and stars while the Ibda' (creativity) Media Student Awards are designed to acknowledge and sponsor young talents both locally and internationally.

DMC now integrates a number of media institutions and activities; its growth is considered to be, in the words of one insider, 'very organic' (Al-Shoush, 2006). Similarly, its organisational structure has evolved from that of a government project to that of a private subsidiary. DMC is now part of TECOM Investments, the parent company of Dubai Internet City, Knowledge Village, Dubai Studio City and the International Media Production Zone. TECOM is one of seven member companies under Dubai Holding established in 2004 to lead Dubai's 'large-scale infrastructure and investment projects' ('About Dubai', 2008). Although Dubai Holding is a private company, it is majority-owned by the ruling al-Maktoum family. Sheikh Mohammad bin Rashed al-Maktoum particularly, Dubai's ruler and the UAE's Prime Minister, envisioned these media free zone areas as 'symbols of the potential of the knowledge economy in the region' ('The Next', 2002, p. 22). The success of TECOM projects is an example of the al-Maktoum family's *modus operandi*: the government builds infrastructure and subsidises its use by private ventures. Investment has typically taken two forms. First, freelance individuals and companies operating in DMC rent space ranging from a desk to a complete building. In return, DMC acts as the point of contact for all government-related activities including visas, work permits and licences. Second, private investors may develop buildings on DMC-owned land, though DMC runs and manages the property.

DMC's success rests on providing a package that capitalises on the free zone setup. Companies or individuals obtain a fifty-year exemption from personal, income and corporate taxes. Unlike in the rest of Dubai, where foreign nationals or companies can own a maximum of 49 per cent, DMC offers 100 per cent business ownership in addition to 100 per cent repatriation of capital and profit. Also, DMC 'partners' enjoy certain freedoms such as the absence of restrictions on customs duties and on Internet sites and flexible labour and residency laws. As a result, DMC relies on comparatively lower operation costs to 'attract big media companies to establish their bases here' (Abbott, 2005a). This translated into offering additional incentives ranging from rent-free packages, discounts on telecommunication bills and the naming of buildings. Mission accomplished, with companies like Saudi-owned MBC and regional offices for Reuters, Associated Press and CNN Arabic's websites. In fact, DMC hopes, as Sa'id al-Muntafiq, former CEO of Dubai Media City was quoted as saying, 'to be one of four or five global bases for broadcasting as we move forward over the next few years' (Sullivan, 2001).

In spite of numerous efforts, the regulatory framework for companies operating in DMC remains ambiguous. DMC often acts as a mediator in labour-related matters with the attempt to maintain a good public image. For example, as part of a restructuring effort in 2006, CNBC Arabiya, a pan-Arab satellite franchise of the US financial cable channel, discharged a number of its employees who started a massive media campaign to claim labour rights. According to a former CNBC Arabiya employee and spokesperson for dismissed workers at the channel, DMC reacted by pushing CNBC Arabiya to settle the matter promptly and quietly (Ahmad interview, 28 March 2008). In matters related to the content of media messages, DMC established the Broadcasting and Publication Standards Tribunal (BPST) in November 2003. On a number of occasions the tribunal was sidestepped in favour of more traditional, local means of mitigation. The tribunal's major achievement was devising a media code that covers issues related to religious sensibilities, alcohol, smoking and sex (Addington, 2006). Whether in print or broadcast, the Dubai government's promise to uphold freedom of speech has been undermined by several cases that underscore the fact that the notion of responsible freedom effectively means self-censorship. Examples abound: the first issue of *Focus On* (FO!) magazine was its last. DMC managed to shut it down for not adhering to its 'business plan': the magazine featured a pullout of a semi-naked model, 'Miss May' (Addington, 2005). Similarly, Geo TV, a Pakistani channel satcasting from Dubai, was shut down after being given two hours' notice from DMC. Accused of violating the code, DMC claimed that Geo has interfered with the politics of another country, Pakistan ('Dubai Shuts', 2007). In many ways, DMC has successfully managed to provide an environment where media corporations can enjoy competitive production costs; however, it has yet to provide an adequate framework for exercising unmitigated freedom of expression (Nicolson, 2006).

Even though the model of DMC has proven difficult to successfully implement elsewhere in the Arab world, it has contributed to changing the pan-Arab media landscape by attracting a high concentration of media industries and stimulating interaction between them. A close examination suggests a number of advantages and disadvantages determined by questions about DMC's economic, social and cultural repercussions on the broadcasting scene. Unlike any other media city, DMC succeeded in simplifying logistics for the establishment of television channels. Because of the ease in finding location, work permits, licences, play-out facilities, television start-ups have gravitated towards DMC. There is no doubt that DMC stands at the centre of the television boom, particularly since 2001. However, after attracting some global and Arab major players, DMC has tempered its initial obsession with the prestige and quality of its partners to focus on the ability of these users to pay regularly increased charges. This has contributed to the proliferation of what are best described as 'boutique' channels, which consist of a small office with a computer server and a handful of employees, with the server playing pre-recorded and pre-loaded programmes. This so-called 'play-out' premise, particularly popular with second-rate music channels, has allowed players with relatively small budgets to have access to satcasting, since most of their investments consist of office leases, operating permits, visa fees and the use of telecommunications' bandwidth. From the DMC's perspective, these small channels diversify the leasing base, offsetting the potential departure of bigger players, especially now that the global financial crisis that began in autumn 2008 has hit Dubai's real-estate and financial industries particularly hard, which is bound to affect the media sector.

In addition to economic attractiveness, DMC has transformed Dubai into a centre – some would argue, *the* centre (though this could change with the current financial crisis) – of creative media activities, competing with cities with historically vibrant media activities like Beirut and Cairo. DMC has discredited the common belief that to enjoy a relatively elevated degree of freedom from direct government intervention, Arab media have to be based outside the Arab world. By relocating to DMC, Arab broadcasters like MBC, international broadcasters like BBC World and news agencies like Reuters and CNN provide concrete recognition of new parameters for media autonomy – though this is relative as the cases previously described indicate. This centralisation of media activity in DMC has affected the development of media cities in the UAE and in the region. It was only when DMC was unable to meet demands for space and facilities that potential broadcasters started looking for alternatives in Jordan, Bahrain and Kuwait. By acting as a catalyst for regional developments, DMC has provided an economic impetus for the deregulation of media industries across the region, with governments hoping to benefit from much-needed direct foreign investments. The Jordanian and Bahraini governments, for example, were able to lure, respectively, Arab Radio and Television (ART) to fund the establishment of Jordan's Media City in 2001, and Orbit to relocate its headquarters to Bahrain in 2003.

In addition to giving a boost to regional television industries, Dubai's grounding of media policy in its economic policy, which has included generous subsidies and lease terms at DMC, exposes these same television industries directly to the impact of economic changes. At the time of this writing, the future growth of DMC is challenged by factors peculiar to Dubai, such as the soaring cost of living, and also to external factors like competition in various parts of the Arab world, in addition to the global economic recession. But Dubai's loss could be another Arab city's gain. For example, if Syrian officials manage to launch a credible media city, which at this time has not been fully realised, the relatively low costs of operating out of Damascus may compel some institutions to relocate from Dubai, though Syrian authorities would have to modify other economic and labour policies. The recent expansion programmes of TECOM, DMC's mother company, focused on developing local talent and investing in Indian production centres, are seen as important attempts to maintain DMC's market lead, a diversification that concentrates on the local (Dubai and the UAE) and the global (Bollywood), instead of emphasising exclusively the pan-Arab sphere (al-Sayegh interview, 30 June 2005). Dubai rulers and DMC executives like to imagine themselves as trendsetters. The extent to which DMC will succeed in inspiring developments in Arab media policy remains to be seen, but DMC's transnational outlook appears to have influenced what can tentatively be described as an emerging pan-Arab television policy regime.

AN EMERGING PAN-ARAB TELEVISION POLICY REGIME?

Clearly, national media policies suffer from several problems. First of all, there is the problem of ambiguously worded, catch-all legal provisions pertaining to 'national unity' and 'national security'. These are powerful control tools for governments who can interpret them instrumentally and implement them arbitrarily to repress political opposition. Second, overlapping jurisdictions make regulation and policy implementation inconsistent and open to manipulation and executive abuse. In various Arab states, royal decrees and presidential fiat trample over legislative development and regulatory agencies. Various ministries compete for jurisdiction over television, typically those of the interior, information, culture and sometimes telecommunications. Since in some cases television regulation is underdeveloped, even non-existent, dated press and publication laws are applied to television. Though there are virtually no laws regulating post-broadcast television content, the 2008 Arab satellite charter and a leaked draft Egyptian television law forecast a hardening regulatory climate with forthcoming laws aimed at controlling television and video distributed through broad-casting, satellite, cable, the Internet (including social networking sites like Facebook, which is very popular in the Arab world) and even mobile phones.

Arab rulers are clearly eyeing the Dubai model, and even 'closed regimes' are on board the 'media cities' bandwagon. As we mentioned earlier, the Syrian gov-ernment a couple of years ago announced the establishment of a media free zone that is struggling to take off, and in May 2006 the first private Jordanian televi-sion began test-broadcasting only to be shut down shortly thereafter. In Saudi Arabia, the focus is on keeping content deemed un-Islamic off the airwaves, in abidance with the Wahhabi foundations of the Saudi government, both to appease establishment clerics and undermine proponents of armed dissent in the name of Islam. In Lebanon, the central challenge of media regulation is to prevent the pluralistic television landscape from fomenting tensions between the country's eighteen officially recognised sectarian groups. In Syria, the govern-ment has, since the rise of Bashar al-Asad, publicly recognised the urgent need to develop television capacities whose ineffectiveness was painfully driven home during the Syrian–Lebanese media wars of 2005 and 2006 and the Syrian–Saudi media wars of 2007 and 2008. In the UAE, Emirate-based media policy has been shaped by the state's desire for political relevance in Abu Dhabi and as a cen-tral part of the economic policy of Dubai's rulers as that city-emirate entered its post-oil era in the 1990s. In Egypt, as we saw in an earlier chapter, the major challenge faced by media regulators is that of navigating the transition from a developmentalist television system whose foundations were laid in the heyday of Nasserism and pan-Arabism, to a system that is increasingly commercial and inescapably embedded in the regional media sphere in which it plays the role of receiver as much as producer of media content.

Most of all, Arab regimes now must take into account powerful commercial interests whose support is vital for regime survival, as they regulate the indus-try. Wealthy governments in the Gulf invest money in entertainment programmes. In addition to fomenting the growth of channels that are politi-cally sympathetic, regimes have fostered the establishment of entertainment programmes that enable them to attract audiences that have deserted govern-ment channels and gravitated towards the more exciting programming grids of privately owned channels such as LBC and MBC. This is clearly visible in Abu Dhabi TV's production of poetry-reality-television shows that resonate with local cultural mores, funded by the Abu Dhabi Cultural Authority, a government agency. (Abu Dhabi TV is owned by the Emirate of Abu Dhabi, the seat of the national capital of the UAE.) Similarly, after causing controversy several years ago by rebroadcasting the Lebanese *Star Academy*, Algerian television took the step of creating a local version of the show, and in Ramadan 2008 satcast a

Table 6.3 Selected Recent and Pending Arab Broadcasting Laws and Regulations

Law	Country	Year
Audio-visual Media Law	Lebanon	1994
Audio-visual Media Law	Jordan	2002
Interim Broadcasting Programme Code of Practice	Iraq	2004
Arab Satellite Television Charter	Pan-Arab	2008
Media Law (National Authority for Audiovisual Broadcast Regulation)	Egypt	(2009, pending)
Media Law (National Media Council)	UAE	(2009, pending)

Koranic recitation contest formatted as a reality-television programme with competitions, nominations and viewers voting via text messaging and the Internet (see Conclusion in Kraidy, 2009).

The emergent pan-Arab policy regime articulates political repression with economic liberalisation, spawning multiple contradictions within and between Arab states. It is one characterised by confusion and the inability to confront challenges posed by a heady combination of new technologies, new content and new audiences. Television is no longer an isolated medium, and through many game, variety, music and reality shows, the mobile phone has become integrated into television programming. Similarly, through blogging, fansites, and value-added services such as ringtones, music and video downloads, and others, the Internet is now linked to both television and the mobile telephone. In addition to being shaped by media convergence, Arab television programmes are characterised by a blurring of genres that puzzles policy-makers long used to a single and rigid distinction between 'political' and 'non-political' programmes: Islamism mixes with personal finance or sexuality, reality shows dabble in politics, infomercials blend news and advertising, talk shows blur politics and entertainment, drama discusses public affairs like AIDS and terrorism. To rein in this media anarchy, states have alternatively used direct repression and the enactment of new laws and regulations that repress and co-opt the television industry. However, Arab states waited nearly twenty years before multilaterally confronting the threat to their authority posed by the transnationalisation of television. The result was the 2008 Arab Satellite Television Charter (ASTC).

On 12 February 2008, Arab information ministers adopted a satellite television charter during an emergency meeting in Cairo. The ASTC document is broad-ranging, covering news, political shows, entertainment and even sports programmes. It is also restrictive, giving Arab governments tools to sanction satellite broadcasters who attack leaders, harm national reputations or air socially unacceptable content. After years of rhetoric about the need for a pan-Arab satellite television framework, what finally compelled Arab states to act?

In the weeks before the meeting, the Egyptian and Saudi information ministers lobbied their colleagues to pass the document, which had been prepared by
a 'committee of experts' during the preceding six months. Momentum towards
action began in the wake of the summer 2006 war in Lebanon. When hostilities
broke out, Egyptian and Saudi leaders first condemned Hezbollah's 'adventur-
ism', but back-pedalled in light of Hezbollah's resilience and the mounting
civilian casualties of Israel's onslaught. In the meantime, as explained in Chapter 4, Hezbollah's television station al-Manar climbed to the top ten in pan-Arab
ratings, and talk-show hosts struggled live to prevent callers from heaping verbal abuse on pro-US Arab regimes. Though not criticised as virulently as the
House of Sa'ud, the Mubarak regime contended with an increasingly
media-savvy Muslim Brotherhood whose influence extended from al-Jazeera to
Hamas's al-Aqsa television to the Arabic-language blogosphere. In that context
a regulatory document that would place 'political restrictions' on Arab airwaves
was a shared Saudi-Egyptian interest.

The ASTC killed several birds with one stone. By penalising content that
allegedly promotes sexual activity, alcohol consumption and alcohol, it placated
socially conservative Islamists, including Egypt's Brotherhood, who for years
had advocated such restrictions. By purporting to protect 'Arab identity from
the harmful effects of globalisation', it appealed to both Arab nationalists and
Islamists. And by prohibiting content that would 'damage social harmony,
national unity, public order, or traditional values', the charter justified authoritarian rule. Finally, the charter has a populist provision, stipulating Arab viewers'
rights to information, including the right to watch sports competitions on free-
to-air government channels even when commercial channels hold exclusivity
agreements. In addition to reasserting the rights of state television channels, this
gives the charter some popular credibility with Arab publics.

The charter resembles Arab media laws, virtually all of which have ambiguously worded language that sanctions libel, slander and any criticism of leaders
and their families. It also affirms current practice: several Arab states have
revoked Arab satellite channels' licences to report from their territories. The
ominous catchall provision against harming 'national reputation' enables a wide
range of repressive measures. The charter in this respect extends to the pan-
Arab sphere provisions already in effect within nation-states.

Implementation has been uneven. Egypt owns NILESAT and Saudi Arabia
controls ARABSAT; in theory they can disconnect undesirable channels, but
such radical action carries political and business risks, especially now that they
have competition from European satellite and since 2005 a privately owned
Bahraini satellite, NOORSAT ('Noorsat Gears', 2005). Qatar declined to sign
the charter, citing potential conflict with its own laws. The Lebanese Informa-

tion Minister stated that the charter was a 'guiding, not binding' document. National journalists' unions were up in arms, and there was widespread suspicion in the Arab press that the charter is intended to silence criticism of US policy and align Arab countries further on the US–Israel axis to counter the rise of Iran. The director of the Saudi Culture and Information Ministry, 'Abdullah al-Jasir, was compelled to explain that the charter 'distinguishes between incitement to violence and resistance to occupation' (al-Barraq, 2008).

Finally, another question worth asking, if only because of the sheer enormity of its ramifications for Arab relations with the world's great powers is: 'Will the charter be applied to foreign Arabic-language satellite channels like the US al-Hurra, the Kremlin's Rusya al-Yawm and Iran's al-'Alam?' If restrictions apply only to 'indigenous' channels, would that not confer an advantage to some of the foreign channels, therefore supporting claims by some Arab journalists that the charter was driven by pro-US motives? Also, commercial channels are likely to sue governments for infringing on their exclusive sports agreements, especially pay-TV channels who pay high premiums for those rights.

With 470 channels (as of April 2009; Abbasi interview, 26 April 2009) peddling fortune-tellers, alternative medicines, Jihadi ideas, titillating bodies, stock-market schemes, and more mainstream news and entertainment, a regulatory framework is not in itself a bad idea. But Arab governments' record on media autonomy is dismal. Even Syria, which at the time was engaged in a media war with Saudi Arabia over the Lebanese situation, signed off on the charter. As the Syrian comedian Durayd Lahham once quipped, 'Arab officials cannot agree unless they are Interior Ministers'. Arab journalists, intellectuals and dissidents are now worried that even when regimes disagree on many things, information ministers agree about muzzling speech. Even if there are no actual implementation mechanisms for the ASTC, the document has become a framework, even if a rhetorical one, for Arab media institutions. For example, the Director of Jordan Media City told the authors in April 2009 that the ASTC was the framework for the work of JMC (Alkhas interview, 30 April 2009; al-Wishah interview, 30 April 2009).

CONCLUSION

This chapter has reviewed various national policies and regulatory frameworks that have shaped the development of Arab television industries, concluding with an analysis of an emerging pan-Arab regulatory regime represented by the 2008 ASTC. Arab television policies have traditionally been motivated by regime self-preservation, the desire to protect cultural, moral and religious values, promoting national unity and socio-economic development, and more recently, by the desire to attract tourism and direct foreign investment in the media industries. As we noted, in spite of shared bases for media policy among Arab states, there are significant differences between them that have given rise to different national media policies that have changed over time.

This chapter explained why and how Arab governments have different policies concerning television: Saudi authorities use television for controlling the Saudi population while at the same time projecting power throughout the Arab world. Lebanese regulators, on the other hand, are concerned with preventing the sectarian-affiliated television channels from undermining internal stability while at the same time enabling them to promote Lebanon's image and lure Arab tourism and investments into the country. The feudal-federal system in the UAE allowed individual Emirates to pursue radically divergent media policies, with Dubai distinguishing itself as a media industries centre through the creation of the Arab world's largest media city, a free-trade zone with attractive conditions for local and global companies. The Syrian regime, caught between a pressing need for economic reform and a desire to maintain an iron grip on political life, spawned a schizophrenic television industry in which drama production thrives while news and public-affairs television wallows in the age of authoritarian state control. These differences between national media policies notwithstanding, Arab regimes for the most part agree about the necessity of a transnational, pan-Arab regulatory framework.

It remains unclear whether the passing of the ASTC by a majority of Arab information ministers in February 2008 was merely a symbolic gesture or whether it constituted a concrete step towards a repressive pan-Arab media-policy regime (though several countries including Lebanon and Qatar expressed concerns about the satellite charter, the Egyptian government moved swiftly to shut down an Islamist satellite channel under cover of the charter). The ASTC is a telling document, less because it has been effectively implemented – it has not – than because it makes visible those actors contending to shape media policy, unmasks their agendas and brings into focus industry and related social and political developments that lead to and shape the emerging Arab policy regime. As the first formal pan-Arab regulatory text, the charter reflects the policy agendas of Arab governments attempting to reassert control over an unwieldy transnational media scene that in addition to television is witnessing an explosion of 'small media' like mobile phones, blogs and social-networking sites like MySpace, Facebook and their local version. With growing harassment and the arrest of bloggers in Egypt, Saudi Arabia and elsewhere, a more sweeping charter regulating the Arab Internet is now to be expected, and a document concerning mobile phones may follow. These developments are relevant to this book since Internet-based video and mobile phone-based text messaging are now important features and revenue generators for the Arab television industries.

As they rush to liberalise the media in aspects conducive to their own survival in power, Arab rulers look at Dubai as a model. Many Arab governments aspire to replicate the model of DMC – Egypt, Jordan and Syria have concretely attempted variations of media cities with mixed results. But Dubai's previously golden model has recently exhibited significant fractures, including cessation of transmission of some DMC-based satcasters by government fiat and the more recent clampdown on 'indecent' behaviour by the Dubai government. A draconian media law proposed in 2008 was scrapped by the ruler under intense criticism and is now under review, and a 2009 decree banned negative reporting on Dubai as the city suffered an exodus of expatriates caused by the global financial crisis and falling real-estate prices. These developments reflect deep contradictions between the economic developments in the media sector, mostly focused in DMC, and the political demographic, social and cultural changes that explosive television-industry growth brings to the table. Overlapping but contradictory pressures to transnationalise and commercialise while respecting political power and social values, will continue to shape Arab and pan-Arab media policy and regulation.

Conclusion

Arab television developed in two stages. During the first stage, beginning in the late 1950s, most Arab governments established national broadcasting systems. For the ensuing four decades, these systems focused on solidifying national unity in newly independent Arab nations, fomenting socio-economic development, and serving as platforms for Arab regimes. The second period, with which this book has been concerned, began in the early 1990s, when a seismic shift occurred from state-owned television stations broadcasting terrestrially towards commercial pan-Arab satellite television industries.

Two decades after it started, the pan-Arab television industry includes approximately 470 news, entertainment and niche channels, led by a handful of industry leaders. Top entertainment channels have led trends of commercialisation and consolidation while articulating local Arab cultures with the global market. As we explained in Chapter 2, channels like LBC and MBC define themselves as family channels, reflecting prevailing social and cultural norms and those institutions' attempts to capture the largest possible multinational Arabic-speaking audience. Institutional profiles of LBC, MBC and Dubai TV described sharply different trajectories of growth, culminating in the emergence of multiplatform conglomerates like LBC Holding, MBC Group and Dubai Media Incorporated. In contrast to the efforts of these media conglomerates to reach a large audience, specialised channels have emerged to claim audiences based on age, gender, religious interest, national identity and even hobbies. Chapter 3 provided an in-depth analysis of niche channels targeting women, youth and pious people, and explained how, by articulating social concerns with niche marketing, these channels foment public discussion about social and cultural issues.

Though entertainment channels continue to drive industry-wide trends, news channels have played an instrumental role in Arab and pan-Arab public discourse. Chapter 4 began with an analysis of al-Jazeera, the Qatari satellite channel whose editorial policies antagonised many Arab and Western governments. As a pioneering pan-Arab news channel, al-Jazeera warrants an analytical approach that eschews both celebrations of the channel as a miraculous creator of a pan-Arab public sphere and ill-informed attacks on al-Jazeera for being an instrument of propaganda for violent radical groups. We hope to have provided that perspective by examining al-Jazeera not only in the geopolitical context of the contemporary Middle East, but by also contextualising the channel within the broader Arab television industries. With that in mind, we analytically pitted al-Jazeera against its main competitor, the Saudi-owned al-Arabiya whose main mission continues to be to contest al-Jazeera's hegemony over Arabic-language satellite television news. We analysed the geopolitical backdrop to the rivalry between the two top news channels, and discussed differences in institutional identity, operational procedures and news reporting. In sharp contrast to these mass-audience news channels, Hezbollah's al-Manar is narrowly focused on combating Israel in addition to promoting the Party of God's agendas in Lebanon and the Middle East. This radical alternative to mainstream players has succeeded in capturing a non-negligible audience and continues to serve as a media model for radical groups in Iraq and Palestine. Finally, we showed how business news channels have emerged to claim the heretofore under-served business audience whose ranks have increased substantially in the last five years courtesy of the increased interest in stock markets in the Gulf states, the boom in energy prices and most recently the global economic recession.

The holy month of Ramadan is central to the Arab television industries. As we explained in Chapter 5, during this thirty-day period the timing of which is determined yearly by the lunar calendar, Muslims fast during the day and enjoy festive meals at dusk, after which they spend hours watching television with their families, friends and neighbours. Large advertising and production budgets, extended viewing hours and special programming reflect the sizeable economic stakes that Ramadan represents for the Arab television industries. As a result, this high-stakes month sets production and programming advertising trends, in addition to highlighting television's crucial links with the pan-Arab advertising industry.

Arab governments have struggled to cope with the explosive growth in the television industry, the transnational scope and commercial underpinning of which makes it difficult to regulate and control. Chapter 6 focused on the policy, regulatory and geopolitical context that shapes Arab television today. We critically surveyed media laws and regulations in key individual Arab countries before analysing the emerging pan-Arab regulatory regime, embodied in the 2008 Arab Satellite Television Charter, the first pan-Arab regulatory document.

Two major trends drive Arab television as the satellite industry enters its third decade. The first is a fluid interplay between the national and regional scales. Until recently, national channels broadcast terrestrially while pan-Arab channels, for obvious reasons, reached viewers via satellite. Recent trends reflect a growing use of satcasting by channels with an essentially national scope. The second trend concerns simultaneous processes of consolidation and fragmentation, with the advent of <u>multiplatform conglomerates</u> coinciding with a marked <u>growth in</u> <u>increasingly specialised channels</u>; specialisation and differentiation is also occur-ring *within* niche markets, for example in Islamic television. The following section summarily explains these two trends.

INTERPENETRATING SCALES

Arab television industries clearly operate on a variety of scales that interpene-trate each other at the levels of ownership, programming and audiences, with wider social and political repercussions. The growth of pan-Arab television is affected by an international context of deregulation, newer technologies and continued media globalisation. Arab television ownership rests on a private–state, local–foreign continuum with various degrees of commercialism and government influence. A wide range of genres fills television schedules, including current affairs and news, drama, comedy, social and women's talk shows, reality shows, music videos and religious programmes. (Two remarks are in order about the latter: first, Islamic programming covers a broad spectrum of affiliations, doctrines and ideologies; second, Christian broadcasting originating from Egypt, Iraq and Lebanon constitutes a niche with pan-Arab and global-diasporic reach.) Though the bulk of Arab and pan-Arab programming is produced in the Arab region, much of it is inspired or adapted from Western programmes, animating public debates about the impact of television on national identity and social values.

This leads to a central question: Has the transnational, satellite-based televi-sion industry created a pan-Arab sense of belonging by increasing cultural identification and economic links between Arab nation-states, as many observers have argued, or is it rather contributing to a resurgence of nation-state-based sentiments and media-consumption patterns? At one level, there is an enhanced awareness by Arabs of all nationalities of broad, pan-Arab issues and concerns. These are discussed daily on the satellite channels, their histori-cal context detailed in various documentaries, and their salience kept alive by channels targeting viewers across national lines. However, even on pan-Arab issues like Palestine or Iraq, the satellite media sphere has reflected various, sometimes competing opinion among Arabs (see Chapter 4). There is a wide spectrum of opinion on the airwaves, with al-Jazeera and al-Arabiya represent-ing competing viewpoints that are relatively close to the centre. Television channels have also been conduits for rhetorical wars between various Arab states and non-state actors – Qatar vs Saudi Arabia; Lebanon vs Syria; Saudi Arabia vs Syria; Egypt vs Hezbollah, etc. Other aspects of the Arab satellite industry highlight international differences rather than fomenting pan-Arab identifica-tion. Though newscasts tend to be presented in *fusha*, or modern standard

Arabic, talk shows, *musalsalat* and variety programmes expose Arab viewers to a variety of accents, styles and cultures. *Musalsalat* like the Syrian *Bab al-Hara* have also rekindled interest in hyper-local identities, in this case that of Damascus. The national provenance of television workers adds a layer of scalar complexity: the majority hails from Egypt, Jordan, Lebanon and Syria, including many Palestinians residing in these countries, a smaller number hails from the Gulf thanks to policies aiming to increase the number of national television workers, and very few are from the Maghreb countries in North Africa. Whether considered from the point of view of media labour and production or markets, Algeria, Libya, Morocco and Tunisia remain relatively marginal in the pan-Arab television industries, though LBC and MBC have in recent years given these countries more attention.

The changing relationship between national and pan-Arab scales has driven a wave of national media reforms through which nation-states have attempted to project their political and economic agendas with a distinct, 'national' voice. Saudi Arabia, Bahrain and Syria for instance, followed a top-down approach to revamping their national television systems, with the state remaining in full control. Even when countries like Egypt, Jordan and Syria allowed privately owned, regime-friendly private satcasters, many of these companies have faced hurdles establishing themselves as a result of constant state interference and policy changes. Other Arab states followed a path of liberalisation and allowed privately owned satellite channels to operate on their territory. This should be understood in the context of regimes' desire to attract viewers to politically friendly channels. Privately owned satellite channels have increasingly targeted national viewers: al-Rai in Kuwait, Dream TV in Egypt and Hannibal TV in Tunisia. In the case of Egypt and some others, the heavy hand of the state, in tandem with business moguls primarily interested in the domestic market, has prevented the development of privately owned Egyptian networks with significant pan-Arab viewership. In the Maghreb countries – Morocco, Tunisia, Algeria – neglect by satellite broadcasters based in the Levant and the Gulf has led to attempts by state broadcasters (e.g. in Algeria) to offer exciting but socially non-controversial entertainment television, while pushing others (e.g. in Tunisia) along a path like Kuwait's, where national channels have used satcasting to circumvent restrictive regulatory measures.

A SIMULTANEOUSLY CONSOLIDATING AND FRAGMENTING INDUSTRY

Market fragmentation is a pervasive trend in the Arab television industries, with emerging patterns pointing to more demographic differentiation, niche programmes and specialised channels. Gulf viewers are known to have more

disposable income than other Arabs, so the priority of most Arab television institutions is to build market share in the Gulf states. Among those, Saudi Arabia
is by far the most important market, not only because of demographic size and
income levels, but also because success with Saudi viewers often opens doors
to Saudi petro-dollars for television production. Not only do Saudi investments
fuel production of drama in Syria, reality television in Lebanon and music videos
in Egypt, but Saudi money sustains the leading production centres in the Arab
world, including media cities in Jordan and Dubai. Increasingly, Arab producers and media owners pursue Saudi financing by tailoring their productions to
the proclivities of Saudi viewers and media moguls alike. On a grand scale, the
influence of Saudi money, tastes and production values is increasingly visible
throughout Arab television industries.

multi platform

A second force driving industry fragmentation is the consolidation of Arab
television industries into multiplatform television operators, which include the
MBC Group, the al-Jazeera network, and the LBC-al-Hayat-Rotana conglomerates. Channels in these conglomerates provide broad news and entertainment
programming while offering a wide gamut of specialised programmes ranging
from Arabic pop music to shows about personal investments, to sports, US
action movies and special programmes for political or religious occasions. The
rise of these groups has a twofold impact. On the one hand, overall it boosted
local production, enhanced programme quality across genres and interests
(which nonetheless remain uneven) and increased advertising revenues. In July
2009, Showtime Arabia and Orbit announced a merger, indicating that the pay-
TV sector was part of the consolidation trend. On the other hand, consolidation
has fomented a commercial race that risks intensifying audience flight to the few
dominant conglomerates, and as a result, weakening production quality and
undermining national production diversity.

A third driver of audience fragmentation is the rise of niche channels focused
on the youth, women and religious market segments (see Chapter 5), in addition to business channels (see Chapter 4) and others specialising in sports,
children and public affairs. In the early years of Arab satcasting programmers
aimed to identify their market in geographical terms of one national audience
and then a secondary area. In contrast today programmers and advertisers target various lifestyle and demographic groups based on age, gender, religion and
income, regardless of geography, with the exception of the Gulf.

A fourth important factor that is intensifying market fragmentation is the
deployment of a widening gamut of new technologies by the main players in the
Arab television industries. In recent years, technology developments have
included the launching of Digital Video Broadcast-handheld (DVB-H) to carry
thirteen channels in Qatar and the UAE; the establishment by Orbit of Media

fragment across exhibition/tech sites

Gates, a company that develops and acquires programmes 'made for mobile'; the introduction by Showtime Arabia of personal video recorders and by ART of video on demand (VOD) for sporting events. Al-Jazeera pioneered news delivery by mobile phone and is now trumpeting HDTV for news and sports. Internet- and mobile-based interactivity has now become a staple of talk shows on al-Jazeera and reality television on LBC.

Market fragmentation threatens to upset established methods of financing. For nearly two decades, Arab pay-TV has struggled for survival and is increasingly considered to be non-viable in the region. A story about Orbit's decision to consider free-to-air satcasting in 2009 posed the question: 'Did the era of encrypted drama channels end?' ('Orbit Free', 2008). Similarly, the traditional advertising model suffers from a lack of trust in audience ratings due to conflicts of interest between television industries and market-research companies. With pay-television and airtime advertising in question, the last five years have witnessed the rise of a third model of financing which combines aggressive corporate sponsorship and product placement with the use of interactivity via the Internet and mobile devices. At the same time, deep-pocketed states remain a vital source of financing for Arab television.

CHALLENGES FOR TELEVISION POLICY AND REGULATION

The Arab satellite industry has stirred heated political and cultural polemics. Political controversies concern complaints and censorship attempts by Arab regimes that come under criticism on screens they cannot control. Government reactions to its loss of control have included retaliation against al-Jazeera and al-Arabiya, whose reporters have suffered harassment, arrest and in some cases death, at the hands of Arab governments in addition to US and Israeli militaries. In Chapter 6 we discussed media law, regulation and policy in selected Arab countries, and explained that governments have moved from direct control of television systems through ownership and operation, to indirect forms of control and influence that rely on enabling the development of privately owned and politically acquiescent satellite channels.

In the near future, it is likely that influential actors, chiefly Egypt and Saudi Arabia, will keep pushing for a regional policy regime. Both these countries have historically dominated pan-Arab politics, both have to contend with media-savvy opposition forces, at home and abroad, and both have been outpaced by smaller states in terms of media dynamism. These small states, such as Qatar and to a lesser extent Lebanon, have been able to exercise a degree of influence that is out of proportion to their demographic, geographical and economic size – politically in the case of Qatar, culturally in the case of Lebanon, and economically in the case of the UAE (via Dubai). These developments upset the regional polit-

ical balance and will subject attempts at a unified policy regime to robust con-
testation.

The dominance of media policy by issues of political control and censorship
has prevented the establishment of broader regulatory frameworks that address
other important aspects of the television industries: channel ownership and
media cross ownership, commercial-break duration, tobacco and liquor advertising. As the Arab television sector becomes more competitive and integrates
further into the global media industry, there is a fear that increased licence fees
for formats, movies and sporting events might accelerate consolidation of the
industry.

The contemporary Arab world has a vibrant, pluralistic and fast-evolving
transnational television industry. Driven by geopolitical instability, petrodollars,
real-estate speculation, and a host of religious and social factors, the Arab television industries reflect a complex mix of business, culture and politics. With
the Arab world's geopolitical and economic importance rising in proportion to
the world economy's needs for energy, the Arab television industries are poised
to continue growing in diversity and quality, in tandem with an ongoing process
of consolidation that might soon leave the industry dominated by a decreasing
number of large conglomerates.

Appendix I: Chronology

1954 French company establishes terrestrial television in Morocco, the first in the Arab world.

1956 Iraq launches first government-owned television channel in the Arab world (2 May); Algeria follows suit.

1959 La Compagnie Libanaise de Télévision (CLT) is established in Lebanon; first indigenous Arab commercial terrestrial channel (28 May).

1961 Kuwait launches terrestrial channel (15 January).

1962 Second commercial terrestrial channel in Lebanon Télé-Orient begins broadcasting (1 June).
Algerian Television begins terrestrial broadcasting (28 October).

1963 Saudi Arabia launches terrestrial channel from Riyadh and Jeddah.
Syria launches terrestrial channel.

1964 British forces establish and supervise Yemeni terrestrial channel (11 September).

1966 Tunisian Television starts terrestrial broadcast (31 May).

1967 First official discussions about owning satellite technology during the Arab information ministers' meeting in Tunisia.

1968 Jordan Television is launched (April).

1969 Arab States Broadcasting Union (ASBU) established in Cairo.
Dubai TV and Abu Dhabi TV start broadcasting in UAE.

1970 ASBU committee considers plans for satellite broadcasting.
Qatar establishes terrestrial television (15 August).

1971 ASBU recommends launching satellite for educational and information purposes.

1972 Saudi Arabia provides satellite feeds of Hajj ceremonies.

1973 Bahrain Television launches terrestrial channel 44.

1974 Oman establishes terrestrial Oman TV.

1975 Saudi Arabia begins receiving satcasts.

1976 Arab Satellite Organization (ARABSAT) established in Riyadh (14 April).

1977 La Compagnie Libanaise de Télévision (CLT) merges with Télé-Orient.
Lebanese government owns 51 per cent of newly formed Télé-Liban.

1980   Dubai Channel 33 restructures to address English-speaking expatriates in the Gulf region.

1983   Saudi Channel 2 launches (9 August) with mostly English-language programmes.

1985   ARABSAT's satellites 1A (8 February) and 1B (15 June) launched.
Dubai Sports Channel begins telecasts and satcasts (2 December).
Lebanese Broadcasting Corporation (LBC) is launched (23 August).

1989   Tunisia announces that the French channel A2 will be rebroadcast for twenty hours every day.
Moroccan government licenses private network broadcasting in Arabic and French. 2M International (later just 2M) is launched from Casablanca.

1990   Egypt Satellite Channel launched (ESC) (12 December) – first Arab government-owned and -operated satellite channel.
Saudi Television channels Saudi 1 and Saudi 2 satcast on ARABSAT.

1991   Baghdad TV satcasts on IntelSat.
Middle East Broadcasting Centre (MBC) satcasts from London (18 September).
Hezbollah's al-Manar Television launches terrestrial broadcast from Beirut (3 June).
Télé-Lumière, a Christian channel launches terrestrial broadcast from Lebanon.
Kuwait TV back on the air after Iraqi occupation ends. Kuwait youth and sports channel goes on the air after the liberation of Kuwait (15 November).

1992   Kuwait Channel 1 initiates satcasts on ARABSAT (4 July).
Dubai TV becomes the first Arab channel to satcast twenty-four hours per day on six satellites covering the world (6 December).
Al-Salam TV and Nablus TV, the first Palestinian channels, are launched.

1993   Dubai Cable Vision Net (cable company) distributes programmes across the UAE.
Arab Radio and Television (ART) begins satcasts from Italy (18 October).
Lebanon-based Future TV launches terrestrial channels (February).

1994   Egyptian Satellite Channel (ESC) broadcasts for twenty-four hours per day.
The Palestinian Authority launches television channel from the Palestinian territories (6 June).
The world's first digital producer and broadcaster Orbit Satellite and

Radio Television Network is launched from Italy (May).

Lebanon-based Future TV tests satellite transmission.

1995   BBC Arabic launched in partnership with Orbit. The channel was stopped in April.

Sheikh Hamad bin Khalefa, Emir of Qatar, signs a decree ordering the establishment of al-Jazeera channel.

1996   Egyptian Satellite Company established to manage NILESAT.

Al-Jazeera goes on the air from Doha, Qatar (1 November).

The Lebanese Broadcasting Corporation International (LBCI) begins satcasting from Italy.

Showtime Arabia established in London (June).

Palestinian Authority Channel goes on air.

1997   ARABSAT 2C satellite in orbit.

Iraq TV satcasts on NILESAT then moves to ARABSAT.

Arab News Network (ANN) satcasts from London on Hotbird (August).

1998   Egypt's NILESAT 101 satellite in orbit.

Egypt launches multiple thematic channels on NILESAT (October).

Iqra' begins satcasts (21 October).

Al-Jazeera increases satcast to twenty-four hours per day.

1999   ARABSAT's 3A satellite in orbit (26 February).

Al-Mustaqilla satcasts from London's West End.

2000   Egypt's NILESAT 102 in orbit.

Dubai Media City opens.

Hezbollah's al-Manar launches satellite channel (25 May).

2001   MBC airs Arabic version of *Who Wants to Be a Millionaire*.

Al-Mehwar channel satcasts from Cairo (31 May).

Privately owned Dream TV Channels 1 and 2 start in Egypt (31 May).

MBC sets up Channel '2' later renamed MBC2.

The Iranian channel al-'Alam is launched from Tehran and Beirut (1 October).

2002   Al-Majd Company launches Islamic pay-TV channel group from Dubai, Riyadh and Amman (6 November).

Israeli TV launches Channel 3 using Hotbird with Arabic or Arabic-subtitled programmes (25 June).

Melody Television's first channel, Melody Hits, begins in Egypt.

2003   Reality TV débuts in the Arab world: *'Ala al-Hawa* (On the Air) win big audiences; protests force *al-Ra'is* off the air. *Star Academy* begins in December. LBC establishes LBC Reality for *Star Academy* – first channel dedicated (four months per year) to reality TV.

Al-Arabiya goes on the air days before the US–UK invasion of Iraq (20 February).

Mazzika TV goes on the air (1 April).

Kingdom Holding launches music channels Rotana Music and Rotana Clips, from Beirut.

Iraq TV ceases broadcasting – Baghdad falls (9 April).

CNBC Arabiya is launched from Dubai Media City under franchise from CNBC US. First Arabic-language business channel, first Arabic franchise of global channel.

2004   Saudi Arabia launches al-Ekhbariya (news) (12 January) and al-Riyadiyya (sports).

US government launches al-Hurra from Virginia (14 February)

Newspaper *al-Rai* launches Kuwait's first independent satellite channel, al-Rai TV, from Kuwait City (14 October).

Al-Aqariya Group launches channels al-Aqariya 1 from DMC (17 December).

DMI launches 'One TV (24 December).

2005   Hannibal TV is launched, the first independent Tunisian channel (13 February).

Al-Jazeera Children's Channel launched (9 September).

2007   Syrian independent channel, Addunia TV (The World) is launched from Damascus Free Zone (October).

Russian ANO TV-Novosti launches Rusya al-Yawm (Russia Today), in Arabic (4 May).

2008   Arab information ministers adopt Arab Satellite Television Charter (ASTC) (12 February).

Fox International Channels and Kingdom Holding launch Fox Movie Channel, a free-to-air movie channel (1 March).

2009   Qatar Foundation for Education Science and Community Development launches second channel dedicated to children Bara'em (Buds).

Number of Arab satellite television channels reaches 470 (April).

Showtime and Orbit announce merger.

Appendix II: Interviews

Abbas, Faisal, Media Pages Editor, *Asharq Al-Awsat*, 9 June 2005, London, United Kingdom [Kraidy interview].

Abbasi, Jawad, General Manager, Arab Advisors Group, 26 April 2009, Amman, Jordan [Kraidy and Khalil interview].

Abdallah, Yasmine, CEO and Managing Director, OTV, 23 April 2008, Cairo, Egypt [Khalil interview].

Abou-Samra, Choucrallah Managing Director, OMD, an Omnicom Media Group, 7 April 2008, Jeddah, Saudi Arabia [Khalil interview].

Ahmad, Eslam, former employee and spokesperson for dismissed staff, CNBC Arabiya, 28 March 2008, Dubai, UAE [Khalil interview].

Al-Bakkar, 'Ammar Group Director of New Media, MBC Group, 4 December 2007. Washington, DC, US [Kraidy interview].

Al-Deeb, Youssef, Chairman and Managing Director of Takhayal, 19 May 2008, Dubai, UAE [Khalil interview].

Al-Ganayni, Tarek Executive Producer and General Manager of T-Vision, 28 April 2008, Cairo, Egypt [Khalil interview].

Al-Hage, Nakhle, Director of News and Current Affairs, al-Arabiya, 29 June 2005, Dubai, UAE [Kraidy interview].

Al-Hajj, Jamil, Head of Business News, al-Arabiya News Channel, 25 May 2008, Dubai, UAE [Khalil interview].

Al-Jasem, Mohammed, Editor in Chief, *Meezan*, 15 November 2005, Kuwait [Kraidy interview].

Al-Khazen, Jihad, *Al-Hayat*, Media and Communication Group, 7 June 2005, London [Kraidy interview].

Al-Meligi, Sherine, Director of Production, Melody Entertainment Ltd, 23 April 2008, Cairo, Egypt [Khalil interview].

Al-Rashed, 'Abdel Rahman, General Manager, al-Arabiya, 27 June 2005, Dubai, UAE [Kraidy interview].

Al-Roueini, Nashwa, Presenter/Executive Producer, MBC/Dubai TV, 3 June 2008, Dubai, UAE [Khalil interview].

Al-Sabeh, Ahmad, Jeddah Office Manager, Optimedia, ZenithOptimedia, 9 April 2008, Jeddah, Saudi Arabia [Khalil interview].

Al-Sahly, Moubarak Faleh, Director, Kuwait Television Channel 4, 15 November 2005, Kuwait City, Kuwait [Kraidy interview].

Al-Sayegh, Abdullatif, CEO, Arabian Radio Network, 30 June 2005, Dubai, UAE
   [Kraidy interview].

Al-Wishah, Waddah, Production Manager, Jordan Media City, 30 April 2009, Amman,
   Jordan [Kraidy interview].

Alavanthian, Sebouh, Director of Programming Department, LBC, 30 June 2004,
   Adma, Lebanon [Kraidy interview].

Ali, Mohammad Nasir, Station Manager, Infinity TV FZ-LLC, 25 May 2008, Dubai,
   UAE [Khalil interview].

Alkhas, Radi, Director General, Jordan Media City, 30 April 2009, Amman, Jordan
   [Kraidy interview].

Atef, Amro Samir, Head Writer for Television Sitcoms, 28 April 2008, Cairo, Egypt
   [Khalil interview].

Bibi, Abdelkader, Head of Marketing and Sales, Dubai Media Inc, 5 June 2004,
   Dubai, UAE [Kraidy interview].

Costandi, Michel, Business Development Director, MBC Group, 3 June 2004, Dubai,
   UAE [Kraidy interview].

Eapen, Joseph, Director–Planning, Brand Connection, 7 April 2008, Jeddah, Saudi
   Arabia [Khalil interview].

Einstein, Peter, Former CEO of Showtime Arabia, Managing Partner Einstein Media
   Capital Partners (UK) Ltd, 29 May 2008, Dubai, UAE [Khalil interview].

Fattouh, Badih, Group Director of Content, MBC Group, 2 June 2008, Dubai, UAE
   [Khalil interview].

Fehmi, Joumana, Programs and Production Director, Al-Rai TV, 16 November 2005,
   Al-Salhiyya, Kuwait [Kraidy interview].

Hammad, Mureed, Media Consultant (previously main anchor at CNBC Arabiya),
   25 April 2009, Dead Sea, Jordan [Kraidy and Khalil interview].

Hamzeh, Samer, Head of News Centre, Dubai Media Inc, 1 June 2008, Dubai, UAE
   [Khalil interview].

Hitti, Paul, Special Projects Manager, Middle East Broadcasting Centre, 22 June
   2005, Dubai, UAE [Kraidy interview].

Ismail, Fadi, Head of 03, MBC Group, 5 June 2008, Dubai, UAE [Khalil interview].

Jazzar, Rony, General Manager, Starwave and AVM, 2 July 2004, Beirut, Lebanon
   [Kraidy interview].

Kattan, Wissam, former Brand Manager, MTV Arabia, 28 May 2008, Dubai, UAE
   [Khalil interview].

Kebbeh, Ziad, Managing Director Endemol Middle East, 24 May 2008, Dubai, UAE
   [Khalil interview].

Khafaja, Amr, founding Manager of Dream TV, 22 April 2008, Cairo, Egypt [Khalil
   interview].

Khalifa, Hesham K., Regional Manager, ARABSAT, 5 January 2008 [Khalil email
   communication].

Khatib, Nabil, Executive Editor, al-Arabiya, 29 June 2005, Dubai, UAE [Kraidy interview].

Kitmitto, Naji, former Executive Producer, Dubai TV, 21 May 2008, Dubai, UAE [Khalil interview].

Koukjian, Roni, Cairo General Manager, Universal Media, part of Universal McCann, 28 April 2008, Cairo, Egypt [Khalil interview].

Koura, Amr, CEO, Al Karma Edutainment, 23 April 2008, Cairo, Egypt [Khalil interview].

Mahfouz, Abdelhadi, President, National Council for Audio-Visual Media, 14 July 2004, Hamra, Beirut, Lebanon [Kraidy interview].

Maskall, Andrew, Senior Channel Marketing Manager, MBC2, MBC4 and MBC Action, 19 May 2008, Dubai, UAE [Khalil interview].

Nour, Karim, Director of Corporate Management, Tarek Nour Communications, 8 March 2008, Cairo, Egypt [Khalil interview].

Sarkis, Karim, Executive Director, Broadcast, Abu Dhabi Media Company, 12 June 2008, Dubai, UAE [Khalil interview].

Stratford, Deborah, Creative Director, CNBC Arabiya, 31 May 2004, Dubai, UAE [Kraidy interview].

Tendler, Clifford, former Channel Director of America Plus, part of the Orbit Communications Network, CEO, GMG Media Group, 21 May 2008, Dubai, UAE [Khalil interview].

Zakaria, Nermine, Business Development Manager, Baraka Media Production, 24 April 2008, Cairo, Egypt [Khalil interview].

Zuraiqat, Hala, Director, Jordan Television, 30 April 2009, Amman, Jordan [Kraidy interview].

Appendix III: Website Addresses of Institutions (Current Names)

BY COUNTRY

Country[1]	Channel[2]	Ownership	Est.[3]	Web link
Algeria	Canal Algérie	L'Entreprise Nationale de Télévision	1962	www.canalalgerie.dz
Bahrain	Bahrain TV	Bahrain Radio and Television Corporation	1971	www.bahraintv.com
Egypt	Channel 1	Egypt Radio and Television Union	1960	www.ertu.org
	Al-Mehwar TV	Al-Mehwar Company – Sama Group	2001	www.almehwar.tv
	Dream 2	Dream Media Company	2001	www.dreams.tv
	OTV	Hawa Limited	2007	www.otvegypt.com
Iraq	Al-Iraqiya	Iraqi Media Network	2003	www.iraqimedianet.net
	Al-Fayha'	Ahlu Al-Bayt TV	2005	www.ahlubayt.com
	Al-Forat	Al-Forat Information Co.	2004	www.alforattv.com
	Al-Sharqiya	Al-Sharqiya Television and Media	2004	www.alsharqiya.com
	Al-Sumariya	Al-Sumariya Iraqi Satellite TV Networks	2004	www.alsumariya.tv
Jordan	JTV1	Jordan Radio and Television Corporation	1968	www.jrtv.jo
Kuwait	KTV1	Kuwait Television	1978	www.media.gov.kw
	Al-Rai TV	Al-Rai Media Group	2004	www.alrai.tv
	Al-Watan TV	Dar Al-Watan Press Printing and Publishing	2007	www.watan.tv
Lebanon	Télé-Liban	Lebanese Ministry of Information	1992	Not available
	Al-Manar Television	Lebanese Communication Group (LLG)	1991	www.almanar.com.lb
	Future TV	Future TV	1993	www.futuretvnetwork.com
	LBC-Sat	Lebanese Broadcasting International Holding	1996	www.lbcgroup.tv
	Orange TV	OTV Holding	2007	www.otv.com.lb
Libya	Al-Jamahiriya	Libyan Jamahiriya Broadcasting Corporation	1968	www.ljbc.net
	Al-Libiya TV	1/9 Media	2007	www.allibiya.tv
Morocco	Al-Maghribiya	Société Nationale de Radiodiffusion et de Télévision	2004	www.snrt.ma

Country	Channel	Ownership	Est.	Web link
Oman	Oman TV	Ministry of Information	1974	www.oman-tv.gov.om
Palestine	Palestine Satellite Channel	Palestinian Broadcasting Corporation	1996	www.psctv.com
	Al-Salam TV	Al-Salam TV	1992	Not available
	Bethlehem TV	Bethlehem TV	1996	www.bethlehem-tv.com
	Nablus TV	Nablus TV Broadcasting	1992	www.nablustv.net
Qatar	Qatar Satellite Channel	Qatar General Broadcasting and Television Corporation	2001	www.qatar-tv.net
Saudi Arabia	Saudi Channel 1	Broadcasting Service of the Kingdom of Saudi Arabia	1965	www.saudi1.tv
Sudan	Sudan TV	Sudan National Broadcasting Corporation (SNBC)	1962	www.sudantv.net
Syria	Syrian Space Channel	General Organization of Radio and TV	1996	www.rtv.gov.sy
	Addounia TV	N/A (Eyad Sharbaji and government cronies)	2007	www.addounia.tv
Tunisia	TV7 Tunisia	Tunisia Radio and TV Establishment	1966	www.tunisiatv.com
	Hannibal TV	Hannibal TV	2005	www.hannibaltv.com.tn
UAE	Abu Dhabi TV	Abu Dhabi Media Company (ADMC)	2007	www.admedia.ae
	Sharjah TV	Sharjah Radio and TV	1989	www.sharjahtv.com
	Dubai TV	Dubai Media Incorporated	2004	www.dmi.ae
Yemen	Yemen Satellite Channel	Public Corporation for Radio and Television	1990	www.yemenrt.com/en/tv1

1 Lacking channels are Mauritania, Somalia and Djibouti.
2 This list includes government- and privately owned channels (where available), with the exception of dynamic markets like Egypt, Iraq, Kuwait, Lebanon and the UAE.
3 Dates provided are for the most recent restructuring or relaunch of the channel.

BY CHANNEL TYPE

Genre	Channel	Ownership	Est.	Web link
News	Al-Jazeera	Al-Jazeera Network	1996	www.aljazeera.net
	Al-Arabiya	MBC Group	2003	www.alarabiya.net
Business news	CNBC Arabiya	Middle East Business News	2003	www.cnbcarabia.com
	Al-Eqtisadiya	Al-Eqtisadiya Business Channel	2006	www.eqtisadia.tv
Business niche channels	Al-Aqariya TV	Al-Aqariya Group	2004	www.alaqariya.tv
	I2tv	Itsalat International Company	2006	www.i2-mobile.tv
General entertainment channels	LBC-Sat	Lebanese Broadcasting International Holding	1996	www.lbcgroup.tv
	MBC 1	MBC Group	1991	www.mbc.net
	Dubai TV	Dubai Media Incorporated	2004	www.dmi.ae
	Infinity TV	Infinity FZ LLC	2004	www.infinitytv.tv
	Al-Aan	Tower Media Middle East	2006	www.alaan.tv
Movie channels	Melody Aflam	Melody Holding	2006	www.melodyaflam.tv
	Rotana Cinema	Rotana Holding Company	2005	www.rotana.net
	MBC2	MBC Group	2003	www.mbc.net
	MBC Action	MBC Group	2007	www.mbc.net
	MBC Max	MBC Group	2008	www.mbc.net
	Fox Movie Channel	Fox International Channels	2008	www.foxmoviestv.com
Music channels	Melody Hits TV	Melody Holding	2002	www.melodyarabia.tv
	Nojoom TV	Nojoom TV	2003	www.nojoomnet.tv
	Rotana Music	Rotana Holding Company	2003	www.rotana.net
	Mazzika TV	Digital Sound Company	2003	www.mazzikatv.com
Sports channels	Al-Jazeera Sports	Al-Jazeera Network	2003	www.aljazeerasport.net
	Gear 'One TV	Global Business Group	2005	www.gearone.tv
	Al-Riyadiyah	Broadcasting Service of the Kingdom of Saudi Arabia	2003	www.alriyadiyah.tv
	Dubai Sports Channel	Dubai Media Incorporated	1998	www.dmi.ae/dubaisports
Western series and shows	MBC4	MBC Group	2005	www.mbc.net
	Dubai 'One	Dubai Media Incorporated	2004	www.dmi.ae/dubaione/
	MTV Arabia	Arab Media Group	2007	www.mtva.com
Children's channels	Spacetoon Kids TV	Spacetoon Media Group	2000	www.spacetoon.tv
	MBC 3	MBC Group	2004	www.mbc.net
	Al-Majd Kids Channel	Al-Majd Satellite Broadcasting Ltd	2004	www.almajdtv.com
	Al-Jazeera Children's Channel	Qatar Foundation for Education Science and Community Development	2005	www.jcctv.net

Genre	Channel	Ownership	Est.	Web link
Religious channels	Télé-Lumière	Télé-Lumière	1991	www.télélumière.com
	Iqra' TV	Arab Radio and Television (ART)	1998	www.iqraa-tv.net
	Al-Resalah Satellite TV	Kingdom Holding	2006	www.alresalah.net
	Al-Majd Holy Qur'an Channel	Al-Majd Satellite Broadcasting Ltd	2004	www.quran.tv
Documentary channels	Al-Jazeera Documentary Channel	Al-Jazeera Network	2007	www.aljazeera.net
Shopping channels	Tamima TV	Tamima Group	2000	www.tamima.com.eg
	Citrus TV	Citrus TV	2005	www.citrus.com
	The Shopping Network	TSN Holding Ltd	2006	www.tsn24x7.com

1 This is an illustrative list of channels, both government and privately owned.

Bibliography

Abbas, F. (2006, 28 March). Arab Media: Finding a Place for 'Product Placement'. *Asharq al-Awsat*, accessed 28 March 2006 at <www.asharqalawsat.com> [Arabic].

Abbott, R. (2005a, 11 September). A City That Never Sleeps, *Campaign Middle East*, accessed 11 September 2005, at <http://campaignME.com/>.

Abbott, R. (2005b, 20 November). Makeover Helps MBC4 Target Saudi Women. *Campaign Middle East*, accessed 20 November 2005 at <campaignME.com>.

Abdel Malik, A. (1995). The ARABSAT Project. *Kuwaiti Arab Journal*. Kuwait City, Kuwait: Kuwaiti Cultural Council [Arabic].

Abou al Naga, S. (2004). Arab Women and the New Media: Empowerment or Disempowerment? *Transnational Broadcasting Studies*, 13, accessed 1 November 2008 at <www.tbsjournal.com>.

About Dubai Holding (2008). *Dubai Holding*, accessed 15 October 2008 at <dubaiholding. com/en/about-dubai-holding>.

About Freej (2009). Accessed 17 May 2009 at <www.freej.ae/main.html>.

Abu Isba', S. K. (1999). *The Challenges of Arab Media*. Amman: Shuruq Publishers [Arabic].

Abu Sheeba, K. (2005, 30 September). Competition between a Number of Productions, Best of Which Is Kuwaiti. *Al-Hayat*, accessed 30 September 2005 at <www.alhayat.com> [Arabic].

Abu-Lughod, I. (1963). The Mass Media and Egyptian Village Life. *Social Forces*, 42 (1): 97–104.

Abu-Lughod, L. (1995). Movie Stars and Islamic Moralism in Egypt. *Social Text*, 42: 53–67.

Abu-Lughod, L. (2003). Egyptian Melodrama – Technology of the Modern Subject? In F. D. Ginsburg, L. Abu-Lughod and B. Larkin (eds) *Media World: Anthropology on a New Terrain*. Berkeley and Los Angeles: University of California Press, 115–33.

Abu-Lughod, L. (2005). *Dramas of Nationhood: The Politics of Television in Egypt*. Chicago, IL: University of Chicago Press.

Abuljadayel, S. (1999, 17 June). A Leading Pay-TV Company in the Arab World. *Arab News*, accessed 1 September 2007 at <www.arabnews.com>.

Addington, T. (2005a, 11 September). Television Rules the Roost in KSA. *Campaign Middle East*, accessed 11 September 2005 at <campaignME.com>.

Addington, T. (2005b, 13 November). Choueiri: 'I Am Not the Godfather'. *Campaign Middle East*, accessed 13 November 2006 at <campaignME.com>.

Addington, T. (2005c, 25 December). 2005: A Year to Remember. *Campaign Middle East*, accessed 25 December 2005 at <campaignME.com>.

Addington, T. (2006, 26 March). Media Tribunal Awaits First Case. *Campaign Middle East*, accessed 26 March 2006 at <campaignME.com>.

Again from Dubai TV in the Show 'Nashwa' (2007, 7 January). *Al-Hayat*, accessed 15 October 2008 at <www.alhayat.com> [Arabic].

Agha, A. H. (1995, April July). Direct Broadcast and Cultural Identity. *Journal of Islamic Studies*, 79 [Arabic].

Ahmadeet, A. (1997). *The Arabs and Satellite Uses: An Experiment or Experimentation*. Beirut: Independent Publishers [Arabic].

Al-Abdallah, K. (2007, 2 April). Al Majd Islamic Channel Receives Employment Applications from Saudi Females. *Elaph,* accessed 15 October 2008 at <www.elaph.com> [Arabic].

Al-Alawi, D. (2003, 12 January). Bahrain Launches New TV Channel. *Gulf News,* accessed 13 November 2006 at <www.gulfnews.com/home>.

Al-Arabiya Finds Tishreen's Campaign Strange. (2005, 28 February). *Assafir*, accessed 28 February 2005 at <www.assafir.com> [Arabic].

Al-Armouti, M. (1982, July). Towards a New Information Order, a Call to Establish an Arab Shared News Market. *The Arab Information, Culture and Sciences* [Arabic].

Al-'Asuj, A. (2006, 12 December). She Recently Moved to Economic Work … Majdulin 'Issa: The Saudi Woman Anchor Taken into Serious Account by Satellite Channels. *Al-Hayat*, accessed 12 December 2006 at <www.alhayat.com> [Arabic].

Al-Bakri, E. S. (1999). *The 2000 War of Satellite Channels.* Amman: Shuruq Publishers [Arabic].

Al-Barraq, N. (2008, 20 February). Abdallah al-Jaser: Satellite Charter Distinguishes between Incitement to Violence and Resistance to Occupation. *Al-Hayat*, accessed 15 October 2008 at <www.alhayat.com> [Arabic].

Al-Bishr, B. (2007). *The Battles of Tash Ma Tash*. Beirut: Arab Cultural Centre [Arabic].

Al-Dossary, S. (2007, 22 July). VP of MTV Worldwide: No One Will Compete with Our Arabic Channel. *Asharq al-Awsat*, accessed 22 July 2006 at <www.asharqalawsat.com> [Arabic].

Al-Dowsari, S. (2006, 19 November). The Head of MBC Group […]. *Asharq al-Awsat*, accessed 19 November 2006 at <www.asharqalawsat.com> [Arabic].

Al-Fardan, A. (2006, 6 August). The War in Lebanon Reveals the Abilities of a Cohort of Arab Female Correspondents. *Asharq al-Awsat*, accessed 6 August 2006 at <www.asharqalawsat.com> [Arabic].

Al-Hakeem, Bassem (2009, 9 March). Starac Friendly Neighbour. *Al-Akhbar*, accessed 9 March 2009 at <www.al-akhbar.com> [Arabic].

Al-Hamamsy, G. (2005, 5 October). Their Eyes Were Watching. *Business Today Egypt*, accessed 15 October 2008 at <www.businesstodayegypt.com>.

Al-Hasan, A. A. H. (2003). Local Drama Series in the Balance of the Viewers and the Experts and the Producers. Riyadh: The Author.

Al-Jammal, R. M. (1991). *Communication and Media in the Arab World*. Beirut: Centre for Arab Unity Studies [Arabic].

Al-Jaza'iri, M. (2005,15 October). Was the Serial al-Hour al-'Ayn a Media Victim? *Asharq al-Awsat*, accessed 15 October 2008 at <http://www.asharqalawsat.com> [Arabic].

Al-Khareef, B. (2007, 11 March). Assistant Manager of al-Majd Satellite. We Are Not a Religious Channel. *Asharq al-Awsat*, accessed 15 October 2008 at <www.asharqalawsat.com> [Arabic].

Al-Khoury, R. (2006, 14 January). Assassination Attempt against May Chidiac Made Her Consider Taking Security Measures ... Mathilda Farjallah: My Professional Success I Do Not Owe to Anyone. *Al-Hayat*, accessed 14 January 2006 at <www.alhayat.com> [Arabic].

Al-Khudr, M. (2006, 4 June). The Artists' Veil. *Al-Hayat*, accessed 4 June 2006 at <www.alhayat.com> [Arabic].

Al-Marashi, I. (2007). The Dynamics of Iraq's Media: Ethno-Sectarian Violence, Political Islam, Public Advocacy, and Globalization. *Cardozo Arts and Entertainment Law Journal*, 25(95): 96–140.

Al-Mesmar, R. (2004, 18 May). A Mix of LBC and MBC Programmes and Resemblance to Its Original Identity. *Al-Mustaqbal*, accessed 17 May 2009 at <www.almustaqbal.com> [Arabic].

Al-Qaradawi. Preachers Don't Know about the Denmark Conference. Amru Khaled: The Conference Is Serious and We Will Not Retreat. (2006, 3 March). *Asharq al-Awsat*, accessed 3 March 2006 at <www.asharqalawsat.com> [Arabic].

Al-Resalah (The Message) Channel Had Made Its Debut Informally on Wednesday. (2006, 7 March). Riyadh: Kingdom Holding Press Release.

Al-Saghir, S. B. M. (2008). *Television and Social Change in Developing Countries*. Jeddah: Shuruq Publishers [Arabic].

Al-Saleh, H. (2005, October 9). The Ramadan Month Taught Saudis the Meaning of 'Seasonal Programming'. *Asharq al-Awsat*, accessed 27 January 2007 at <www.asharqalawsat.com> [Arabic].

Al-Saleh, H. (2006, 29 January). Hamed El Ghamdi ... the Face of Saudi Television. *Asharq al-Awsat*, accessed 1 October 2007 at <www.asharqalawsat.com> [Arabic].

Al-Saleh, H. (2007, 27 January). Arab Islamic Channels ... between Its Rejection of Commercials and Advertising's Rejection of Them. *Asharq al-Awsat*, accessed 27 January 2007 at <www.asharqalawsat.com> [Arabic].

Al-Sarraf, N. and Jasem, H. (2005, 9 April). The Iraqi Media Gets out of the Box with More Than 20 Channels and 260 Newspapers. Asharq al-Awsat, accessed 3 March 2006 at <www.asharqalawsat.com> [Arabic].

Al-Shafi'i, M. (2006, 1 March). Amru Khaled: We Will Go to Denmark in Spite of al-Qaradawi's Opposition. *Asharq al-Awsat*, accessed 15 October 2005 at <www.asharqalawsat.com> [Arabic].

Al-Sham Satellite Channel (2005, 9 September). *Assafir*, accessed 9 September 2005 at <www.assafir.com> [Arabic].

Al-Shaoush, E. (2006, 20 September). The Tunisian Television Punishes Arabic Productions. *Elaph,* accessed 20 September 2006 at <www.elaph.com> [Arabic].

Al-Sheikh, 'A. (2007). *Kuwait Television from Dubai*. Dubai: The Author [Arabic].

Al-Sheikh, B. (2006, 20 January). The Arab Woman and Her Confused Image. *Al-Hayat*, accessed 20 January 2006 at <www.alhayat.com> [Arabic].

Al-Shoush, M. (2006, 20 March). Number of Dubai Media City Partners Rises by 20% in 2005. *Gulf News*, accessed 20 March 2006 at <www.gulfnews.com>.

Al-'Utaybi, B. (2006, 18 April). Very Bold Mathilda Farjallah. *Al Rai*, accessed 7 September 2009 at <www.alraimedia.com> [Arabic].

Al-Zein, H. (2006, 1 June). Dubai TV Harvests What Future TV Planted. *Assafir*, accessed 1 June 2006 at <www.assafir.com> [Arabic].

Al-Zern, J. (2007). *The Internationalization of Arab Media, the Container and the Realization of Identity*. Damascus: Press Publishers [Arabic].

Alessar, D. (1973). *A Report on the Experiment of News Exchange via Satellite between the Levant and Maghreb Centres*. Amman: Jordanian Television [Arabic].

Allison, A. (2008, 1 February). Pierre into the Future. *Communicate*, accessed 18 October 2008 at <www.communicate.ae>.

Alsumaria TV Goes Terrestrial in Iraq (2007, 13 February). Dubai: ASDA'A Public Relations Press Release.

Alterman, J. B. (2003). The Information Revolution and the Middle East. In N. Bensahel and D. L. Byman (eds), *The Future Security Environment in the Middle East: Conflict, Stability, and Political Change*. Santa Monica, CA: Rand, 227–47.

Ambah, F. S. (1995a, 24 May). Arabs Channel-surf past State-run TV. *Christian Science Monitor*, 1.

Ambah, F. S. (1995b, 3 June). Saudi Regime Prepares to Dish out Censorship. *The Irish Times*, City Edition, 10.

Ambah, F. S. (1998, 21 October). Islamic TV Channel Aims to Combat Western 'Decadence'. *Associated Press*, accessed 15 October 2008 at LexisNexis Academic online database.

Amin, H. Y. (2000). The Current Situation of Satellite Broadcasting in the Middle East. *Transnational Broadcasting Studies*, 5, accessed 1 December 2001 at <www.tbsjournal.com>.

Amin, H. Y. (2001). Arab Women and Satellite Broadcasting. *Transnational Broadcasting Studies*, 6, accessed 1 December 2001 at <www.tbsjournal.com>.

Amin, H. Y. and Boyd, D. A. (1994). The Development of Direct Broadcast Television to and within the Middle East. *Journal of South Asia and Middle Eastern Studies*, 18(2): 37–50.

Anderson, B. (1983). *Imagined Communities: Reflections on the Origin and Spread of Nationalism*. London and New York: Verso.

Andijani, N. (2006, 12 November). Saudis Reconsider Their Ads. *Asharq al-Awsat*, accessed 9 September 2005 at <www.asharqalawsat.com> [Arabic].

Arab Human Development Report 2003: Building a Knowledge Society (2003). New York: United Nations Development Program, accessed 15 October 2007 at <hdr.undp.org/en/reports/regionalreports/arabstates/Arab_States_2003_en.pdf>.

Arab Satellite TV Channels: The Future Is Promising but … (2005, May) *ArabAd*, 12.

Arab World's MBC TV Moves Base from London to Dubai Media City (2001, 20 March). Paris: *Agence France Presse*, accessed 15 October 2007 at LexisNexis Academic online database.

Arabic Online Portals Featuring News Content (2006). Amman: Arab Advisors Group.

Arabs Should Let in Direct Satellite (1998, 25 February). *Gulf Daily News*, accessed 1 September 2007 at <www.gulf-daily-news.com/home.asp>.

ARABSAT Says French Channel Ban over Porn Is Final (1997, 24 July). *Beirut Times*, 7.

ARABSAT Second Generation Satellites (1997). Riyadh: ARABSAT.

ARABSAT's General Manager: We Have Pointed CFI's Attention since 1993 on Their Violation of Our Contract. (1997, 27 July). *Asharq al-Awsat*, 16 [Arabic].

Armbrust, W. (1996). *Mass Culture and Modernism in Egypt*. Cambridge: Cambridge University Press.

Armbrust, W. (2002). The Riddle of Ramadan: Media, Consumer Culture, and the 'Christmasization' of a Muslim Holiday. In D. Bowen and E. Early (eds) *Everyday Life in the Middle East*, Bloomington: Indiana University Press, 335–48.

Armbrust, W. (2005). Synchronizing Watches: The State, the Consumer, and Sacred Time in Ramadan Television. In B. Meyer and A. Moors (eds) *Religion, Media and the Public Sphere*, Bloomington: Indiana University Press, 207–26.

Awad, M. (2006, 11 December). Advertising Equations. *Assafir*, accessed 8 October 2008 at <www.assafir.com> [Arabic].

Ayish, M. I. (1997). Arab Television Goes Commercial: A Case Study of the Middle East. *International Communication Gazette*, 59 (6): 473–94.

Azmashli, S. (2005, 2 April). Al-Madina FM Facing Lebanese Stations … Syria Gambles on Private Radio Stations, *Al-Hayat*. accessed 2 April 2005 at <www.alhayat.com> [Arabic].

'Azour, S. (2006, 7 October). And They Ask You about the Veiling of Serials Featuring Veiled Actresses … Say It's the Quandary. *Al-Quds-al-Arabi*, accessed 15 October 2008 at <http://www.alquds.co.uk> [Arabic].

Badr, A. (2005, 22 March). Will Tendency towards Feminization Save Syrian Media from Its Crisis? *Al-Quds Al-Arabi*, accessed 22 March 2005 at <www.alquds.co.uk> [Arabic].

Badran, A. R. B. (1991). Christian Broadcasting in the Eastern Mediterranean: The Case of Middle East Television. *Gazette*, 47: 33–46.

Barkey, M. (1996, January). Satellite TV: On the Eve of Revolution. *Arab Ad*: 12–14.

Battah, H. (2006a, February). Arab Television and Mobile Phones: True Interaction. *MENA Region: Mobility for One Language, Diverse Cultures*. An MTC Report: 61–5.

Battah, H. (2006b, February/March). The SMS Invasion. *Middle East Broadcasting Journal*, 6: 18–22.

Big Brother Show Suspended (2004, February 20). Dubai: MBC Group Press Release.

Blanford, N. (2001, 28 December). Hezbullah Sharpens Its Weapons in Propaganda War. *Christian Science Monitor*, accessed 15 October 2008 at <www.csmonitor.com>.

Boehm, E. (1996, 15–21 April). Docu Disagreement Pushes BBC out of Arabian Orbit. *Variety*: 52.

Boucher, R. (2004, 17 December). US State Department Spokesman Washington, Daily Press Briefing DC, accessed 19 December 2004 at <www.state.gov/r/pa/prs/dpb/2004/39934.htm>.

Boulos, J. C. (1996). *La télé: quelle histoire*. (The TV: What a Story). Beirut: Fiches du Monde Arabe [French].

Bouqanoun, I. (2005, 20 October). Al-Jazeera Kids ... A Reading of the Notion and a Critique of the Vision. *Aljazeera.net* website, accessed 20 October 2005 at <english.aljazeera.net>.

Boyd, D. A. (1991). Lebanese Broadcasting: Unofficial Electronic Media during a Prolonged Civil War. *Journal of Broadcasting and Electronic Media*, 35(3): 269–87.

Boyd, D. A. (1993). A New 'Line in the Sand' for the Media. *Media Studies Journal*, 7(4): 133–40.

Boyd, D. A. (1999). *Broadcasting in the Arab World: A Survey of the Electronic Media in the Middle East* (2nd edn). Ames: Iowa State University Press.

Boyd, D. A. (2001). Saudi Arabia's International Media Strategy: Influence through Multinational Ownership. In K. Hafez (ed.) *Mass Media, Politics & Society in the Middle East*. Crisskill, NJ: Hampton Press, 43–60.

Browne, D. (1975). Television and National Stabilization: The Lebanese Experience. *Journalism Quarterly*, 52: 692–8.

Browne, D. (1999). *Electronic Media and Industrialized Nations: A Comparative Study*. New York: Blackwell.

Burkeman, O. (2003, 24 April). Norm Pattiz, Chairman of the Mideast Committee of the Broadcasting Board of Governors (BBG) Arab World Now Faces Invasion by American TV. *Guardian*, accessed 1 September 2007 at <www.guardian.co.uk>.

Burnett, K. (1996, December). The Scramble for Satellite Viewers, *Arab Ad*, 6: 166.

Byerly, C. M. and Ross, K. (2004). Introduction. In C. M. Byerly and K. Ross (eds) *Women and Media: International Perspectives*. Oxford: Blackwell, 1–9.

Byrne, C. (2003, 17 April). *Towards Freedom* Broadcasts Democracy to Iraq. *Guardian*, accessed 1 September 2007 at <www.guardian.co.uk>.

Cazes, S. (2003, February). *The Iraqi Media: 25 years of Relentless Repression*. Reporters without Borders Report, accessed 1 September 2007 at <www.rsf.org>.

Chaddock, G. R. (2003, 21 April). Next, Iraq's Cultural Regime Change. *Christian Science Monitor*, accessed 1 September 2007 at <www.csmonitor.com/2003/0421/p01s01-woiq.html>.

Chinni, D. (2003, 13 May). Whose Chaos Is It, Anyway? Iraq's or America's? *Christian Science Monitor*, accessed 1 September 2007 at <www.csmonitor.com/2003/0513/p09s01-codc.html>.

Clark, J. and Palmer, R. (1994, 7 February). Orbit Sat TV to Launch. *Daily Variety*, 14.

Curtin, M. (2007). *Playing to the World's Biggest Audience: The Globalization of Chinese Film and Television*. Berkeley: University of California Press.

Dabbous-Sensenig, D. (2002). The Arab World and the Challenge of Introducing Gender-Sensitive Communication Policies, Presentation to the Expert Group Meeting of the United Nations Division for the Advancement of Women, Beirut, 12–15 November, 2002, accessed 27 December 2002 at <www.un.org/womenwatch/daw/egm/media2002/reports/OP5Dabbous.PDF>.

Dabbous-Sensenig, D. (2006). To Veil or Not to Veil: Gender and Religion on Al-Jazeera's *Islamic Law and Life*. *Westminster Papers in Communication and Culture*, 3(2): 60–85.

Daher, R. (2009, 26 April). Hala Serhan on al-Libiya. *Elaph*, accessed 29 April 2009 at <www.elaph.com> [Arabic].

Dalati, R. (2005, November/December). The Great Call-in Giveaway. *Middle East Broadcasting Journal*, 4: 33–5.

Deloire, C. and Berretta, E. (2004, 2 December). Al-Manar Television: Channel of Hatred. *Le Point*, accessed 15 October 2008 on LexisNexis Academic online database.

Director of Dubai Media Incorporated: There Are No Specialized Cadres in the Arab World (2006, 6 July). *Asharq al-Awsat*, accessed 15 October 2008 at <www.asharqalawsat.com> [Arabic].

Divine Inspiration (1997, March). *Cable & Satellite Europe*, 159: 20.

DMI Mission and Vision (2008). Dubai Media Incorporated, accessed 15 October 2008 at <http://www.dmi.gov.ae/vision_En.asp>.

Dore, L. (2007, 11 February). UAE Advertising Spent Crosses $1 Billion in '06. *Khaleej Times*, accessed 15 October 2008 at <www.khaleejtimes.com/index00.asp>.

Downing, J. (1996). *Internationalizing Media Theory: Reflections on Media in Russia, Poland, and Hungary*, 1980–95. London: Sage.

Dr Abd al-Halim al-Hajjaj [...] on Plans for Reception of Satellite TV in Iraq (1999, 13 November) *Al-Iraq*: 4 [Arabic].

Dramatic Changes in Arab Television Ratings – 'Al Manar' Climbs from Nowhere to the Top 10 (2006, 23 August) *MENA Report* news portal website, accessed 23 August 2006 at <www.menareport.com/en/business/202216/&mod=print>.

Dubai Media City Profile (2009), accessed 17 May 2009 at <ae.zawya.com/cm/profile.cfm/cid1000167>.

Dubai Media Inc. Re-launches Dubai Sports Channel with New Identity (2005, 28 December). Dubai: Dubai Media Incorporated (DMI) Press Release

Dubai Shuts Down Independent Pakistan TV Station under Pressure (2007, 17 November). *Associated Press*, accessed 15 October 2008 at LexisNexis Academic online database.

Dubsky, A. (2007, 25 April). Population Boom Threatens Mideast Stability. *MEED*, accessed 15 October 2008 at <www.meed.com>.

Echchaibi, N. (2007). From the Pulpit to the Studio: Islam's Internal Battle. *Media Development*, 1.

Egypt TV Viewership. (2005). Cairo: TNS.

El-Baltaji, D. (2008, May). I Love My MTV. *Arab Media and Society*, accessed 1 June 2008 at <www.arabmediaandsociety.com>.

El-Emary, N. (1996). L'industrie du feuilleton télévisé Egyptien à l'ère des télévisions transfrontières (The Industry of Egyptian Television Series during the Era of Trans-border Televisions). *Revue Tiers Monde*, 37(146): 251–62 [French].

El-Nawawy, M. and Iskandar, A. (2003). *Al-Jazeera: The Story of the Network That Is Rattling Governments and Redefining Modern Journalism*. New York: Basic Books.

Emerging Dubai 2006 – Media and Advertising, 2006 (2006). London: Oxford Business Group.

Fakhreddine, J. (2000). Pan-Arab Satellite Television: Now the Survival Part. *Transnational Broadcasting Studies*, 5, accessed 15 March 2000 at <www.tbsjournal.com>.

Fandy, M. (1993, 15 December). Who Is Afraid of the Satellite Dish? *Christian Science Monitor*, 23.

Field, N. and Hamam, A. (2009). Salafi Satellite TV in Egypt. *Arab Media and Society* 8, accessed 15 May 2009 at <www.arabmediasociety.com/article=712>.

Forbes Arabia Compiles List of Top 40 Arab Brands. (2006, 19 October). Dubai: Forbes Arabia Press Release.

France Seeks EU Debate after Banning Hezbollah-linked TV Channel (2004, 15 December). *Agence France Presse*, accessed 15 October 2008 at LexisNexis Academic online database.

Francis, T. (2007, July 18). Media … in Arabic. *Al-Hayat*, accessed 18 July 2007 at
   <www.alhayat.com> [Arabic].

Franklin, S. (1996, November/December). The Kingdom and the Power. *Columbia
   Journalism Review*, accessed 20 January 2000 at
   <backissues.cjrarchives.org/year/96/6/saudi.asp>.

Gaetner, G. (2004, 28 June). Les Ultimes affaires de Khalifa, *L'Express*, accessed
   15 October 2008 at <www.lexpress.fr>.

GCC Advertising Expenses Rise by 464 Percent in Ten Years (2005, 30 November).
   Kuwait News Agency (KUNA), accessed 30 November 2005 at <www.kuna.net.kw/
   newsagenciespublicsite/homepage.aspx?language=ar> [Arabic].

General Manager of MBC Group Ali al-Hudaithy: I Dream of the Day the
   Governments Lift Their Hands off the Channels (2006, 19 December). *Al-Hayat*,
   accessed 19 December 2006 at <www.alhayat.com> [Arabic].

General Organization for Information, The (1998). NILESAT. Cairo: Ministry of
   Information [Arabic].

Ghorab, W. (1994, 25 October). ART Not for Sale Now, Says Kamel. *Arab News*,
   accessed 1 September 2007 at <www.arabnews.com>.

Gourevitch, A. (2003, 23 October). Exporting Censorship to Iraq, *American Prospect*:
   34–5.

Guaaybess, T. (2005). *Télévisions arabes sur orbite. Un système médiatique en mutation*
   (1960–2004). Paris: CNRS Éditions.

Gulf Buddies (1996, May). *Cable & Satellite Europe*, 149: 24.

Habib, Vicky (2006, 7 August). From 'Closer to the Truth' to 'So You Know More'…
   Al-Arabiya Changes Its Slogan but Says Professional Essence Does Not Change.
   Al-Hayat, accessed 15 October 2007 at <www.alhayat.com> [Arabic].

Haddad, S. (2002, 19 April). Entretien: Le responsable de l'information au Hezbollah
   parle d'un équilibre de la terreur avec Israel. (Interview: The Hezbullah
   Information Executive Talks of a Balance of Terror with Israel). *L'Orient-Le Jour*,
   accessed 19 April 2002 at <www.lorientlejour.com>.

Haddad, V. (2006, 7 May). Anchors' Make-up […] Simple Touches between the
   Rhythm of Events and the Nature of the Job – Accomplishing the Difficult Balance
   between Appropriate Appearance and Respect for the News. *Asharq al-Awsat*,
   accessed 7 May 2006 at <www.asharqalawsat.com> [Arabic].

Haddad, V. (2008, 22 February). Women of the Small Screen Transform 'Bakery's
   Women' into a Memory: On MBC, LBC and al-Hurra, Arabized Copies of *The
   View. Asharq al-Awsat,* accessed 22 February 2008 at <www.asharqalawsat.com>
   [Arabic].

Hajj Abdi, I. (2005, 28 April). Diana Jabbour: Why Don't We Make the Screen a
   Bridge between Citizens and the State? *Al-Hayat*, accessed 28 April 2005 at
   <www.alhayat.com> [Arabic].

Hallin, D. and Mancini, P. (2004). *Comparing Media Systems: Three Models of Media and Politics*. New York: Cambridge University Press.

Hamadeh, D. (2008, 3 September). TV Ad Rates Rise up to 25% during Ramadan. *Emirates Business* 24/7, accessed 15 October 2008 at <www.business24-7.ae/pages/default.aspx>.

Hamidi, I. (2005, 3 September). Programs for the First Privately Owned Syrian Satellite Television Channels Are Produced in Damascus and Transmitted from Dubai at a Cost of US $12 million ... Al-Sham Channel Wants to Confront Suicidal Thought without Video Clips. *Al-Hayat*, accessed 3 September 2005 at <www.alhayat.com> [Arabic].

Hammoud, A. H. (2008). *Al-Jazeera: A Role Bigger than a Station*. Beirut: al-Hadi Publishers [Arabic].

Hammoud, A. H. (2008). *Reality Television, the Human in The Cage of picture*. Beirut: al-Hadi Publishers [Arabic].

Hamzeh, N. (2004). *In the Path of Hezbollah*. Syracuse, NY: Syracuse University Press.

Haneyneh, R. (2005, 25 September). The Director of Dubai Channel: The Star of Daoud al-Sharyan Shines with Us. *Asharq al-Awsat*, accessed 25 September 2005 at <www.asharqalawsat.com> [Arabic].

Hardaker, D. (2006, 4 January). Amr Khaled: Islam's Billy Graham. *Independent*, accessed 4 January 2006 at <www.independent.co.uk>.

Haress, S. (2008). *The Arab Media and the Media Cultural and Political Globalization*. Cairo: Arab Publishers [Arabic].

Harmon, M. (2008, September). Arab Youth, TV Viewing and 'Affluenza'. *Arab Media and Society*, accessed 15 October 2008 at <www.arabmediaandsociety.com>.

Hasan, E. E. M. *et al.* (2007). The Media in the Arab World between Liberation and the Reproduction of Hegemony. *Issues and Reform Series*, 15. Cairo: Cairo Centre for Human Rights Studies [Arabic].

Hassan, J. and Al-Shehri, N. (2006, 7 March). Saudi Arabia: Al-Resalah Launched. *Arab News*, accessed 7 March 2006 at <www.arabnews.com>.

Haugbolle, S. (2007) That Joke Isn't Funny Any More: Bas Mat Watan's Nasrallah Skit and the Limits of Laughter in Lebanon. *Arab Media & Society*, (3), accessed 15 May 2009 at <www.arabmediasociety.com>.

Hazeen, G. (2005, 28 September) Ramada Screens Do Not Lack of Them ... Jordanian Drama in Search of Success. *Al-Hayat*, accessed 18 July 2007 at <www.alhayat.com> [Arabic].

Head of MBC Group al-Waleed al-Ibrahim: We Are Studying the Establishment of Alliances with Arab and Global Groups (2006, 19 November). *Asharq al-Awsat*, accessed 19 November 2006 at <www.asharqalawsat.com> [Arabic].

How Television Was Established in Lebanon (1974, January). *Al-Dustur*: 6 [Arabic].

Hussein, S. (1988). *The Gulf Television Media and Complete Development*. Riyadh: Gulf Television Unit [Arabic].

I Almost Left MBC and My departure Is Possible at Any Moment ... and the Broadcast of *al Hour al-Ayn* Was a Mistake (2006, 26 September). *Asharq al-Awsat*, accessed 26 September 2006 at <www.asharqalawsat.com> [Arabic].

Information Minister Calls on Journalists to Defend 'Freedom of Expression' and Give up on 'Vocabulary of Confrontation' ... Syria Moves to 'Control' Electronic Publishing in a New Media Law (2005, 16 August). *Al-Hayat*, accessed 16 August 2005 at <www.alhayat.com> [Arabic].

Interview with Tareq al-Suwaidan, General Manager of al-Resalah Channel (2006). *Transnational Broadcasting Studies*, 16, accessed 12 December 2006 at <www.tbsjournal.com>.

Iraq Television Viewership Poll (2003, 16 October). US Department of State, Office Intelligence and Research, accessed 19 December 2004 at <stanhopecenter.org.iraqmediapoll.shtml>.

Ishtar Satellite: Particularity amidst Media Chaos (2005, 15 September). *Al-Hayat*, accessed 1 September 2007 at <www.alhayat.com> [Arabic].

Jaafar, Ali. (2005, 24–30 October). Rockin' Iraq. *Variety*, News: 1.

Jaber, H. (1997). *Hezbollah: Born with a Vengeance*. New York: Columbia University Press.

Journalists Killed in Iraq, 2008 (2008). Committee to Protect Journalists (CPJ), accessed 22 April 2009 at <www.cpj.org/reports/2008/07/journalists-killed-in-iraq.php>.

Kannawee, M. (2006, 1 September). Advertising Agencies Pressure to Control the Ramadan Map. *Asharq al-Awsat*, accessed 1 September 2006 at <www.asharqalawsat.com> [Arabic].

Karam, I. (2007). Satellite Television: A Breathing Space for Arab Youth? In N. Sakr (ed.) *Arab Media and Political Renewal: Community, Legitimacy and Public Life*. London: I. B. Tauris, 80–95.

Kazan, N. (1996, November). A Winner in the Booming Satellite Industry. *Arab Ad*, 6–12.

Kelaita, K. (2001, 4 June). Dubai Investing in Information Trade. *Time Magazine*, 157, accessed 15 October 2007 at <www.time.com/time/interactive/business/dubai_np.html>.

Khalaf, R. (1994, 16 November). Saudi Businessmen Reach for the Media Stars. *Financial Times*: 4.

Khalil, J. F. (2004). Blending In: Arab Television and the Search for Programming Ideas. *Transnational Broadcasting Journal*, 13, accessed 1 December 2008 at <www.tbsjournal.com>.

Khalil, J. F. (2005). To Pay or Not to Pay? Free Western Entertainment Channels Seek Pay Package Audiences. *Transnational Broadcasting Studies*, 14, accessed 1 December 2008 at <www.tbsjournal.com>.

Khalil, J. F. (2006a). Inside Arab Reality Television: Development, Definitions and Demystification. *Transnational Broadcasting Studies*, 1(2).

Khalil, J. F. (2006b). News Television in the Arabian Gulf ... Period of Transitions. *Global Media Journal, American Edition*, 5(8), accessed 15 June 2006 at <lass.calumet.purdue.edu/cca/gmj/index.htm>.

Khalil, J. F. and Abughaida, D. (2004). Appealing to the Hearts and Minds: How the Arab Channels Fought for the Gulf War Audience. *Transnational Broadcasting Studies*, 12, accessed 1 December 2004 at <www.tbsjournal.com>.

Khouri, R. G. (2005, 13 August). Media in the Lives of Young Arabs: Mirror or Monster? *Daily Star*, accessed 13 August 2005 at <www.dailystar.com.lb>.

KIPCO Asset Management Company (KAMCO.KSE) (2008). *Zawya Industry Classifications* (ZIC), accessed 18 October 2008 from <www.zawya.com/cm/profile.cfm? companyid=1000192>.

KIPCO Chief Looks Back with Pride: Showtime on Right Track (2000, 13 September). *Kuwait Times*, accessed 1 September 2007 at <www.kuwaittimes.net>.

Kishani, Y. (2002). *Arab Satellite communication in the Era of Open Skies* (1st edn). Beirut: Special Publication [Arabic].

Kooley, J. K. (1980, 2 September). Libya Offers Oil to Cyprus for Propaganda Base. *Christian Science Monitor*, 10.

Kraidy, M. M. (1998a). Satellite Broadcasting from Lebanon: Prospects and Perils. *Transnational Broadcasting Studies*, 1, accessed 15 December 2005 at <www.tbsjournal.com>.

Kraidy, M. M. (1998b). Broadcasting Regulation and Civil Society in Post-war Lebanon. *Journal of Broadcasting and Electronic Media*, 42(3): 387–400.

Kraidy, M. M. (1999a). The Global, the Local, and the Hybrid: A Native Ethnography of Glocalization. *Critical Studies in Mass Communication*, 16(4): 458–78.

Kraidy, M. M (1999b). State Control of Television News in 1990s Lebanon. *Journalism and Mass Communication Quarterly*, 76(3): 485–98.

Kraidy, M. M. (2000a). Transnational Satellite Television and Asymmetrical Interdependence in the Arab World: A Research Note. *Transnational Broadcasting Studies*, 5, accessed 15 December 2005 at <www.tbsjournal.com>.

Kraidy, M. M. (2000b). Television and Civic Discourse in Postwar Lebanon. In L. A. Gher and H. Y. Amin (eds) *Civic Discourse and Digital Age Communications in the Middle East*, Stamford, CT: Ablex, 3–18.

Kraidy, M. M. (2001). National Television between Localization and Globalization. In Y. Kamalipour and K. Rampal (eds) *Media, Sex and Drugs in the Global Village*. Lanham, MD: Rowman & Littlefield, 261–72.

Kraidy, M. M. (2002). Arab Satellite Television between Regionalization and
    Globalization. *Global Media Journal*, 1(1), accessed 15 December 2005 at
    <lass.calumet.purdue.edu>.

Kraidy, M. M. (2003). The Shutdown of Lebanon's MTV: Political and Legal
    Dimensions, Unpublished manuscript.

Kraidy, M. M. (2005). *Hybridity, or the Cultural Logic of Globalization*. Philadelphia,
    PA: Temple University Press.

Kraidy, M. M. (2006a) Reality Television and Politics in the Arab World (Preliminary
    Observations) *Transnational Broadcasting Studies* [peer-reviewed paper edition]
    2 (1): 7–28, electronic version available at <www.tbsjournal.com/Kraidy.html>.

Kraidy, M. M. (2006b, 7 November). Islamic Popular Culture. *Common Ground News
    Service*, accessed 1 June 2008 at <www.commongroundnews.org>.

Kraidy, M. M. (2006c, May). Syria: Media Reform and Its Limitations. *Arab Reform
    Bulletin*, 4(3). Carnegie Endowment for International Peace, Washington, DC,
    accessed 1 June 2008 at <www.carnegieendowment.org/publications>.

Kraidy, M. M. (2006d). Governance and Hypermedia in Saudi Arabia. *First Monday*, 11(9),
    accessed 15 October 2007 at <firstmonday.org/issues/special11_9/kraidy/index.html>.

Kraidy, M. M. (2007). Saudi Arabia, Lebanon, and the Changing Arab Information
    Order. *International Journal of Communication*, 1(1): 139–56, accessed 1 June 2008
    at <ijoc.org/ojs/index.php/ijoc/article/view/18/22>.

Kraidy, M. M. (2008a). The Arab Audience: From Activity to Interactivity. In K. Hafez
    (ed.) *Arab Media: Power and Weakness*, New York: Continuum, 77–8.

Kraidy, M. M. (2008b). *Arab Media and US Policy: A Public Diplomacy Reset*. [Policy
    brief]. Muscatine, IA: Stanley Foundation, accessed 1 June 2008 at
    <stanleyfdn.org/publications/pab/PAB08Kraidy.pdf>.

Kraidy, M. M. (2008c, March). Arab States: Emerging Consensus to Muzzle Media?
    Arab Reform Bulletin, 6(2). Washington, DC: Carnegie Endowment for
    International Peace, accessed 1 June 2008 at
    <www.carnegieendowment.org/publications>.

Kraidy, M. M. (2008d). Al-Jazeera and Al-Jazeera English: A Comparative Institutional
    Analysis. In M. Kugelman (ed.) *Kuala Lumpur Calling: Al Jazeera English in Asia*.
    Washington, DC: Woodrow Wilson International Centre for Scholars.

Kraidy, M. M. (2009). *Reality Television and Arab Politics: Contention in Public Life*.
    Cambridge and New York: Cambridge University Press.

Kraidy, M. M. and Khalil, J. F. (2007). The Middle East: Transnational Arab
    Television. In L. Artz and Y. Kamalipour (eds) *The Media Globe: Trends in
    International Mass Media*. Lanham, MD: Rowman & Littlefield, 79–98.

Kraidy, M. M. and Khalil, J. F. (2008). Youth, Media, and Culture in the Arab World.
    In S. Livingstone and K. Drotner (eds) *International Handbook of Children, Media
    and Culture*. London: Sage, 330–44.

Labeeb, S. (1990). *The Arabs and Television: Direct Broadcast Satellites*. Riyadh: Gulf Television Unit [Arabic].

Lamloum, O. (2004) *Al-Jazira, miroir rebelle et ambigu du monde arabe*. Paris: Découverte.

Launch of MTV Arabia Channel in 2007 (2006, 31 December). *Elaph*, accessed 31 December 2006 at <www.elaph.com> [Arabic].

Leading Middle East Pay-TV Platform Builds New Broadcast Centre at Dubai Media City (2004, 16 February). Dubai: Showtime Arabia Press Release.

Lebanon Bans Satellite News Broadcast by Private Stations (1998, 7 January). *Xinhua News Agency*, accessed 15 October 2008 at the LexisNexis online database.

Lebanon Satellite to Add to Crowded Mideast Skies (1996, 5–11 February). *Variety*, accessed 15 October 2008 at the LexisNexis online database.

Levine, J. (2006, 25 June). Al-Jazeera, as American as Apple Pie. *Washington Post*: B03.

Malik, A. (2001, 13 November). Al-Jazeera Kabul Office Destroyed by US Missile. *Associated Press*, accessed 15 October 2007 at the LexisNexis online database.

Malik, Z. (2006, November). New Emotions, New Products. *Gulf Marketing Review*, accessed 1 October 2007 at <www.gmr-online.com/httpdocs>.

Matar, D. (2007). Heya TV: A Feminist Counterpublic for Arab Women? *Comparative Studies of South Asia, Africa and the Middle East*, 27: 513–24.

Mauris, M. (2002). *Female Television Creatives*. Cairo: Higher Council for Culture [Arabic].

MBC and Dubai Media City Signed an Agreement (2001, 21 March). London: MBC Group Press Release.

MBC Celebrates Its Five-year Anniversary (1996, 30 September). London: MBC Press Release.

MBC Completed Its Relocation (2002, 27 April). Dubai: MBC Group Press Release.

MBC Moves to Dubai (2002, 28 April). Dubai: MBC Group Press Release.

MBC Opens Dubai Media City Headquarters (2002, 30 April). Dubai: MBC Group Press Release.

MBC to Launch Subscription Package (1993, 21 October). *New Media Markets*, accessed 15 October 2008 at the Business Wire online database.

McCarthy, R. (2003, 28 May). Unrepentant Propaganda Chief Sticks to the Baath Party Line. *Guardian,* accessed 1 September 2007 at <www.guardian.co.uk>.

Measuring Security and Stability in Iraq (2006, May). Report to Congress in accordance with the Department of Defense Appropriations Act 2006 (Section 9010), 13, accessed 15 October 2008 at <www.defenselink.mil/pubs/pdfs/9010_March_2007_Final_Signed.pd>.

Media Cities in the Arab World (2004, April). Amman: Arab Advisors Group.

Mernissi, F. (2004). The Satellite, the Prince, and Scheherazade: The Rise of Women as Communicators in Digital Islam. *Transnational Broadcasting Journal*, 12, accessed 15 June 2008 at <www.tbsjournal.com>.

Miles, H. (2006). *Al-Jazeera: The Inside Story of the Arab News Channel That Is Challenging the West*. New York: Grove Press.

Millichip, J. (1996, April). Sand Castles: Special Satellite Middle East. *TV World*, 45–50.

Mohamad, J. (1975, 22 January). A Study about the Franco-Lebanese Negotiations about the Two Television Channels in Lebanon. *Assafir*, 12 [Arabic].

Muawad, M. (2000). *The Arab Satellite Channels and the Future of Arab Relations after the Liberation of Kuwait*. Kuwait City: Modern Book Publishers [Arabic].

Na'ameh, M. (2007). *The Syrian and Arab Media Scene*. Damascus: Orient Printing and Publishing [Arabic].

Napoli, J. J., Amin, H. Y. and Napoli, L. R. (1995). Privatization of the Egyptian Media. *Journal of South Asian and Middle Eastern Studies*, 4, 39–57.

Nashwa al-Rouayni Starts in February with Ma' Nashwa (2007, 6 January). Dubai: Dubai Media Incorporated Press Release.

Nassar, S. (2006, 13 February). The 'Arab Woman's Channel': The Absence of Fundamental Issues. *Assafir*.

Neimat, K. (2007, 31 January). Jordan: Advertising Expenditure Hits $215m Record High in 2006. *Jordan Times*, accessed 31 January 2007 at <www.jordantimes.com>.

New Identity: Al-Arabiya, A (2003). *Tasmeem: The Arabic Design and Creativity Magazine*: 3–6. [Arabic]

New Research Sheds Light on Changing Media Landscape in the Arab World (2003, 10 March). Amman: Arab Advisors Group Press Release.

Next Generation, The (2002, April). *Gulf Business*: 22–3.

Nicolson, A. (2006, 13 February). Boom Town. *Guardian*, accessed 15 October 2008 at <www.guardian.co.uk>.

Noorsat Gears up for Increasing Demand for Satellite Television Broadcasting in the Middle East (2005, 20 September). Manama: Noorsat Press Release.

Noun, F. (2009, 29 April). Une 'cité médiatique' verra le jour au Kesrouan, à l'initiative de Télé-Lumière. (A Media City Will See the Day in Keserwan, Upon the Initiative of Télé-Lumière). *L'Orient-Le Jour*, accessed 29 April 2009 at <www.lorient-lejour.com.lb>.

Nyouf, H. (2004, 14 April). Kuwaiti Information Officer: We Ban. *Al-Arabiya*, accessed 14 April 2004 at <www.alarabiya.net>.

Ohrstrom, L. (2005, 7 December). New Kids' Channel Navigates 'Edutainment'. *Daily Star*, accessed 7 December 2005 at <www.dailystar.com.lb>.

Omar, R. (2008, 16 September). Nostalgic Revolution Brings Television Back to the Foreground. *Al-Mustaqbal*, accessed 16 September 2008 at <www.almustaqbal.com> [Arabic].

Omran, S. (2006, 24 October) Egyptian Ramadan Drama in the Accusation Pit. *Al-Hayat*, accessed 18 July 2007 at <www.alhayat.com> [Arabic].

Online Presence of FTA Satellite Channels in the Arab World, The (2006). Amman: Arab Advisors Group.

Orbit Free-to-Air Beginning of Next Year (2008, 27 October). *Al-Akhbar*, accessed 27 October 2008 at <www.al-akhbar.com> [Arabic].

Orbit Satellite Television Terminates Pact with BBC Worldwide Television (1996, 11 April). Rome: Orbit Press Release.

Otterman, S. (2006). Fatwas and Feminism: Women, Religious Authority, and Islamic TV, *Transnational Broadcasting Studies*, 16, accessed 1 December 2007 at <www.tbsjournal.com>.

Otterman, S. (2007, May). Does the Veiled Look Sell? Egyptian Advertisers Grapple with the Hijab. *Arab Media and Society*, accessed 15 June 2007 at <www.arabmediaandsociety.com>.

Overview: The Arab States (2006). New York: United Nations Population Fund.

Oxford Business Group (2006, 14 June). *Egypt: Sharpening the Ad Edge*, accessed 18 October 2008 at <www.oxfordbusinessgroup.com>.

Pan Arab TV Quantitative Monitoring (2005). Dubai: STATEX/Ipsos-STAT.

Peterson, J. (2008, January). Sampling Folklore: The 'Re-popularization' of Sufi Inshad in Egyptian Dance Music. *Arab Media and Society*, accessed 15 October 2008 at <www.arabmediaandsociety.com>.

Pintak, L. (2007a, 8 January). Al-Zawraa and Egypt's On-air Ambiguity. *Daily Star*, accessed 15 October 2008 at <www.dailystar.com.lb>.

Pintak, L. (2007b, 11 January). War of Ideas: Insurgent Channel Coming to a Satellite near You. *Arab News*, accessed 15 October 2008 at <www.arabnews.com>.

Pond, C. (2006). The Appeal of Sami Yusuf and the Search for Islamic Authenticity. *Transnational Broadcasting Studies*, 16, accessed 1 December 2007 at <www.tbsjournal.com>.

Prince al-Waleed bin Talal Raises His Stake in LBC Sat to Around 85% with a Value of US $78 million (2008, 8 July). Riyadh: Kingdom Holding Company Press Release.

Qandeel, H. (1989). *ArabSat: The Arab Satellite Network and Communication Issues in the Arab Nation.* Cairo: General Commission of Books [Arabic].

Qeeshani, Y. (2002). *Arab Satellite Communications in the Age of Open Skies.* Beirut: Private Publication [Arabic].

Quick Overview (2008, 13 October). *Al-Akhbar*, accessed 13 October 2008 at <www.al-akhbar.com> [Arabic].

Radwan, A. F. (2005, 21 December). They Demand Access to Broadcast Channels ... 'Our Voice' Is Made by Children. *Al-Hayat*, accessed 21 December 2005 at <www.alhayat.com> [Arabic].

Rahman, S. (2003, 21 February). Dh1.1b News Channel in Arabic Takes off at DMC. *Gulf News*, accessed 15 October 2007 at <www.gulfnews.com/home>.

Ramadan's Drama Fever: Arabic Mini-Series Production during Ramadan 2004 (2004, 28 October). Amman: Arab Advisors Group.

Ramadan Kareem (2006, September). *Gulf Marketing Review*, accessed 1 October 2006 at <www.gmr-online.com/httpdocs>.

Ramadan Productions, Stars Fees Cut Third of the Budgets (2006, 4 October). *Al-Kifah el-Arabi*, accessed 4 October 2006 at <www.kifaharabi.com> [Arabic].

Ramadan Sheikhs ... the Bet of Ramadan 2008 (2008, 26 August) *Al-Akhbar*, accessed 9 March 2009 at <www.al-akhbar.com> [Arabic]

Rawnsley, G. D. (1996). Cold War Radio in Crisis: The BBC Overseas Service, the Suez Crisis and the Hungarian Uprising, 1956. *Historical Journal of Film, Radio and Television*, 16 (2): 197–219.

Reaching the Modern Arabic Woman – MBC4 Goes On-air with a Totally New Look (2005, 23 November). Dubai: MBC Group Press Release.

Reality Shows in the Arab World (2004). Amman: Arab Advisors Group.

Refuses Earning Money from the Pockets of the Audience through SMS and Reality Television (2006, 8 October). *Al-Riyadh*, accessed 8 October 2006 at <www.alriyadh.com> [Arabic].

Religious Programmes Compete with Television Drama in Ramadan (2007, 13 September). *Al-Riyadh*, accessed 9 March 2009 at <www.alriyadh.com> [Arabic].

Return of the Comedy Series for the Screen during Ramadan, The (2006, September 12). *Al-Hayat*, accessed 12 September 2006 at <www.alhayat.com> [Arabic].

Richter, F. and El Senussi, K. (2005, November). Consumer Alert. *Business Monthly*, accessed 15 December 2005 at <www.amcham.org.eg/publications/businessmonthly>.

Rugh, W. A. (1980). Saudi Mass Media and Society in the Faisal Era. In W. A. Beling (ed.), *King Faisal and the Modernization of Saudi Arabia*. Boulder, CO: Westview Press, 125–44.

Rugh, W. A. (2004). *Arab Mass Media: Newspapers, Radio, and Television in Arab Politics*. Westport, CT: Praeger.

Russell, P. (1994, November). Roman Roads Lead to New Orbits. *TV World*: 28–9.

Sa'ate, A. (1992). *Media Policy in the Kingdom of Saudi Arabia. Cairo: Saudi Centre for Strategic Studies* [Arabic].

Saadé, J. (1997, 11 November). LBCI Faces Legal Quiz over Tamraz Talk Show. *Daily Star*, accessed 11 November 1997 at <www.dailystar.com.lb>.

Sabeh, B. (1997, 24 December). Compliance with a Unified Political Discourse and Allowing Télé-Liban to Broadcast via Satellite. *As-Safir*: 7 [Arabic].

Sabeh, B. (1997, 22 January). No Censorship on Media Freedom and Satellite Issue Will Enjoy 'Home' Treatment. *An-Nahar*: 4 [Arabic].

Saddam's Sacked Media Workers Demand Jobs Back (2003, 1 June). *Jordan Times*, accessed 1 September 2007 at <www.jordantimes.com>.

Sakr, N. (2005). Women, Development, and Al-Jazeera: A Balance Sheet. In M. Zayani (ed.) *The Al-Jazeera Phenomenon: Critical Perspectives on New Arab Media*. London: Pluto, 127–50.

Sakr, N. (2007). *Arab Television Today*. London: I. B. Tauris.

Salamandra, C. (2005). Television and the Ethnographic Endeavor: The Case of Syrian Drama. *Transnational Broadcasting Studies*, 14, accessed 30 September 2005 at <www.tbsjournal.com>.

Salamandra, C. (2008). Through the Back Door: Syrian Television Makers between Secularism and Islamization. In K. Hafez (ed.) *Arab Media: Power and Weakness*. New York: Continuum, 252–62.

Satellite Generations (2002, September). *ARABSAT*, accessed 15 October 2002 at <www.arabsat.com/satgen/index.asp>.

Satellite Programs and the Telephone Calls They Generate Are the Reason (1997, 23 January). *Annahar*, 6 [Arabic].

Sa'ud, Fahd (2005, 3 November). Religious Programmes during Ramadan … Divided Audience. *Elaph*, accessed 15 October 2008 at <www.elaph.com> [Arabic].

Saudi Arabia: Media Survey (2004). Amman: Arab Advisors Group.

'Saudi Arabia', Media Survey (2004, October), *Arab Ad*, no details available.

Saudi Media (1986, 27 October). *'Okaz*, 7426: 13 [Arabic].

Saudi 'Ulemas Demand the Total Prohibition of Women Appearing in the Mass Media (2009, 25 March). *Al-Quds al-Arabi*, accessed 25 March 2008 at <www.alquds.co.uk> [Arabic].

Saudis Clamp Down on Satellite Viewing (1996, December). *Arab Ad*, 6: 167.

Sbeihi, M. A. (1987). The Television of the Kingdom of Saudi Arabia and Its Stages of Development. Jeddah: The Author [Arabic].

Schleifer, S. A. (1998). Media Explosion in the Arab World: The Pan-Arab Satellite Broadcasters. *Transnational Broadcasting Studies*, 1, accessed 15 October 2002 at <www.tbsjournal.com>.

Schleifer, S. A. (2000a). Does Satellite TV Pay in the Arab World Footprint? Exploring the Economic Feasibility of Specialized and General Channels. *Transnational Broadcasting Studies*, 5, accessed 15 October 2002 at <www.tbsjournal.com>.

Schleifer, S. A. (2000b). The Dubai Digital Broadcasting Miracle, *Transnational Broadcasting Studies*, 5, accessed 15 October 2002 at <www.tbsjournal.com>.

Schleifer, S. A. (2001). Looks Are Deceiving: Arab Talk Shows and TV Journalism. *Transnational Broadcasting Studies*, 6, accessed 15 October 2002 at <www.tbsjournal.com>.

Sha'ban, S. (1998). The Egyptian Satellite NILESAT. Cairo: General Commission of Books [Arabic].

Shadid, A. (2006, 1 May). A Newsman Breaks the Mold in Arab World. *Washington Post*: A01.

Shams, D. (2007, 16 July). The Story of Al-Manar's Survival Told by Its News Director. *Assafir*, accessed 16 July 2007 at <www.assafir.com> [Arabic].

Shapiro, S. (2005, 2 January). The War inside the Arab Newsroom. *New York Times Magazine*, accessed 15 October 2007 at <www.nytimes.com/2005/01/02/magazine/02ARAB.html>.

Sheikh Hamad bin-Mohammad al-Ghammas on al-Huda New English language Islamic Channel (2005, 28 October). *Al-Watan*, accessed 30 October 2008 <http://www.alwatan.com.sa>.

Shobokshi, H. (2007, 22 January). The Most Difficult Issue. *Asharq al-Awsat*, accessed 22 January 2007 at <www.asharqalawsat.com> [Arabic].

Showtime Fully Switched On. (2004, 24 April). Dubai: Showtime Arabia Press Release.

Siebert, F. S., Peterson, T. and Schramm, W. (1956). *Four Theories of the Press*. Urbana: University of Illinois Press.

Sinno, A. M. (2001). *Television in Lebanon and the Arab World*. Beirut: Al-Nahda Publishers [Arabic].

Sirri, O. (2003, 9 January). The Oracle in the Desert: Can Dubai's Media City Deliver on Its Promise of Freedom of the Press? *Cairo Times*, 6 (43).

Sixteen Satellite Channels to Start Working at Jordanian Media City within a Month (2004, 4 August). Amman: Jordan Media City Press Release.

Sreberny, A. (2000). Television, Gender, and Democratization in the Middle East. In J. Curran and M. J. Park (eds) *De-Westernizing Media Studies*. London: Routledge, 63–79.

Steiner, L. (1992). The History and Structure of Women's Alternative Media. In L. Rakow (ed.) *Women Making Meaning: New Feminist Directions in Communication*, London: Routledge, 121–43.

Sullivan, S. (2001). Dubai Media City Prepares for Next Phase. *Transnational Broadcasting Studies*, 7, accessed 15 October 2002 at <www.tbsjournal.com>.

Swank, A. (2007, May). Sexual Healing: How Big Is Kalaam Kibeer? *Arab Media and Society*, accessed 15 July 2007 at <www.arabmediaandsociety.com>.

Syria to Create the Largest Media City in the Arab Region (2007, May). *Forward Magazine*, accessed 15 July 2007 at <222.fw-magazine.com/print/375>.

Tawil, F. (1997). Saudi Media Scene Evolution. *Arab Ad*, 7, 8–10.

Telecoms and Media TV International Sourcebook 2008 (2008). London: Informa.

Temko, N. (1984, 7 March). The Battle of the Broadcasts in the Gulf War. *Christian Science Monitor*, 1.

Temko, N. (1984, 14 August). Why Ordinary Arabs Faithfully Turn to the Voice of the 'Enemy'. *Christian Science Monitor*, 1.

Terzis, G. (2007). *European Media Governance: National and Regional Dimensions*. London: Intellect.

TNS–Egypt Insight Services and Solutions, accessed 30 October 2008 at <www.tnsglobal.com/global/alm/egypt>.

TNS Ratings (2005) *Ramadan* 2005. Cairo: TNS.

Toutounji, I. (2006, 1 December). 385 Channels are Fighting on the Remainders … 85% of the Ads Are for Five Television Groups. *Al-Hayat*, accessed 22 February 2007 at <www.alhayat.com> [Arabic].

Toutounji, I. (2007, 22 February). Dubai Television Establishes a Distribution Company for Television Series. *Al-Hayat*, accessed 22 February 2007 at <www.alhayat.com> [Arabic].

Trends in Middle Eastern Arabic Television Series Production – Opportunities for Broadcasters and Producers (2007). Dubai: Booz Allen & Hamilton.

Trofimov, Y. (2007). *The Siege of Mecca*. New York: Doubleday.

TV Trend Analysis KSA January 2009 (2009, January). Jeddah: Business Compass Research and Brand Consultancy.

UAE Vital Statistics (2008). *FDI Magazine*, accessed 15 October 2008 at <www.fdimagazine.com>.

US Bureau of the Census (International Database), accessed 18 October 2008 at <www.census.gov/ipc/www/idb>.

US Warplanes Bomb Al-Jazeera Office in Baghdad, Kill Journalist (2003, 8 April). *Al-Jazeera.net*. Doha: Al-Jazeera, accessed 15 October 2007 at <Aljazeera.net> [Arabic].

Van Zoonen, L. (1992). The Women's Movement and the Media: Constructing a Public Identity. *European Journal of Communication*, 7: 453–76.

Waleed al Ibrahim Receives the Award of the Knight of the Arab Media (2006, 12 November). *Al-Hayat*, accessed 20 February 2008 at <www.alhayat.com> [Arabic].

Wedeen, L. (1999). *Ambiguities of Domination: Politics, Rhetoric, and Symbols in Contemporary Syria*. Chicago, IL: University of Chicago Press.

Who Wins, Saudi Arabia with New Production or MBC with Steady Steps (2005, 11 October). *Al Jazirah*, accessed 9 March 2009 at <www.al-jazirah.com> [Arabic].

With a Warning, French Media Watchdog Agency Grants License to Hezbollah-linked Network (2004, 19 November). *Associated Press,* accessed 15 October 2007 at LexisNexis Academic online database.

World Economic Outlook Database (2007, September). Washington, DC: International
    Monetary Fund, accessed 18 October 2008 at
    <www.imf.org/external/pubs/ft/weo/2008/01/weodata/index.aspx>.

World Population Prospects, the 2002 Revision Highlights (2003). Geneva: United
    Nations, accessed 18 October 2008 at <www.unpopulation.org>.

Yasin, S. (2006, 3 February). Egyptian Women Writers and Directors Present More
    than 20 Drama Series during 2006 ... Women's Television Drama Triumphs for the
    First Time on Patriarchy. *Al-Hayat*, accessed 22 February 2007 at
    <www.alhayat.com> [Arabic].

Yasin, S. (2006, 13 April). A Study Rings the Alarm Bell ... 'The Video Clip Woman':
    An Organized Industry Promoting Sensationalism and Superficiality. *Al-Hayat*,
    accessed 13 April 2006 at http://www.alhayat.com> [Arabic].

Yassine, S. (2007) Lebanese Seek Smiles from Political Satire. *Middle East Online*
    (10), accessed 15 May 2009 <http://www.meo.tv/english/>.

Yehia, R. (1998, 24 February). Hizbullah Calls for Hebrew Satellite TV. *Daily Star*,
    accessed 24 February 1998 at <www.dailystar.com.lb>.

Yehia, R. (2000, 2 November). Hezbullah Broadens Its Airwaves Battlefront.
    Al-Manar's Satellite Television Channel Moves into Palestinian Homes for an Extra
    14 Hours a Day. *Daily Star*, accessed 2 November 2000 at
    <www.dailystar.com.lb>.

Yunes, N. (2001, 25 January). State Media or Regime Media. *Annahar*, accessed
    25 January 2001 at <www.annahar.com> [Arabic].

Yussef, H. (1997, September). NileSat and the Challenge of Existence. *Radio Art
    Journal*, 1(46). Cairo: Radio and Television Union [Arabic].

Zayani, M. and Sahraoui, S. (2007). *The Culture of Al-Jazeera: Inside an Arab Media
    Giant*. Jefferson, NC: McFarland & Company.

Index